THE ART OF
TAXIDERMY

ENLARGED ILLUSTRATED
SPECIAL EDITION

BY JOHN ROWLEY

The Art of Taxidermy
Illustrated Enlarged Special Edition

by John Rowley
Cover design by Mark Bussler

More Books at
CGRpublishing.com

1939 New York World's Fair: The
World of Tomorrow in Photographs

The Complete Ford Model T Guide:
Enlarged Illustrated Special Edition

The Aeroplane Speaks:
Illustrated Historical Guide to
Airplanes

PLATE I.

GROUP OF DUCK HAWKS.

Designed to illustrate the nesting habits. From a photograph of
a group in the American Museum.

TO

Dr. J. A. ALLEN,

CURATOR OF THE DEPARTMENT OF VERTEBRATE ZOÖLOGY
IN THE AMERICAN MUSEUM OF NATURAL HISTORY,

THIS BOOK IS RESPECTFULLY DEDICATED

AS A TOKEN OF SINCERE PERSONAL REGARD,

AND ALSO IN RECOGNITION OF HIS VALUED ASSISTANCE

AND ADVICE TO THE DEPARTMENT OF TAXIDERMY

DURING THE PAST TEN YEARS.

THE ART
OF TAXIDERMY

BY

JOHN ROWLEY

CHIEF OF THE DEPARTMENT OF TAXIDERMY IN THE
AMERICAN MUSEUM OF NATURAL HISTORY, NEW YORK CITY ;
MEMBER OF THE NEW YORK ZOÖLOGICAL SOCIETY,
LINNÆAN SOCIETY OF NEW YORK,
AMERICAN ORNITHOLOGISTS' UNION, ETC.

"Into a perfect work time does not enter"
HENRY D. THOREAU

*ILLUSTRATED WITH TWENTY FULL-PAGE PLATES
AND FIFTY-NINE DRAWINGS IN THE TEXT*

1898

PREFACE.

TAXIDERMY, a name formerly applied to the trade of most inartistically upholstering a skin, has of late years made such enormous strides toward perfection—as much, perhaps, by improvement in methods as by any superior skill on the part of the taxidermist—that I am emboldened to describe in the following pages the results of a number of years' study, experiment, and practical work in the taxidermic field.

It is a fact much to be regretted that many taxidermists, by reason of their extreme jealousy and narrowness of mind, are exceedingly loath to communicate new ideas and discoveries to their fellow-workers. But, thanks to the more general enlargement and increase in number of scientific museums of late years, a number of men of genius and education have taken up the study of the art. It is largely owing to their exertions that the taxidermy of the present day is so far in advance of what it was a decade since; and the few works on the subject that they have written have been eagerly devoured by every progressive taxidermist in the country.

Some of the methods described in the following pages may seem to involve considerable time and expense. Let it be said, in answer to this, " If a thing is worth doing, it is worth doing well." I should advise the preparator to consider, before starting to mount a specimen for exhibition, whether or not the material in hand warrants it; and should he decide in favour of preparing the specimen—

v

which will doubtless happen if he be imbued with the proper degree of energy and enthusiasm—then let him give the specimen all the time it demands. When we consider that an experienced modeller may take *months* to prepare one model, why should an ambitious taxidermist feel at all discouraged at the expenditure of a few *weeks* upon a large specimen?

In writing this work it has been my aim to eliminate all extraneous matter, and to stick as closely to the subject of taxidermy as lay in my power. Nothing is further from my thoughts than to claim that the methods here recommended are beyond improvement. I simply give the results of my own experience, coupled with that of other taxidermists with whom I have come in contact, in the hope that fellow-workers who have not had the benefit of the experience of others, nor the time and means necessary to experiment on new lines of work, may reap some new ideas and be benefited thereby.

My thanks are due to Dr. J. L. Wortman, the late Mr. I. N. Travis, Jr., Mr. John Fitze, Mr. William M. Richardson, and especially to Mr. Frank M. Chapman, all of the American Museum of Natural History, for kind assistance rendered in the preparation of the following pages; and I here take pleasure in recording an expression of my appreciation of their valued service.

Mr. Charles R. Knight kindly volunteered his assistance in the preparation of a number of the illustrations; and to Mr. Ernest W. Smith, an assistant in the Department of Taxidermy in the American Museum, is due the credit for the drawings and diagrams, to both of whom I here extend my thanks for their faithful delineations. The original photographs used were, with but two exceptions, made by myself.

JOHN ROWLEY.

AMERICAN MUSEUM OF NATURAL HISTORY,
    NEW YORK CITY, *February, 1898.*

CONTENTS.

THE ART OF TAXIDERMY.

CHAPTER I.

COLLECTING.

As an introduction to the following chapters it would seem that a few hints on collecting would not be without value. A detailed account of the hunting of all varieties of game is of course out of the question, and the methods employed in capturing various game animals may be found fully described in our journals and works more especially treating of the subject.

A description of a short collecting trip, in a locality where both large and small game is to be found in reasonable numbers, would perhaps best serve to illustrate this chapter and give the reader a general idea of the methods employed in securing and caring for specimens in the field.

Before starting, read up all accessible literature bearing upon the section it is proposed to visit, and, if possible, correspond with people who are or actually have been in the precise locality. A letter, inclosing a stamped envelope for reply, addressed to the postmaster of the town nearest the proposed collecting ground, is generally fruitful in result.

Having decided upon the locality, the next thing to be considered, barring the funds, is the outfit, and this must of course be adapted to suit the locality and season. Passing over the subject of tents, camping outfit, wearing apparel, sleeping bags or hammocks, etc., we come to the outfit *actually* necessary to enable us to secure and properly prepare our specimens.

THE OUTFIT FOR COLLECTING BIRDS AND MAMMALS.

Guns and Ammunition.—The choice of guns and ammunition is a point upon which opinions vary, and much must be left to the individual, who will in any case probably suit his own fancy. A twelve-gauge, moderate choke, hammerless breech-loading shotgun, of any reliable make, fitted with a .32-calibre auxiliary barrel, is, to my mind, the best all-round collecting gun. A paper cartridge, loaded in a special way for ten and twelve gauge shotguns, with a round ball which will pass easily through the choke-bored barrel, is now regularly manufactured in this country and is for sale at first-class gun houses. This cartridge works remarkably well, and with a number of paper shells loaded with shot varying in size from buckshot to No. 12, in connection with the auxiliary barrel to be used for shooting small specimens, enables the collector to be prepared for almost any game he may chance to meet. A .22-calibre auxiliary barrel, to shoot the shot-cartridge manufactured by the Winchester Repeating Arms Company, does very effective work at comparatively short range, but has been discarded by the best collectors in favour of the .32-calibre. Extra long, brass, cylindrical cartridges, centre fire, are now made by the same firm, and these may be recapped and reloaded an indefinite number of times. A .32-calibre, bottle-necked shot-cartridge, also manufactured by the Winchester Company, is well adapted to the auxiliary barrel, but, although it shoots stronger than the cylindrical shell, is not reloadable. A few ball-cartridges to fit the auxiliary are also convenient to have, in case a large animal is wounded; and at close range, rather than to further disfigure the skin by again shooting the animal with a large load, these may be used to advantage.

The choice of a rifle will of course depend upon the

game to be hunted. For an animal as large as the moose, a .45–90 rifle is none too large, but for deer a .44–40 is better adapted, and has the advantage of greater lightness and facility of handling. A half-magazine, .44–40 "take-down" rifle, manufactured by the Marlin Repeating Arms Company, has given very satisfactory results on deer. A full-magazine gun gives more weight at the muzzle, which is perhaps an advantage on a long standing shot; but for

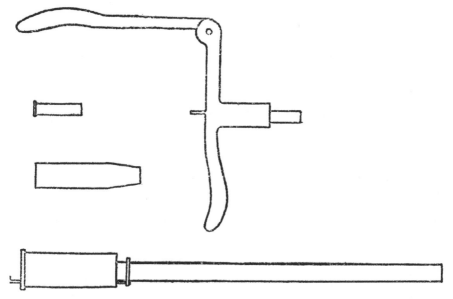

Fig. 1.—Auxiliary Barrel and Reloading Outfit.

quick work on a running deer I prefer the half magazine. Furthermore, the full-magazine gun is generally loaded to its utmost capacity at the beginning of a trip into the woods, and about one half or more of the same cartridges are still found there at the end of the hunt. This rifle is made to " take down "—that is, the gun lifts apart at the breech, and may be stowed away in an ordinary trunk—a great advantage over the non-" take-down " rifles, which are too long to be accommodated thus.

The Winchester smokeless cartridges fitted with the copper-jacketed ball give perfect results, and have been used by a friend successfully upon walrus, where the soft lead ball seemed to have little or no effect.

The Moth-proof Can.—A necessary incumbrance on a collecting trip to the collector who takes pleasure in bringing home good specimens of small birds and mammals is the "moth-proof can." This is simply a square-cornered tin can, eighteen by eighteen by thirteen inches, with the top arranged to lift off, and the interior filled with trays of soft, thin pine. These are made to set one on top of the other, and the whole to so fill the can that when the cover is clamped on the trays will not jolt about in moving. Soft pine makes the best bottom for the trays, as a specimen can be readily pinned to it, which gives it an advantage over cardboard. It will be found advantageous to have a wooden box constructed of seven-eighth-inch pine to receive the can in shipping, and when at work in the woods the box may, in a hurry, be used as a work-table upon which to prepare small specimens. On starting out, the trays may be packed full of ammunition, tools, etc., well packed with cotton or tow, a padlock adjusted, and the whole will be found to be a most convenient receptacle in which to ship much of the paraphernalia. Upon returning, the can may be used in the laboratory for storage for small bird and mammal skins.

Traps.—A good assortment of traps for mammals is the next consideration. Steel traps, No. 0, inside springs, with chains, for animals of the size of the muskrat, and larger sizes with the outside double springs, will give satisfaction for larger specimens. For field-mice, shrews, etc., the "cyclone" and the "climax" mouse traps are perfect in their action. Another trap of more recent manufacture is found fertile in results; this is the "out-o'-sight." The base of the "out-o'-sight" is, however, made of wood, and the whole should be well steeped in hot paraffin to render it waterproof, otherwise it will warp and twist out of shape from dampness. These traps are all made collapsible, are very light, and so compact that a dozen or more of either may be readily carried in a side pocket. They may be arranged for use on runways or with bait. A larger size of the "climax," called the "climax rat-trap," and also of the "out-o'-sight," are manufactured and are well adapted for animals of the size of squirrels. These larger sizes are much too strong for a mouse, and not infrequently will cut a mouse quite in two. A variety of bait may be used with these traps. Shrews, which are mainly insectivorous in their diet, may be taken by baiting with pieces of meat. Rolled oats are used for mice by a number of our experienced collectors, and any combinations may be used to tickle the palates of the little rodents, varying the bait according to the locality. On a recent trip I baited with a "*table d'hote.*" It consisted of hickory-nut meats, black-walnut meats, cheese, rolled oats, chestnuts, roasted peanuts, and sweet corn. These were chopped up fine and kept in air-tight boxes, and a few drops of oil of anise added occasionally to perfume the whole. This proved to be a "stunner," as shrews as well as mice would devour portions of it, upward of one hundred shrews and numbers of mice having been taken during a three-weeks' trip.

These traps all work on the "dead-fall" system, and must be visited frequently in a warm climate, as a mouse or shrew will peel off on the belly in a few hours after death, and quicker still if exposed to the direct rays of the sun on a hot day.

Tools and Materials.—A small belt hatchet, to be used in setting traps and "blazing" trees.

A small emery stone to sharpen axes and knives.

A couple of shoe-knives, the ends ground down to a point, for skinning large game.

Two small scalpels (microscopic) and two medium-sized scalpels for birds and mammals.

One whetstone.

Two pairs of scissors.

One pair of small cutting pliers.

2

One pair of 4-inch forceps.

One pair of 8-inch forceps.

One hand scraper for removing the flesh and fat from greasy hides.

One small and one large scraper.

One small three-cornered file.

One steel comb.

One surgeon's saw.

One pocket compass.

One aneroid barometer for taking altitudes.

Barbour's linen thread, Nos. 60, and 25.

Three-cornered glover's needles, Nos. 000, 0, and 3.

A couple of papers of pins.

A pencil and note-book, with a small calendar pasted on the inside of the cover.

One millimetre rule, to measure small mammals; or, in default of this, an ordinary 2-foot rule, and give the measurements in English inches and fractions.

A number of small tags, strung, for birds and small mammals.

A triplicate set of numbers, stencilled in lead, reaching from 1 to 25, to number the skin, skull, and limb bones of large mammals.

One tape measure.

One blow-pipe and egg-drill.

Twine, heavy and light.

Alum and arsenic, dry, mixed in equal parts, in a tin box with a screw top.

A small bag to hold traps, arranged to sling over the shoulder.

A stout tin box, with a hinged cover, eight by six by six inches high, to hold all the small tools, the arsenic can, etc.

Partially annealed brass wire, wound on spools, sizes 16, 18, and 22, for placing in the tail sheaths of small mammals.

A needle case, with a small square of emery cloth pasted on the inside of the cover, to be used for cleaning rust from needles.

A quantity of matches, previously soaked in hot paraffin to render them perfectly waterproof.*

---

* These are a great boon to the hunter. I am indebted to Mr. I. N. Travis, Jr., formerly an assistant in the Department of Taxidermy

A good supply of candles, or a couple of lanterns and oil. These are a necessity, as much of the material collected must be cared for at night, and small mammals, if left until the next day, are apt to spoil.

Common table or dairy salt, for preserving large hides.

An Agassiz tank (a copper tank, eight by thirteen inches by ten inches high, with a screw top), or, in default of this, a couple of large preserve jars, full of dry plaster of Paris, to be used in taking plaster casts of noses, or difficult parts of the external anatomy of large mammals.

One copy of Ridgway's Manual,* to enable the collector to note and afterward reproduce the colours of the bills and legs of birds and the parts of some animals and reptiles.

An Agassiz tank, a duplicate of the one used for plaster, filled with a seventy-per-cent solution of alcohol and water, for alcoholics.

Corn meal, for absorbing blood and moisture in skinning birds and small mammals.

A toothbrush, to use with the meal in cleaning the blood from fur or feathers.

If possible, in addition to all this, I recommend every collector to take with him a four-by-five camera, of any reliable make, with the necessary outfit for taking photographs. Views of heads, and parts of large mammals, sometimes photographs from life, may be made with the camera, which, when enlarged, will afterward be of great service in mounting. An accurate sketch is perhaps a safer and surer method. But, aside from its utility in this respect, the camera is a wonderful record keeper, and views of camp scenes, etc., neatly mounted in an album, are a constant source of admiration to your friends and a pleasure to yourself. I have always taken a camera into the field with me on my collecting trips, and the numbers of fine photo-

---

in the American Museum, for this method of waterproofing matches, which method has since been patented by him.

* A Nomenclature of Colors for Naturalists, and Compendium of Useful Knowledge for Ornithologists. By Robert Ridgway. Boston: Little, Brown & Co., 1886.

graphs which have resulted have more than repaid me for the many pains and aches endured while " packing " the outfit over a long " carry." *

OFF ON A COLLECTING TRIP.

We will pass over the details of preparation for the trip, the long, almost endless journey on the cars, and it is with a feeling of relief that our party, two in number, hears the name of our station called out by the railroad porter.

As the roar of the train dies out in the distance, we inspect our baggage to see that everything has arrived and is in good condition. A rough-looking woodsman has been standing on the station platform meanwhile, seemingly very much interested in what is going on. He finally steps up and asks our names. We at once recognise in him the man we have been corresponding with for some time past, and who arranged to meet us at the depot and go on a hunt with us.

We are escorted to a hotel, where arrangements are soon made with the proprietor to hold our trunks and certain articles of wearing apparel not needed in camp until our return from the trip. A bargain is soon struck with a teamster to haul our outfit to the point we have chosen— the shore of a small lake a number of miles off—and, after purchasing a supply of food and other articles needed about camp, we are soon on the road.

After a long and tiresome journey over rough logging roads, many times wondering how it will be possible for the wagon to proceed farther in such a country, we finally reach the spot decided upon as headquarters during our stay in the woods.

A good level camping site is selected a few rods from

---

* To the collector who must develop his plates in a hot climate, it may be well to state that flowing the plate with a strong solution of formalin just after developing will effectually prevent frilling in the subsequent operations of fixing and washing.

the shore of a lake, and the canoe and outfit are soon un-
loaded. After bidding our teamster good-bye, with instructions to return for us at a certain time, we apply ourselves
to the work of pitching the tent and making things snug
for a few weeks' stay. A rude table is constructed upon
which to prepare our bird and mammal skins, the floor of
the tent carpeted with the tips of fir boughs, a few stones
set in position for a fireplace, the guns inspected and oiled,
and our paraphernalia generally arranged for business.

As night is fast approaching, a supply of firewood is cut
and supper prepared. After eating we stretch ourselves at
full length on the fir boughs, and, in the full glow of the
camp-fire, spin yarns and talk over the plans for the hunt.
At length we conclude to " turn in." The sleeping bags
are unrolled and spread upon the boughed floor of the tent,
a fresh supply of fuel is added to the fire, and we are soon
sleeping, dreaming of the morrow.

The next morning we are up and about long before daybreak. After a hasty breakfast we pocket a light lunch
for the noonday meal, gather up our bag of traps, strap on
our belts, not forgetting our little spotting hatchet, shoulder
our guns, and start off to " run out a line of traps."

But, as we are surrounded by wilderness, first let us take
a glance at the topography of the country, and get a few
bearings and see how the land lies.

The compass is taken out and laid upon a stump. Due
east rises that bold mountain, about seven miles distant.
This is a first good landmark. To the south the ground
rises from the lake and forms a series of hills, which trend
generally from east to west. By keeping these and other
similar landmarks which we note in mind, we soon learn to
navigate the woods, and are always able to tell by a glance
at the compass, or the sun on bright days, in which direction we should travel to reach camp.

Setting a Line of Traps for Small Mammals.—That
rising ground to the south offers a fine chance for a line of

traps, as by starting in at the water's edge and keeping right on up the slope we not only strike a varying growth of timber, but also a varying altitude, and a small mammal that might be found living in the rank grass at the edge of the lake might never be found at the summit of the hill, and *vice versa*. At a future day we will set out a line of traps up the side of the high mountain yonder.

As we proceed along the shore of the lake, looking for a suitable spot from which to make a start, we see numerous signs of muskrats and minks, and occasionally a branch cut off on a bevel as if done with a knife, and bereft of every particle of its bark. These we at once recognise as " beaver signs," and upon examination find them to be fresh. This is certainly very encouraging, and we proceed with renewed vigour. At the base of an old stump which juts out into the water we begin our line of traps, and as there is a perfect "landing place" of muskrats here, with a sufficient depth of water to drown the animal when caught, we set a No. 0 steel trap a couple of inches under the water in front of the landing, and fasten the end of the chain by means of a piece of stout wire to a root which juts out from the bank under the water. We have been so busy setting our muskrat trap that not until now, when too late, did we notice that heron which has flown right over us. " Don't shoot; he is now too far off; but have your eyes about you next time." A small brook empties into the lake at this point, and we will set a No. 0 steel trap on that flat rock, which comes up almost to the surface of the water, near the bank. Minks have a habit of following water courses, and indeed on that mud flat there are to be found marks of his little feet. All around the rock the water is quite deep, and a stick is driven down out in the pool and the end of the chain attached. " Let's see. We have no bait. Put your auxiliary in your shot gun and shoot that chickadee. He is just what we want." A piece of fish would answer better, but the bird will do. Some of the feathers are plucked out of the bird and strewn about on the bank. The body is well swabbed around the ground close to the edge of the water, so that the mink may get a good scent of the game, and the bird tucked into a small hole at the water's edge close by the trap. When the mink comes along he can not fail to notice the feathers and smell the carcass, and at once, being a semi-aquatic animal, is bound to slide into the water, and before he knows it, in his efforts to dig out the bait, his hind foot touches the pan of the trap and in his struggles he soon drowns. A few branches thrown into the water in the vicinity of the trap also tend to further entangle the animal in his efforts to escape and hasten drowning. Now for our line of mouse traps. Right here in this heap of brush grown up with long weeds is an excellent spot to set a trap, and upon close examination a number of small runways are found leading off into the long grass. A number of "cyclone" and "climax" mouse traps are set in the brush heap and out in the grass; on the runways a number of the "out-o'-sight" traps are placed, each trap being tied with a piece of twine to some adjacent object. Where no tree or shrub is found that can be "spotted" with the hatchet to mark the spot, a strip of white cotton cloth is tied to a twig or weed stalk. The spot where each individual trap is set must be marked, and well marked too, otherwise, being so inconspicuous and such a number being put out, a great many would escape notice when going the round of the traps and be lost. So we proceed, "spotting" a line through the woods as we go, and placing traps baited with different materials in every convenient nook—in a pile of rocks, in a brush heap, upon logs, under logs, at the entrance to holes, and so on up the hill until we find our stock of traps exhausted. We have set an occasional trap for a mink or sable, some of them being steel traps and some wooden "deadfalls." We have also set on the crest of the ridge some of the larger "climax" and "out-o'-sight" rat traps for chipmunks and squirrels, and in a cedar swamp which we passed through a number of rabbit snares were set on the runways which crossed our line. "But here! what has torn that stump down in that style?" We examine, and see the marks of claws where bruin has been at work searching for grubs. How lucky we brought a bear trap into the woods with us! A bear trap should always be taken on a collecting trip in a locality infested by bears, if only for self-protection, for if a bear once gets the run of a line of traps it will generally be found that bruin has visited the traps just before you. Since our line of mouse traps is all carefully placed, we can not do better than to examine for further signs of the bear. Let's follow down the ridge into that heavy beech growth, as bears are fond of beech nuts, and if he visits this neighbourhood frequently the freshest signs will be found there.

That large beech tree over there seems to have quite a number of nuts still hanging to the twigs; and—yes, see the broken branches hanging down with the dead leaves dried on, where the bear has been feeding! As we near the tree we find the unmistakable marks of bears' claws on the trunk. Further examination of the surrounding trees shows that they, too, have been resorted to by the bears in search of their favourite food. These are evidences enough that this is the bear's feeding ground, and to-morrow we will build a " coop " and try to catch the old rascal. "Hark! what is that snort?" "There it goes again!" That was only a deer. See the marks in the newly fallen leaves where he has been pawing for beech nuts! There goes his trail leading right into that fallen tree-top. He was lying down in there and heard us coming and stole out on the other side without our knowledge, and when at a safe distance snorted at us. Don't try to follow him. Without the aid of a good tracking snow, and in the dry loose leaves, it is of no earthly use. Deer are plentiful, and we shall have no difficulty in securing all we wish.

Deer-hunting.—Let us take a short cut to camp, as it

has taken longer to set our traps than we anticipated, and it is getting well on toward evening. No talking, no cracking of twigs—walk as quietly as possible, and we may get a shot at a deer. See that great owl sitting up in that spruce yonder! Let me kill him. No, it is better not to shoot. We want fresh meat in camp, and do not wish to spoil our chances of getting a deer by startling them with the noise of a gunshot. Suddenly to the left—crash! crash! thump! thump! thump! There he goes, a fine buck. He was lying down in that clump of low spruces and heard our voices and jumped. Here is an old lumber road going in the direction of the lakes, and by following this we will be enabled to walk more silently. Carefully we steal along, avoiding a blow of the moccasined foot against stones or roots, and lifting the feet well over the logs and branches. We stop at intervals to look and listen. Suddenly a slight movement in the bushes ahead catches the eye. There, see that deer's head and neck! He is browsing on the tips of the twigs of that low fir tree. There is a fine shot! The whole head and neck are exposed to view from behind that large spruce, and, though it is a small mark, you are sure of the game if hit. Crack! goes the .44 smokeless cartridge. The deer instantly wheels about in its tracks and faces the direction from which the sound came, riveted to the spot. Did you not see that small fir twig drop just over the deer's neck? You missed as clean as a whistle. Another cartridge is pumped into the barrel instantly, and a bullet, square into the chest, low down, brings the animal to its knees. Don't shoot again; it is unnecessary, and the less the hide is mutilated the better for our purpose. As we rush forward to examine our prize a thumping of hoofs and crashing of brush greet our ears. We were a little too fast. Had we been more cautious we might have obtained a shot at the second deer. Our animal proves to be an old buck. Don't slash his throat to bleed him, as it will ruin the hide for mounting. As he breathes his last, a knife is introduced at the peak of the brisket and the skin neatly cut, in a straight line, along the centre of the belly as far back as the root of the tail. As we need the flesh for food, the belly walls are now cut through and the viscera removed. The liver is cut out for consumption at camp, and since there is no gall sac found in the liver of the *Cervidæ*, we will not bother to cut it out. The animal is rolled over on its belly, the fore parts lifted up, and the blood allowed to drain out from the inside. The inside of the carcass is not washed out, as the meat keeps better if the blood is allowed to dry and crust over it. This incrusting of the blood also allows the blowflies less chance to deposit their eggs in the flesh. As it is now late in the afternoon, we will not stop to measure and skin the carcass, but will hang it up out of the reach of foxes and leave it till morning.

Hanging up a Dead Buck.—With the spotting hatchet three straight poles ten or twelve feet in length are cut, one end crotched, the other roughly sharpened. As we have no heavy twine with us, a piece of white cedar bark is stripped from the trunk of a neighbouring tree and the hind legs lashed firmly together, just above the hock or gambrel joint. The crotched end of one of the poles is introduced between the hind legs just above the thong, and while the hind parts are lifted well into the air the other two poles are placed in position so as to form a tripod of the three, with the deer's carcass hanging from the centre. The bases of the poles, sharpened to prevent their slipping on the ground, are brought closer together one after the other, until the nose of the deer hangs well beyond the reach of foxes or the smaller carnivora. By this means one person may in a short time hang a heavy buck, whereas were he to try to lift the whole carcass and hang it over a projecting limb or stub out of harm's way, it would prove a troublesome job.

As the carcass hangs close by the old logging road, it is unnecessary to further mark the spot in order that we may find it in the morning. As darkness is now fast approaching, we hasten to get out of the woods before it becomes too dark to find our way. At last we come in sight of the lake, and, rather than make a short cut to camp through the woods, we follow the open shore of the lake, where the travelling is better, until camp is reached. There is still light enough left to see to cut firewood, and this is soon done—one chopping while the rest carry the pieces in. A fire is soon going and supper prepared. After eating, wearied with our first day's work in the woods, we soon turn in, and oblivion follows.

Before daybreak we are moving, and as soon as possible are again on the road. We have with us the skinning knives, tape, and notebook to enable us to care for our deer, and an axe, a bear trap, and a quantity of bait to reset our small mammal traps. We have also not forgotten to bring with us a small vial of powdered strychnine. We strike the old lumber road and follow it out to the scene of our labours of the previous evening. A number of Canada jays clear the spot at our approach, and—yes, the foxes and wildcats have also been there and commenced work on the mass of viscera lying upon the ground. Get your shotgun and auxiliary barrel ready, and as the jays come back one by one they may be secured. These are local or resident birds, and, since they are distinctively northern in distribution, a series will be desirable. Here comes one now. He sails in and alights upon a dead stub near by. Good shot! Wipe the blood off the plumage with a fluff of cotton batting, and insert a small plug of cotton in the mouth to keep the fluids of the stomach from running out and soiling the feathers. We have with us, in the back pockets of our hunting coats, a number of sheets of stiff paper. A sheet is rolled into a cone or cornucopia, and the bird dropped in head foremost and settled well into the cone. The top is then folded over so the bird will not drop out, care being used that the fold is not made too low, otherwise the quills of the tail feathers will be bent over and perhaps broken. A number of the birds having thus been secured, we proceed with the buck. He is lowered to the ground, the poles thrown aside, and the cedar lash that bound the hind legs together severed.

Measuring a Deer for Mounting.—Where it is not convenient to make a cast of one side of an animal for future reference, to enable us to mount our deer and construct a properly proportioned manikin upon our return, measurements of the animal in the flesh are taken and the manikin

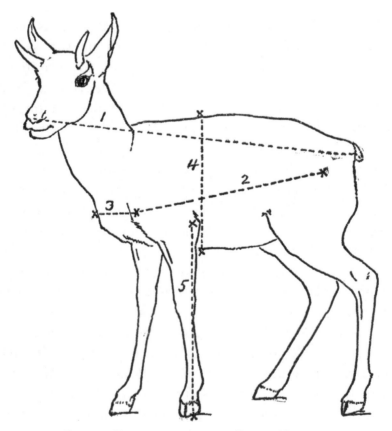

FIG. 2.—MEASUREMENTS OF A LARGE MAMMAL.

built according to them. Measurements are entered in the notebook as made. These are always taken in straight lines, the tape being tightly stretched from one point to the other and not allowed to sag or follow the contour of the body or limbs. The measurements really necessary are but few, and in the case of a deer are the following:

1. *Total Length.*—End of nose to end of tail vertebræ.

2. *Femur to Humerus.*—Head of the femur to head of the humerus, with the humerus resting in the position occupied in standing.

3. *Distance between Humeri.*—Across the chest, from the extreme outsides of the heads of the humeri. Allowance will here be necessary for the slight flattening of the carcass and consequent reduction of space between the humeri by reason of the removal of the viscera. In other cases bloating of the carcass may tend to increase this distance.

4. *Depth of Body.*—This is the distance in a straight line from the top of the back, just behind the shoulder, to the brisket.

5. *Height at Shoulder.*—As this is a measurement which may be made to vary according as the foreleg is pushed up or drawn out, there is but one way out of it. If the centre of the elbow belongs just even with the line of the brisket, place it there. Measure in a straight line from the centre of the elbow to the flat (not the point) of the hoof. This measurement, added to the depth of the body behind the shoulder (No. 4), will give the standing height at the withers. In other species, if the elbow belongs below or above the line of the brisket, measure the distance from the centre of the elbow to the line of the brisket, and add this to or subtract it from, respectively, the sum of the two former measurements.

Colours of the Eye and Places devoid of Hair.—These may be noted by the use of a colour chart—that is, a paper on which are small squares of different colours, each numbered. Ridgway's Nomenclature of Colours,* and Chap-

---

* See page 7, footnote.

man's Handbook of Birds of Eastern North America *
each contain a colour chart and are admirably adapted for
this work. They should be found in the outfit of every
scientific collector.

Skinning a Buck for Mounting.—Having previously
made a cut from the point of the brisket to the anus with
a shoe knife ground down to a point at the end, the cut is
continued backward along the under side of the tail to the
very tip. The next incision is made at the back of the hind
foot and continued up the back of the leg over the centre
of the hock or calcaneum along the top of the large tendon
(*Achilles*) and so on up the back of the leg, keeping the
knife in the centre of the ridge of long hair here, which will
afterward conceal the opening cut when sewed up on the
manikin. When cut up the back of the hind leg to within
about six inches of the central or belly cut, the line of direction goes forward between the hind legs so as to meet the
longitudinal belly cut at a right angle. The other hind leg
is treated similarly. A foreleg is now taken. Starting at
the back of the hoof, as in the hind limb, the opening cut
is continued up the centre of the back of the leg to the
elbow. From here the opening cut runs inside the leg,
following along the centre of the line of the humerus and
meeting the belly cut between the forelegs at a right angle,
as in the case of the opening cut of the hind legs. The
other foreleg is treated likewise. All the necessary body
cuts having been made, we will give the head our attention.
The point of the knife is dug into the thick skin at the
centre of the top of the head, just back of the horns, and an
opening cut made running down the centre of the back of
the neck for about half its length. From the starting point
of this cut on the top of the head two short cuts are made,
each reaching to the base of a horn. The cuts thus made

* Handbook of Birds of Eastern North America. By Frank M.
Chapman. D. Appleton and Company, New York, 1895–1898.

form a Y, the arms terminating at the bases of the horns and
the body extending about halfway down the centre of the
back of the neck. All the opening cuts are now made.

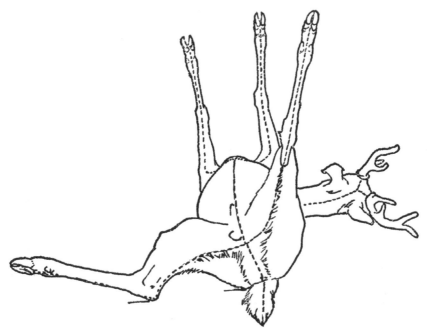

Fig. 3.—Opening Cuts on a Deer.

The skinning of the body is a simple matter. When possible, the skin is peeled off the carcass by pressure with the
fist, and where it refuses to yield the knife is called into
requisition, cutting always as close to the skin as possible,
to avoid leaving fat and chunks of flesh adhering to the
skin. The vertebræ of the tail are completely skinned out
from the sheath of skin, and the feet disjointed from the
leg bones at the junction with the first phalanx. The skinning of the body, limbs, and tail having been completed,
the skin is pulled up about the neck and the neck skinned
up as far as possible from behind. The neck is further
skinned by working with the knife through the opening cut
at the back, and the ears severed close to the skull. The
skin is detached around the base of the horns with the point
of the knife, and the skull separated from the spinal column

at the first vertebra or *atlas*. The body and neck, with the skin removed, is now pulled aside, and the skinning of the head completed. Care is used in skinning around the eyes not to cut the lids. By introducing the fingers of the left hand underneath the skin they serve as a guide in cutting. The skinning is proceeded with as far as the mouth, and the lips severed close to the bone all around, leaving the lips attached to the skin. The head is now skinned with the exception of the nose, which is attached to the skull by the cartilage. This is severed and the skull is freed entirely from the skin. The hoofs are separated by continuing the opening cut at the back down between them, when the two hoofs separate like an opening oyster. The point

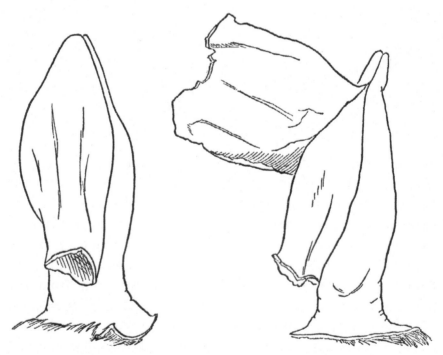

FIG. 4.—SKINNING A DEER'S EAR,   FIG. 5.—SKINNING A DEER'S EAR, THE
     THE EAR INVERTED.   CARTILAGE HALF OUT.

of the knife is worked well down into each hoof, completely encircling the phalanges, in order to admit the salt which is to be put on the skin to cure it after we arrive at camp.

The ears are now skinned from the inside by inverting them. If the ears are not skinned and salted the hair is apt to pull, although this is not always the case. Before mounting, the ears must be skinned and the cartilage removed, and they will never again skin so easily as when fresh. The lips are split from the inside, *not shaved off* entirely from the skin. The nose is also carefully skinned and the surplus flesh and cartilage cut off.

After sponging with water to remove the blood from the hair, the skin is ready to receive the salt. These latter details are left until camp is reached. The entire limb bones are now cut out of the flesh, each limb bone being kept entire with the ligaments attached to the joints. The shoulder blades and pelvis are also roughed out, and with the limb bones made into a compact bundle. As there are three in the party, we naturally make three parcels of the luggage. The skin is rolled up, hair side in, to prevent the hair from being broken and worn in travelling through the woods, and securely tied with a piece of light rope brought along for the purpose. The skull is not mutilated in any way, and, with the horns attached, forms the third parcel. In cleaning the skull the bulk of the muscle is cut away and the lower jaw detached. The brain is removed through the opening at the base of the skull (*foramen magnum*) by means of a small green stick. The stick is splintered on the end and pounded upon a stone till a decided burr is formed. This makes a first-class brain hook. After the bulk of the brain is removed the interior of the skull, or brain cavity, is well rinsed out with water. The lower jaw is tied into place with twine, and the skull after drying is ready for shipment. Should insects attack it a good coating of arsenical soap will check their ravages.

The flesh of the deer desired for camp use is hung up, to be called for at a future day. The balance of the carcass and viscera are well poisoned by sprinkling them with powdered strychnine, and by sifting the powder into gashes cut in the flesh. Chunks of the flesh are also cut off, split, well poisoned, and placed about in convenient places. The contents of the stomach or paunch of the deer are now turned out, some pieces of flesh placed inside the stomach, the whole tied up compactly, and we have a most inviting bait for our bear.

Setting a Bear Trap.—Arrived on the crest of the ridge, in the heavy beech growth, where the bear signs are the most plentiful, we search for a desirable spot to place our bear trap. The upturned roots of a large tree offer special facilities, and we accordingly proceed to gather a number of old stumps and dead limbs, which are placed leaning against the face of the upturned roots in such a way as to make a sort of coop, open only in the front. The deer's paunch, with some scraps of venison inside, is hung on a root in the back of the coop. The bear trap is now set by placing it lengthwise upon the ground alongside of a heavy log. Two stout poles are cut and used as levers to press down the stout springs. The heavy chain which is attached to the trap is made fast to a "clog." This is simply a green, hard-wood stick five or six inches in diameter, with the butts of the lopped branches bristling in all directions. The trap is bolted fast to this clog by means of a clevis. The trap is now placed at the entrance to the coop, and strewn with moss and leaves and made to resemble the surrounding ground. A small dead stick is placed horizontally a little in advance of the trap and slightly elevated, so that the bear, when stepping into the coop for the bait, lifts his foot over the slight obstruction and steps into the trap.

Having set the bear trap, we now proceed toward camp, going backward over the line set the previous day. We find that nearly every trap has been tampered with by mice or other animals. Our first ones—some of the larger "climax" and "out-o'-sight" traps—contain ground squirrels and red squirrels. In our smaller traps we find numbers of small mice and shrews. Some of the more common species which we find mutilated and partially eaten by their associates, we discard. *Save always the first specimen of a kind secured, no matter in what condition it may be, so long as there is enough left to identify it.* A second specimen might not be secured. The traps are reset and rebaited as we go along, and occasionally a bird is met that is desirable as a specimen. These are of course shot when possible.

At last we reach the lake, and, as we suspected, a muskrat is found in our trap here, drowned. The trap is reset. The mink trap remains undisturbed. We again reach camp in the afternoon, and while the cook makes preparations for night, we proceed to care for our specimens.

Curing a Deer Skin.—As formerly directed, the deer skin is thoroughly sponged with water and combed with a steel comb while sponging to remove clots of blood from the hair. The water is wrung out and the skin spread out on the ground, flesh side up. Common table salt is spread evenly over the surface of the skin and well rubbed in with the hand. The ears and feet are well salted, and the skin of the head and neck and limbs folded over on the body skin, flesh to flesh, and the skin rolled up. It is then placed, rolled up, in the fork of a tree, or, in fact, anywhere out of the way where stray dogs or other animals will not molest it, and allowed to remain there till morning. Next day the skin is examined for soft spots, where, by reason of too great thickness, the salt has not struck through. If any such spots are found, they are shaved down from the inside with the shoe knife and the spots again rubbed with salt. The skin is now hung over a convenient limb or tent rope in the shade, and allowed to partially dry out. It is then given a thin coat of arsenical soap all over the inside, to keep bugs out, and again dried out. When nearly dry it is tagged with a lead number corresponding with the number attached to the skull and limb bones, and also with the same number in the notebook. The skin is now rolled up compactly, hair side in, to prevent the hair from being worn in transportation, and tightly corded. If kept dry, the skin will now keep well for an indefinite period in fine shape for mounting. If the skin gets wet it is simply dried out again as before, and re-corded.

We will now proceed to take care of our smaller specimens, the ones that are most apt to spoil being first prepared; these are the shrews and mice. For convenience sake in writing this description we will take as an example one of the ground squirrels (*Tamias*) secured, the mice and shrews all being prepared in precisely the same manner.

Making a Small Mammal Skin for Study.—The tools and materials necessary to prepare skins of small mammals are the following:

A millimetre rule, or, in default of this, an ordinary two-foot rule, a small scalpel, a pair of small scissors with sharp points, a small scraper (Fig. 15, Plate IV), pins, a pair of six-inch forceps, needle and thread (No. 60), notebook and pencil, labels, annealed brass wire for tails, a soft toothbrush, corn meal—kiln-dried meal is preferred—arsenic and alum (dry, in equal parts), and cotton batting.

MEASUREMENTS.

But three measurements are necessary, these being made as follows:

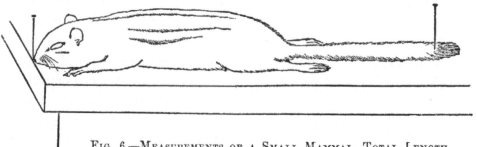

FIG. 6.—MEASUREMENTS OF A SMALL MAMMAL, TOTAL LENGTH.

Total Length.—The specimen is laid upon the table, resting flat upon its belly, and straightened out. A pin is driven into the table just at the tip of the nose, and another at the tip of the tail vertebræ (not the ends of the hairs). The carcass is pushed aside and the distance between the two pins measured in a straight line.

Length of Tail.—The body is allowed to hang over the edge of the table, with the base of the back of the tail at the upper corner or edge of the table. The back of the tail

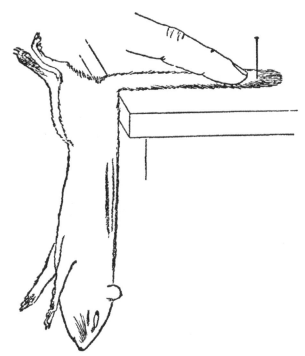

FIG. 7.—MEASUREMENTS OF A SMALL MAMMAL, LENGTH OF TAIL.

lies flat along the top of the table, and is pulled slightly to get the upper edge of the table to fit snugly to the body of the specimen where the tail joins. A pin is driven into the table at the end of the tail vertebræ, and the distance measured from the pin to the edge of the table.

Hind Foot.—This is the distance from the heel or end of the *calcaneum* to the tip of the longest claw. The foot is bent at a right angle and held just at the edge of the table, the foot flattened out, and a pin driven into the table at the point of the longest claw. A pencil mark may be used instead of the pin. This distance is measured as before. Compasses may be used instead of the pins, if desired.

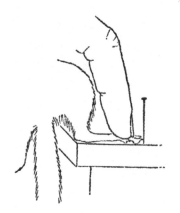

Individual collectors have their own pet methods for measuring and making up bird and small mammal skins, but the results obtained are the same. These measurements, with the sex, date, and locality, are all recorded in the notebook and numbered 1, No. 1 being afterward written on tags and attached to the skin and skull. The next specimen would of course

FIG. 8.—MEASUREMENTS OF A SMALL MAMMAL, LENGTH OF HIND FOOT.

be No. 2, and so on.

Skinning. — With the small scalpel an opening cut is made in the skin at the centre of the abdomen, reaching back to the root of the tail, care being used not to cut through into the abdominal cavity.

With the thumbs the skin at the sides of the cut is pushed aside and detached from the flesh of the abdomen. Corn meal is now applied liberally to absorb the moisture. When the skin has been loosened from the body sufficiently, so that the upper part of the hind leg is exposed to view from within, the hind leg is detached from the body as close to the pelvis as possible, using the scissors for this cut. Corn meal is thrown on the spot at once, as the blood runs freely if the specimen is fresh. The other hind leg is treated similarly. The flesh about the base of the tail is cut away with the scalpel and the root of the tail exposed to view. The skin of the base of the tail is seized with the thumb and finger of one hand, and the vertebræ, attached to the body, gripped with the other hand. By pulling and coaxing, the tail vertebræ slip out of the skin or sheath of the tail.

The skin is now inverted over the body, and the body is skinned easily until the shoulders are reached. These are cut, as in the case of the hind legs, as close to the body as possible (at the junction of the humerus with the scapula), using the scissors as before.

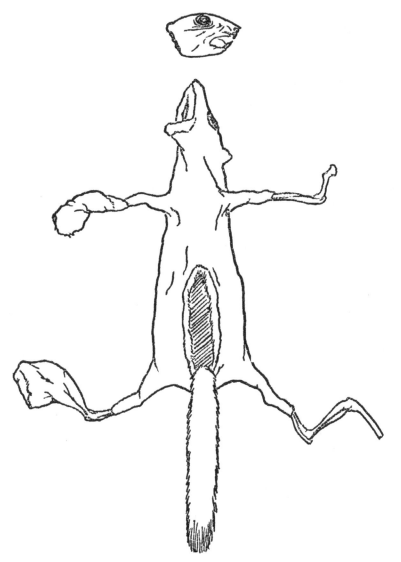

Fig. 9.—Skinning a Chipmunk, the Skin inside out.

The skin again peels off easily until the bases of the ears are reached. These are severed with the knife close to the skull, and the eyes are soon reached. Care is required to avoid cutting the lids, but a little practice will enable the operator to accomplish this successfully.

The lips are severed close to the bone, and the skull is entirely detached from the skin.

The skin of the legs is now inverted over the flesh and these members skinned down to the toes. The flesh is cut away from the limb bones, but the bones themselves are left intact and not disarticulated.

Making up a Small Mammal Skin.—When the limb bones are all thoroughly cleaned of flesh, the whole inside of the skin is well dusted with powdered alum and arsenic, dry, in equal parts, being applied with a bristle brush or a fluff of cotton batting. Cotton batting is wrapped about the limb bones to replace the muscle, and the legs are turned right side out. No wires in the legs are necessary in this case. The hair is now examined for blood spots. If any exist, the blood is sponged off with water and the hair dried off with corn meal. The meal is thrown on the wet hair and the part well beaten and brushed with the tooth-brush. The meal works quicker and absorbs more readily if heated. More dry meal is heaped upon the skin, and the beating and brushing continued until the fur is perfectly dry and fluffy. Hot sand will answer, if meal is not at hand.

A stitch is now taken at the nose to draw the front of the lips together and keep the mouth closed. A piece of soft brass wire is cut long enough to reach from the tip of the tail to a third of the way up into the body. A little cotton batting is wound around the wire, tapering, making the artificial tail assume somewhat the shape of the natural tail, which has been withdrawn. The wire with the cotton wrapped upon it is swabbed over with a wad of wet cotton and the dry preservative dusted over it, enough of the preservative hanging fast to the wet cotton to thoroughly poison the tail.

The artificial tail is worked down into the sheath of

the tail clear to the tip. It is absolutely necessary that the point of the wire shall go *clear* to the tip of the tail skin; otherwise, when dry, the tip of the tail is apt to be broken off in handling. If the wire itself is too large to admit of entering the extreme tip of the tail sheath, the end of the wire must be tapered off with a file.

The legs having been filled and turned right side out and the tail wire inserted, nothing now remains but to fill the body skin. This is best done with a roll of cotton batting or fine long-fibred tow. If wads or pads of cotton or tow are pushed in one after the other, a lumpy exterior will result, which roughness will be intensified as the specimen dries. A roll of cotton or tow of about the length and girth of the head and body is formed and grasped firmly with the large forceps, grasping the roll lengthwise, with the points well up toward the end of the roll.

The roll is inserted into the skin of the body and forced well up into the head, keeping the filling tightly squeezed with the forceps until the head skin and limbs are properly arranged upon the roll. The forceps are then withdrawn, when the cotton fluffs out, filling the interior of the skin fully and evenly.

The proximal ends of the bones of the hind legs and the tail wire should rest upon the upper or belly side of the filling, and a small flat pad of cotton covered over them to keep them from coming in contact with the skin. The opening along the belly is now neatly sewed up and brushed lengthwise with the toothbrush.

The skin is turned right side up and made to conform in length with the carcass which lies upon the table. The skin, if too full, is also compressed. The front paws are made to lie side by side along the sides of the head, and the hind limbs are drawn out behind so as to lie alongside the tail, which projects straight behind. The hair is slightly brushed with the toothbrush to render it smooth and to keep the colour pattern. A tag with the number written upon it is attached to a hind leg, and the specimen pinned down into a tray from the collecting can by driving a pin down through each foot into the soft pine bottom, the soles of the feet resting flat upon the wood, with the toes spread.

The skull is twisted off the neck vertebræ and the brain removed through the occipital opening or spinal orifice without in any way injuring the bones of the skull. A small stick is better than a wire for this purpose, and a small syringe and water may be used to advantage. The bulk of the muscle is cut away from the skull, but not so close as to scrape and injure the processes. Skulls of very small mammals, such as mice and shrews, are better not cleaned at all. The brain may even be left to dry in, as in removing it the small bones of the base of the skull are liable to injury. A tag is now attached to the skull and numbered, and the skull simply allowed to dry, when it is placed in a small box kept for this purpose. When the specimen is thoroughly dried, the pins are removed from the feet, and the skin is ready to be packed and shipped.

Fig. 10.—Chipmunk Skin, completed.

Mammals larger than a gray squirrel are better salted and dried flat. These may be relaxed and made up afterward in the laboratory.

Being constructed somewhat differently, bats require different treatment. The measurements to be made are the same as for other mammals, with the additional measurement of extent of wings. This is the greatest spread from tip to tip of the extended wings. The opening cut is always made along the back, instead of on the belly. The skinning and filling is done in the same general way as with the ground squirrel. In pinning the specimen out to dry, the bat lies upon its back, with the wings nearly closed, the pins entering at the joints. If the wings are extended they are liable to be broken off in handling when dry.

We will now proceed to make up the skin of a blue jay secured while visiting the traps. The same set of materials used in preparing the ground squirrel will answer for the jay.

Making a Bird Skin.—The colours of the eye, bill, and legs are carefully recorded, in order that these parts may be properly rendered when the specimen is mounted at some future day. No measurements are necessary. The jay is laid upon the table, belly up. With the scalpel a straight cut is made through the skin of the abdomen, reaching from the posterior end of the breastbone to the anus, care being used that the point of the knife does not cut through the belly walls into the abdominal cavity and release the intestinal fluids, which will run over and disfigure the feathers.

The skin at the sides of the cut is loosened from the flesh, using the finger nails or the end of the scalpel handle for this purpose. The skin is separated from the sides of the body until the knee joint is exposed to view. The leg, inside of the skin, is disarticulated at the knee joint by cutting through it with the scissors. The other leg is treated similarly. Corn meal is liberally applied all through the process of skinning to absorb the blood and juices that flow, and which otherwise would soil the feathers. The vertebræ at the base of the tail are cut through with the scissors, care being used not to cut so close to the tail feathers as to sever their bases, or they will drop out. The skin is now inverted over the body, and the skin of the back worked carefully to prevent its tearing. After this the skin peels off easily until the butts of the wings are reached. The wing bones are severed close to the body, the scissors being stout enough for this purpose in a bird of this size. In larger birds the bone snips are used. The skin again peels off easily over the neck until the base of the skull is reached. By gentle manipulation, and pulling the skin by pressing it against the skull with the thumb and fingers and drawing forward at the same time, the base of the skull is gradually forced through the skin of the neck, until the ears are reached. The skin of the ears is deeply rooted into the cavity of the skull at this point. With the forceps, the skin is picked up and pulled out of the cavity. This is much better than cutting through the skin at this point. The eyes are next reached. Great care is here necessary to avoid cutting the lids, or cutting too deep with the point of the scalpel and puncturing the eyeball. The eyeball is covered with a thin bluish-coloured membrane. This membrane is cut in two, exposing the eyeball in the socket. The other eye is of course treated similarly. The skull is now skinned right on to the base of the bill.

With the scalpel the base of the skull is cut completely through, laterally, severing the skull from the vertebræ and exposing the brain. The tongue is now drawn out.

With the points of the scissors a V-shaped cut is made on the under side of the skull, or roof of the mouth, the sides of the V running parallel with the inner sides of the mandibles, and the cuts reaching deep into the brain cavity. Another cut is made with the scissors across the apex of the V and the V-shaped piece of bone drawn out, bringing with it a mass of brain and muscle. These cuts are quickly made, three sharp strokes of the scissors being all that are necessary.

The balance of the brain is now picked out of the skull

with the point of the scalpel, and the eyes, if they have not come out with the V-shaped mass, as they sometimes do, are easily picked out of their sockets. The bulk of the remaining muscle upon the skull is scraped off, and corn meal applied to keep the moist skull from sticking to the feathers.

The flesh surrounding the remaining leg bones is removed by inverting the skin over the leg and cutting away the flesh with scissors and scalpel.

The base of the tail is well cleaned of flesh, especial care being used to remove the oil sac at the top of the root of the tail.

The wings are now cleaned by peeling the skin over the bones from the inside as far back as the elbow joint, and removing the flesh. The secondaries should never be stripped from the bone under any circumstances. This trick of cleaning a bird's wing by stripping down the secondaries, to save time, and removing all the bones in sight save the *ulna*, is much practised by professional collectors who know that they will never be called upon to mount their skins. The muscles of the forearm in small birds can be removed from the inside without any difficulty. In large birds an opening is made inside the wing, lengthwise of the bones, and afterward sewed up.

The wings having been well cleaned, the skinning process is completed, provided no fat adheres to the inside of the skin. Should any fat exist, it must be scraped off with a large scraper, liberal quantities of dry corn meal being used during the scraping process to absorb the oil.

The skin, wrong side out, is now well dusted all over the inside with dry alum and arsenic applied with a fluff of cotton batting or a bristle brush. A wad of cotton batting is forced into the eye sockets, the cotton being pushed in through the opening at the base of the skull with the forceps and packed against the finger, which is pressed against the outside of the eye socket. This method of filling the eye sockets is much better than to fill the socket from the outside.

The skin of the head is now worked back over the skull until right side out again. As the feathers of the head are

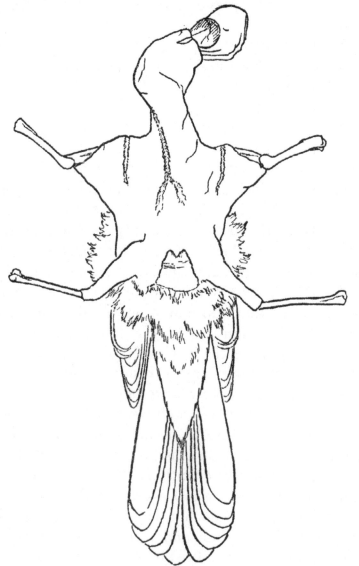

Fig. 11.—Skinning a Bluejay. The Skin inside out, Ready to be Poisoned.

apt to be more or less ruffled, a knitting needle or piece of stiff wire is introduced through the eyelids and worked upon the skull, between the skin and bone, thus lifting up the feathers and ádjusting them properly. The skin is now blown with the breath the way of the feathers to settle them into place, and also to remove any loose meal or poison that may be on the outsides of the feathers.

If any blood stains show on the feathers, they must be removed by sponging with lukewarm water and drying the feathers again with corn meal. The meal is heaped upon the wet feathers and beaten and pounded with a toothbrush, more meal being applied and the beating continued until the feathers have again resumed their fluffiness. This is a slow and laborious process, and is only used in the field, where all the appliances necessary for quickly and perfectly cleaning plumage are not available. Directions for this will be found in a succeeding chapter. Should the shafts of any of the wing or tail feathers be bent, if the bent feathers are held in a jet of steam for a few seconds they will straighten out perfectly, so long as the shaft is not actually broken.

A fluff of cotton batting is wound around the leg bone, and the leg turned right side out.

The distal ends of the humeri are brought about as close together inside the skin as they would be in life when the wings are closed, and tied together with a thread.

A fluff of cotton batting is now wound about the end of the knitting needle or stiff wire, the extreme tip being made small and pointed, and the balance of the wad being shaped by pressure to imitate roughly the body and neck of the bird.

The end of the wire with the cotton upon it is now worked up inside the neck through the opening in the body skin until the point of the wire is driven firmly up into the throat and wedged between the mandibles. The body skin is worked forward to reduce the length of the neck, and the skin held up on the wire and the wings adjusted. The skin is now laid upon its back and the wire withdrawn, leaving the cotton filling, all in one piece, reaching from between the mandibles to the base of the tail. Wooden toothpicks are used by some collectors in place of the wire, the toothpick being left in the skin. If too much cotton has been rolled up, a portion may be subtracted. If more filling is required, more cotton may of course be added. The skin should be well filled out and rendered plump,

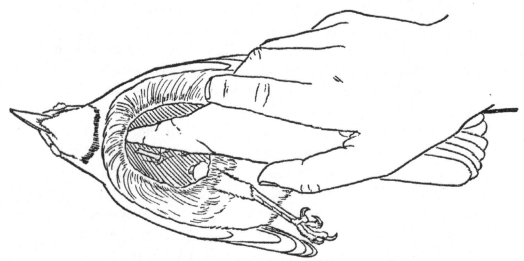

FIG. 12.—" MAKING UP " A JAY'S SKIN. PUTTING IN THE FILLING.

when the opening in the skin is sewed up with a few stitches. A hard wound body should never be introduced into a bird skin that is intended to remain in the shape of a skin, as, if it is ever necessary to mount the specimen, it is a difficult task to remove the filling.

If cotton is not at hand for filling, tow, excelsior, or any dry, fibrous vegetable matter may be used. Animal products, such as hair or wool, are better avoided.

Should the mandibles show a disposition to open, a stitch may be taken through the nostril and the thread tied together underneath the bill. A pin is sometimes used for this purpose.

The legs are crossed and lie flat upon the tail, which is slightly spread.

A label bearing the number of the specimen is now attached to the legs at their point of crossing and the skin is ready for wrapping.

COLLECTING.

A sheet of cotton batting (of as long fibre as is available, Dennison's absorbent cotton being the best) is split by carefully drawing it apart until a thin sheet of cotton is obtained large enough to envelop the skin. The feathers of the breast are neatly arranged by lifting them up in bunches with the thumb and finger and allowing them to drop back into position. The bird skin is now laid, breast down, upon the centre of the sheet of cotton, and the wings and feathers of the back and tail arranged. The cotton projecting beyond the bill is brought up over and laid down upon the head. The cotton at one side is served in the same way, and then the other side is drawn up and allowed to overlap on the other side. In this way the bird skin is neatly enveloped in a thin sheet of cotton, through which the shape of the skin can be perfected. This is by far the best method of wrapping bird skins of this size. For large birds a sheet of stiff paper is used, the skin being laid upon its back upon the centre of the sheet, and the sides brought up over the breast and pinned together, thus keeping the wings in place while drying. A piece of cheese cloth or burlaps answers even better than paper, as paper materially retards the drying out of the skin.

The skin is now laid away to dry, resting upon its back in one of the wooden trays from the collecting can.

The sex of the bird is determined by cutting with the scalpel through the ribs of one side in order to expose to view the inside of the " small of the back."

If a male, two round, whitish-coloured bodies (whitish in most birds) will be found bound in close to the bone. If a female, a mass of small, whitish-coloured matter, the ovaries, or in the breeding season the immature eggs themselves, will be found in the same situation.

Among naturalists the sign of the planet Mars (♂) is used to designate a male, while the sign of Venus (♀) answers for the female.

The sex, date, locality, colours, and any further notes

4

desired, are now written in the notebook, these data corresponding with the number written on the label affixed to the bird's legs. The label should always be firmly tied on a specimen, and not loosely attached with a flimsy half-hitch, ready to drop off at any moment.

FIG. 13.—JAY'S SKIN COMPLETED.

Calling a Woodpecker.—While at work on the jay a loud, cackling note is heard, which we at once recognise as that of the pileated woodpecker. Just what we want, as his head must be skinned by a different process from that used in preparing the jay. " Get the shotgun and a No. 8 shot-shell. He is a strong bird, and will require to be hit pretty hard. Come, let's get in good range of that dead stub, conceal ourselves well in the bushes, and call him up." By clapping with the hands in imitation of the noise produced by a woodpecker at work on a hollow stub, we at once arouse his curiosity. He calls louder than ever. The clapping is continued, and again the bird calls, this time much nearer. " Now, look out—he will soon sail in! " The irresistible clapping is still continued, and at last we catch a glimpse of a black and white streak passing through the trees, and before we are hardly aware of it he dips in and alights upon the dead stub we had selected for him. He at once starts his call-note, but it is cut short by the roar of the gun, and the grand bird falls fluttering to the ground.*

---

* This method of calling woodpeckers was suggested to me by Mr. Frank M. Chapman, Assistant Curator of the Department of Vertebrate Zoölogy in the American Museum, and, if properly executed, will almost invariably call up not only the pileated woodpecker, but other species of woodpeckers as well.

COLLECTING.

Examine the large head and small neck, and it will at once be seen that the skull is much too large to be forced through the neck in skinning without tearing the skin. Therefore an opening is made with the scalpel along the centre of the top of the head, reaching back a little past the base of the skull. The skin is worked loose on top of the skull with the end of the scalpel handle, the skull disjointed at the base and cleaned as in the case of the jay. After poisoning and filling, the edges of the opening are brought together with needle and thread, and the feathers adjusted. The wings, too, being larger than the jay's, require different treatment. Instead of cleaning from the inside by peeling the skin loose from the front of the bone of the forearm, a longitudinal opening is made on the under side of the wing from the first to the second joints, and the sinews and muscles removed. The inside of the wing is then thoroughly poisoned with alum and arsenic, a little cotton or tow spread over the bones, and the edges of the opening brought together with stitches. In other respects the bird is treated precisely the same as the jay.

Ducks and other water birds are better opened along the back instead of on the belly, as it is often difficult to make the breast feathers meet over the cut and properly conceal it.

After Beavers.

The next morning we decide to split up our party and divide the scene of our labours. While one goes out on the old lumber road and brings in a quarter or two of the venison and afterward goes over the line of mouse traps, the other two members of the party take a rifle and a batch of heavy double-spring traps, jump into the canoe, and go on a cruise for beaver, the signs of which were found on the shore of the lake the first day. We will follow the canoe.

We shall of course be compelled to do more or less

PLATE II.

AT WORK IN THE WOODS.

hunting to find the beaver dam, if one exists, which we are by no means sure of.

Beaver, when much molested, will discard the old-time way of living, and will simply dig a burrow in the bank like a muskrat, and continue their existence there.

The canoe proceeds to the head of the lake, where a stream puts in. There is also a long "dead-water," as it is called; that is, the stream gradually widens out on approaching the lake, flowing through flat, boggy ground, and becomes so sluggish finally that it is difficult to tell where the stream ends and the lake begins. A tributary of the main stream comes in here, and we decide to follow this up. As we paddle silently along, a small white stick is noticed floating upon the water, and upon examination proves to have been freshly cut and peeled by a beaver. As we push up the stream we notice more of these peeled sticks, and conclude that we are on the right track. As we turn a bend in the stream we come fairly into view of an old beaver house that has been reconstructed for the coming winter. We at once paddle to it. The fresh supply of branches brought together by the beavers for food, and other signs, are evidence that the beavers are living here, and we noiselessly proceed to lay our plans for their capture. Going off to a safe distance from the beaver house, in order that we may not disturb the inmates, a green spruce sapling is cut, small enough at the base to allow the ring at the end of the trap chain to slide easily back and forth.

The branches, except the ones at the top, are cut off smoothly, and the butt end of the pole split and wedged so that the ring encircling the pole can not be forced over. We then paddle over silently to the beaver house, and, having selected a landing place used by the beavers in climbing upon the bank, with a sloping bottom running off into deep water, we shove the end of the pole out into the deep water and allow the top to rest against the bank at an acute angle.

COLLECTING.

The trap, already set, is placed under the water, just in front of the landing place, where the beaver in going ashore is likely to touch the pan and be caught by a hind foot.

As soon as he finds himself caught the beaver will at once make for deep water, and, in floundering about in his struggles to escape, the ring on the end of the chain gradually slides down the pole, and soon the beaver is unable to come to the surface of the water to breathe, and drowns. We retire as noiselessly as we came, without having stepped out of the canoe and in no way having disturbed the beavers.

We follow up the main stream, and, although we find moose and caribou signs plentiful, there are no further signs of beaver. We proceed down the lake to camp, and find the third member of our party at work on the small specimens he secured during the day.

A couple of days are now spent in collecting specimens of both birds and small mammals. The line of traps is gone over daily—sometimes twice—the game secured, and the traps rebaited. Birds are shot and made into skins, and notes on habits, etc., entered in the diary.

At last we find ourselves on the road to the bear trap, fully equipped to skin and cut him up. But as we near the coop we find the clog undisturbed, and at once know that bruin has fooled us. Ah, the sly rascal! See how he has torn a hole in the side of the coop and stolen the bait without entering from the front! The coop is not disturbed by us. We simply shift the trap around to the opening made by the bear and rebait the coop and retire.

The balance of the day is spent in collecting. A number of deer are seen, but none secured. On the road to camp, as we near the spot where our buck was dissected, we search the ground and are rewarded by finding a fine red fox and some Canada jays that have succumbed to our strychnine. The next morning we conclude to visit the beaver trap, and all get into the canoe and paddle silently up the lake. As we near the beaver house we see the bank has been scratched and worn in the vicinity of our trap, and know at once that our beaver has been caught. Yes, the trap is gone from its position, and as we look down into the clear water we see the beaver, completely submerged, drowned.

We lift him into the canoe, dripping with water, loosen the trap from his hind foot, and reset the trap and paddle off, congratulating ourselves upon our success.

We again resolve to paddle up the main " dead-water " to look for moose or caribou, and, with guns ready, silently we glide around the numerous crooks and turns of the stream. Fresh signs of moose are plentiful, but we reach the head of canoe navigation without a sight of any game. As the canoe grates upon the gravelly bottom of a sand bar and finally comes to a dead stop, we involuntarily listen. We have about made up our minds to return to camp, when a steady splash ! splash ! is heard, as of some large animal walking in the water. Our ears catch the direction, and we look, eagerly expecting the animal to come in sight around the bend of the stream. The splashing continues, and, to our surprise, an enormous bull moose comes in sight, the water dripping from his ill-shaped nose and mouth, and a long piece of pond-lily root dangling down, upon one end of which he is chewing.

As the animal comes in sight he stops, pricks up his ears, and looks intently in our direction.

As the wind is drawing slowly toward the animal, we do not hesitate to shoot. We draw the sights low down on his shoulder and press the trigger. As the reports of the smooth bore and rifle ring out simultaneously, the bull makes a great leap and disappears into the bushes that fringe the stream.

We hasten to the spot and find the tracks in the soft moss. We follow them for a short distance and are finally rewarded by a sight of blood upon the leaves. As we proceed, the trail of blood is more easily followed, and here, where the poor beast stood still for a short time, there is quite a pool of clotted blood.

Evidently the animal is badly hurt, and we resolve to return to the canoe and skin our beaver, and leave the moose to succumb to his wounds, rather than to follow too hastily and again start him while he has sufficient strength to run.

Skinning a Beaver.—As we have neglected to bring our tape with us, a straight branch is cut, one side is flattened with the knife, and the measurements—the same as those taken for the deer—marked off on the flattened and whitened side of the stick, and the stick placed in the canoe. When camp is reached we will measure and record the measurements from the stick.

As the beaver is to be mounted in the same manner as the ground squirrel—that is, by soft filling—it is skinned in practically the same manner, a description of which has already been given. The feet, being larger, are split underneath, on the sole of the foot from the junction of the middle toe to the centre of the *calcaneum*, or heel, in the hind foot, and from the middle toe to a short distance beyond the wrist in the forefeet.

The feet are skinned down to the toe nails by inverting the skin over the toes and cutting and pulling alternately until the nail is reached, the webs between the toes being separated or split during the process. The tail is also split with the knife down the centre, on the under side, in its entire length, in order to properly clean it, as the tail can not be stripped as in the squirrel. The ears and lips are treated precisely as in the buck. When camp is reached, the skin, after having been salted and rolled up over night, will require to be scraped inside with the skin scraper to remove the fat, when the skin is again salted and rolled up and left for another day. The skin is then shaken out, painted on the flesh side with arsenical soap, partially dried, as in the deer skin, and finally rolled up and tied tightly with twine. The skin and skull are then tagged, and are ready to ship.

TRAILING A MOOSE.

The skinning of the beaver having occupied some time, we now proceed to take up the trail of the wounded moose.

There is the spot where we stopped following the tracks and trail of blood. Although the moss has fluffed out some in the tracks, and as a consequence these are not so distinct as at first, still, with the aid of the blood spots, we have no difficulty in keeping on the right track. Here is a spot where the moose lay down to rest for a time, until the pain from the wounds became too severe. And see this great pool of clotted blood in the centre of the bed! See where he crashed through that pile of brush instead of going around it! The spots of blood on the trail are now less and less frequent, the blood having probably clotted and dried over the wound and prevented its flow. As we continue to follow on the trail a strange odour suddenly smites our nostrils, and we at once know that we are close to the animal.

Bull moose at this season have a strong odour, and if the wind is right this may be detected for quite a distance. We now proceed cautiously, with guns cocked and ready, expecting the moose to jump at every step. There he lies beside that moss-covered log. A closer inspection assures us that another shot is unnecessary, as the beast lies prone upon his side, dead.

As the fact dawns upon us that this huge beast is really ours, the forest echoes with our yells of delight.

And what a mighty pair of antlers!—and all secured through the blindest luck.

We sit down upon a log and congratulate ourselves upon our phenomenal luck.

An inspection of the wounds proves that the round ball from the shotgun did the work. The .44–40 rifle ball simply struck the centre of the humerus, glanced, and came out at the chest, making only a flesh wound. The round ball, aimed a trifle too high, had passed through the lungs and out the other side, going clear through the body. Had the ball gone a trifle lower, death would have been almost instantaneous.

Skinning a Bull Moose.—As this is by far too valuable a skin to leave in the woods all night at the mercy of bears and other carnivorous animals, we at once proceed to skin the moose.

A straight road is " spotted " back to the canoe by one member of the party, to facilitate carrying out the hide, while the other members proceed with the skinning.

Measurements are taken as in the buck, the same opening cuts made, and the body and limbs skinned out. The neck is skinned in the usual way and disjointed where it joins the skull, as in the case of the buck. We will not skin the head until we arrive at camp, as we wish to make some photographs and a cast of the nose, to assist us in modelling the nose on the manikin when we return to the laboratory.

The skin, with the enormous skull and horns attached, is tightly rolled up and lashed to the centre of a stout pole. The carcass is disembowelled and left until the next day, when some of our party return and rough out the limb bones, pelvis, and shoulder blades, and take such portions of the flesh as are required for camp use.

When ready to proceed to the canoe, the ends of the pole are lifted upon the shoulders of two of the party, and we start off. Our progress is slow owing to the great weight of the skin and skull and the great spread of the antlers, which persist in catching and becoming snagged in every possible way in the brush.

Frequent rests are taken and many pet names indulged in while on the way to the " dead-water." But as the work must be done, and as we understood before starting on our trip that much drudgery and hardship must be endured, we grit our teeth and proceed. At last, with a feeling of relief, we reach the water and deposit our load in the centre of the canoe and start for camp, where we arrive long after darkness has set in.

Casting a Moose Nose.—The next morning we proceed to take a cast in plaster of the moose nose.

A rude table is constructed and the moose head placed upon it, and a number of photographs taken from different points of view. The head is then turned over on its side upon a bed of moss placed on the table and secured with ropes to steady it.

Some of the tallow of the animal is melted in a small frying pan and applied to the hair of the upper part of the nose with the hand, and the hair smoothed down in order to keep the plaster from sticking to and pulling it out.

Clay will answer for this purpose, but tallow is better, as when cool it holds the hairs down wherever placed, and the plaster also draws more freely from tallow than from clay. When the nose, back as far as the eyes, has been thoroughly greased over the upper half, damp sand from the beach is gathered and, with a shoe knife, laid on the moss around the nose, care being used to build up the sand so as not to leave more than a lateral half of the nose above the sand.

When the sand is built up and smoothed down around the whole nose, a wall of sand about half an inch in height is built up, running across and over the face just in front of the eye, to prevent the plaster from running upon the ungreased hair and taking in more surface than we wish.

The dish-pan is now called into requisition, a bucket of water brought from the lake, and a tin drinking cup borrowed from the camp kit.

Water is poured into the dish-pan to the depth of about an inch, and dry plaster—taken from the Agassiz tank with the screw top, where it has kept perfectly dry—sprinkled in until it rises in a cone about an inch high above the surface of the water. With the hand the plaster is now thoroughly mixed, and should be of about the consistence of thin cream. With the drinking cup the liquid plaster is ladled out and poured over the greased surface of the nose, blowing stoutly with the breath in order to destroy all " bridges " or bubbles that may form. When all covered with a thin layer of plaster, this is allowed to harden before applying more, as a thick layer of soft plaster is apt by its weight to sag and press the nose out of shape. What little plaster remains in the dish-pan is thrown away and another batch mixed up thicker than before, with a pinch of salt thrown in to make it set more rapidly.

This batch is laid on the first coating evenly all over to the depth of half an inch, and is allowed to remain until set. When setting, plaster heats up. This is allowed to occur, and then the whole head is turned upside down upon the table without disturbing or removing the half mould from the nose.

When the head is properly adjusted, and the shell of plaster, now on the under side of the nose, lies well embedded in the moss so that it will not break, the sand is brushed away from the edges of the mould, and the edges shaved and worked down smooth with the knife.

A few holes are cut with the knife on the upper surface of the edges of the mould, large enough to admit the end of the thumb, to act as " keys " for the projecting knobs of the other half of the mould, when completed, to set in.

The sand is carefully brushed from the hair on the upper or exposed half of the nose, and the hair well greased with hot tallow as before, this time greasing the edges of the mould as well, to prevent the two halves of the mould from sticking.

A wall of sand is built as before, running across the face in front of the eye, the ends of the wall terminating on the edges of the plaster half mould already on. A quantity of plaster is mixed as before, sufficient to cover the remaining half of the nose with a thin layer, and the plaster thrown on and blown as before.

When sufficiently set, another layer of about half an inch is added as before.

When the plaster has set and cooled off, the head, with the moulds in position on the nose, is lifted down upon the ground and allowed to rest upon the backs of the antlers with the nose in the air.

The edges of the moulds are trimmed with a knife until the seam where the two halves of the mould join is plainly visible all around.

The mould is gently tapped all over with a stick of wood until the moulds show a disposition to loosen, when they are pried apart with wooden wedges, the nostrils being flexible enough to allow the plaster to draw away from the cavity of the nose.

The two half moulds, when joined together, form a perfect mould or reverse of the moose's nose. If we were short of plaster the moulds would be allowed to dry and then be tied up and packed in moss to prevent breakage, and taken to the laboratory and the cast made there.

But as we have used our plaster economically and still have left a sufficient quantity, we will proceed to run out the cast. All particles of dirt are dusted out, and the whole inside of the mould oiled thinly with the hot tallow. If we wished a very fine impression a thinner oil would be necessary—one that would not harden and fill up detail. But for this purpose tallow does very nicely.

The two halves of the mould are adjusted and tied firmly by wrapping them about with twine, a small quantity of plaster is mixed, the whole poured into the mould, and the mould rocked about in all directions so that the liquid plaster is distributed about evenly over every portion of the interior, wave upon wave. This thin coating is allowed to set, and, when hard enough to work on, another batch of plaster is mixed and wisps of tow, submerged and

PLATE III.

CASTING A MOOSE'S NOSE.

saturated with the liquid plaster, lined up inside the mould evenly all over to the depth of half an inch. If tow can not be procured, cotton batting, or a hemp rope chopped up with a hatchet, will answer. The whole is now set aside and allowed to harden up before we again commence work upon it.

As we have no mallet, the spotting hatchet is made to take its place. A pointed shoe knife is used as a chisel, and the outside layer of plaster chipped away. This, thanks to the greasing of the mould, comes off in great chunks and is soon cut entirely away, and we have as a result a complete counterpart in form of our moose nose.

The cast, being hollow and lined with tow, is light and strong—very much better than if we had run the mould solid full of plaster and allowed it to set. We now have a perfect model to be used in reconstructing the nose when we mount our specimen upon our return to the laboratory.

The cast is placed in the sun to dry, and afterward well packed in moss to prevent breakage in transportation.

Our attention is now given to the skinning of the head and feet and the salting of the skin. This is all done in precisely the same way as in the deer, which has already been given. Especial care is, however, given to the skinning of the nose. All the flesh and cartilage is shaved away from inside, nothing save the lips and the skin of the nostrils remaining on the skin.

TRAPPING A BEAR.

We now proceed to look after our bear trap. Once more we find ourselves on the old lumber road, and pass the spot where the buck met his death. The ground for some distance around is searched for animals that may have been poisoned with our strychnine. With the exception of a sable and a few more jays, nothing further is found to reward us. Undoubtedly other specimens have succumbed to our poison and wandered off and died, never to be found.

In due time we come in sight of the bear coop, and at once notice that the clog is missing. Aha, old fellow, we have been too cunning for you! Having eaten the first bait, the bear could not resist the temptation to again inspect the coop and see if perchance another dainty morsel awaited him. Having been so successful in stealing the first bait through the hole torn in the side of the coop, the second bait must come out the same way. But that is where bruin made a mistake, and as a result found his left hind foot clasped in the toothed jaws of the iron trap. The bait still remains intact, and trap and clog are gone, but where? No signs are to be seen in any direction, and we start and circle, widening the circle as we go. Ah! here are his claw marks on this young spruce, and there the lower branches are clawed and broken by the bear. Here, farther on, is where the bear climbed a small fir and cleaned the branches and bark off for a distance of twenty feet from the ground.

The trail leads on, the marks of the trailing clog becoming more plainly visible as we proceed. Here the bear became entangled in this brush heap, and, after reducing the mass to kindling wood, freed the trap and clog from the entanglement, and proceeded. We now move on cautiously, making as little noise as possible, and finally come in sight of a ball of black fur, partially hidden between the limbs of a mass of fallen timber. As we draw nearer, the bear simply raises his head and sniffs at us. When within about twenty yards, a rifle ball through the neck quickly despatches him, and, after hauling the carcass to an open place to facilitate the work, preparations are made for skinning.

Skinning and Skeletonizing a Bear.—As the bear is a fine adult male and the foot but little injured by the trap, we will save both skin and skeleton, each to be mounted separately, thus making two exhibits of one specimen.

After measuring, the skin is removed as in the case of

the deer, the opening cuts at the back of the head and neck being omitted and the belly cut being allowed to extend up the throat to between the angles of the jaws. Before making the opening cuts it is a good plan, if possible, to decide upon the position or attitude the animal is to assume when mounted. In this case, if we wished to mount the bear standing upon his hind legs, breast on, it would be better, in order to show no seams from the front, to allow the opening cut to extend from the back of the neck straight down the centre of the back to the tail, and omit the opening cuts on the belly and at the backs of the limbs. The bottoms of the feet will have to be opened whichever way the opening cuts are made, in order to invert the legs. Afterward, in mounting, the manikin is lifted off the pedestal and the skin drawn on like a pair of trousers, and the manikin again placed on the pedestal and bolted fast. But as our bear is to assume an ordinary walking posture when mounted, the opening cuts are made as usual.

In disarticulating the skull from the vertebræ care is used not to sever the hyoidean apparatus of the throat, as the bones form a part of the skeleton, and this we wish to save entire. The skin having been removed, with the bones of the feet still in position in the skin, the hide is thrown aside while the skeleton is roughed out.

The limbs are first disarticulated and the flesh cut off roughly, being careful not to throw away the knee-pans. The viscera are next removed and the belly walls cut off. The ribs are disarticulated one by one, both from the vertebral column and from the breastbone or sternum, being particular to strike the point of the knife between the joints and not to unnecessarily hack or nick the bones. The slender-bladed, pointed shoe knife is admirably adapted for this work. Having a large, round, wooden handle, it does not gall the palm of the hand like the cartilage knife usually adopted for skeletonizing.

The ribs having all been taken off and laid carefully in

a pile along with the skull and limb bones, the sternum, all entire, is next roughed out. Lastly, the vertebral column is cut into three or four sections for convenience in handling. The muscles of the skull are cut away and the tongue and brain removed. The skin and the skeleton are now tied up separately as compactly as possible, the discarded remains well poisoned with strychnine, and a line spotted back to the coop, where the trap is reset. We carry the skin and skeleton of the bear to camp, going back over the line of mouse traps, which are carefully reset where needed, and the game taken out and pocketed.

Snaring a Grouse.—As we proceed, a fine male "spruce" or Canada grouse flies up from our path and alights upon a limb just out of reach. As we have not as yet saved one of these for a skeleton, we will secure him. Don't shoot him, as the shot is apt to shatter the bones and spoil the skeleton. Don't be in a hurry; the bird is not apt to fly off for some time yet. See, he has settled himself, and having got over his scare—if, indeed, such a thing is to be found in any portion of his anatomy—is actually preening his feathers!

Cut a small switch from that bush and attach a noose of this soft copper wire to the end of it. Now step up close and throw the noose over the bird's head as carelessly as you choose. See! the saucy bird actually pecks at the noose and has partly closed it. Re-adjust the noose, and don't lose so much time. There! you have the noose well over the bird's head; now yank! The poor "fool bird," as it is rightly named, comes fluttering to the ground. As the bird is not dead, the thumb and fingers are pinched tightly together on opposite sides, just under the butts of the wings over the ribs, and by pressure the lungs are closed, and the bird soon suffocates.

Large birds of prey which are but slightly wounded and full of fight may be killed in the same way, by clamping the ribs together with the fingers. Simply noose or lasso the feet, and tie the end of the string to any adjacent object. The butt of the gun or a crotched stick may then be pressed upon the neck to hold the head down, and the fingers tightly clamped upon the ribs, thus compressing the lungs until death ensues.

This may seem a cruel method, but to shoot the specimen again may ruin it, and a knife blade stuck into the base of the skull from the outside or through the roof of the mouth has its disadvantages. I have never met a collector who had enough regard for the sufferings of a bird to take the trouble to carry along a bottle of chloroform for use in these cases. They are a bloodthirsty crew, and their main object seems to be to secure material, no matter by what means.

Skeletonizing a Bear (continued).—Arrived at camp, after duly caring for the more perishable material, the bones of the bear are more carefully cleaned of flesh and tendons, the skull well rinsed out, and the toe bones cut out of the foot by inverting the skin of the toes over them. In order to get the whole skeleton of the foot, it is necessary to cut around each toe nail and detach it from the skin, leaving the nails fast to the bones of the foot.

The nail is afterward macerated off by soaking in water, and replaced on the manikin in mounting the skin.

In the case of a hoofed animal, the point of the knife is worked from the inside down to the point of the hoof, the bone completely encircled with the knife and loosened. With the aid of a screw-driver the last phalanx may be wedged out without detaching the hoof from the skin. When the bone is too obstinate and refuses to come out in this way, a hole is cut in the bottom of the hoof and the bone further loosened from below and forced out. Having the complete skeleton well roughed out, the whole is put into an ordinary feed bag and anchored out in the lake, where it is allowed to remain for a few days in order to soak out the blood. The bones are then dried and packed for shipment.

5

Curing a Bear Skin.—The skin of the bear now demands our attention. The lips having been split from the inside, the ears inverted or turned wrong side out, and the skin well washed to remove blood stains, the skin is spread out upon the ground and salted and rolled up, flesh to flesh. Next morning a sapling butt about six inches in diameter and about six or eight feet long is placed with one end resting upon the ground and the other end resting in a crotch driven into the ground to raise it about three feet, thus constructing a temporary " beam."

The bear skin is thrown over the beam, flesh side up, and the fat thoroughly scraped off with the hand scraper (Plate 4, Fig. 5). In the laboratory we would use the fleshing knife for this purpose, but as this tool is somewhat cumbersome we omit it from our collecting outfit on short trips.

When thoroughly cleaned of fat, the skin is again salted and rolled up until the next day, when it is hung up and partially dried, painted on the flesh side with arsenical soap, and allowed to dry further, when it is rolled up and tightly corded, a lead number of course being attached.

Skeletonizing a Grouse.—Ordinarily the first specimen of a species secured is made into a skin for mounting, and a subsequent one reserved for skeletonizing. It is not practicable or necessary ordinarily to mount the bird and save the skeleton entire separately.

The bill and legs must go with the skeleton, and to cast or model these artificially for use in connection with the mounted skin involves an amount of labour not to be bestowed upon a bird unless extremely rare.

Part of the plumage may be saved for a more perfect identification of the skeleton if the collector is not certain of the species. The bird in this case is skinned as usual, detaching the skin at the knee in the case of birds with a naked tarsus, and at the toe nail in birds which are feathered to the claw. Care must be taken to avoid cutting

COLLECTING.

the vertebræ at the base of the tail, and the skin should be detached about the base of the bill. The wings may be opened underneath and the skin peeled and cut off to the first joint.

In the case of the grouse this is, however, unnecessary. The plumage is got rid of in the quickest manner possible by plucking and cutting with the scalpel and scissors. The viscera are removed and the flesh cut from the breast-bone. The primaries and feathers of the spurious wing are left on, or clipped with the scissors in about half their length. If any of the tendons of the leg have ossified just above the knee they are allowed to remain. The legs and wings are not disarticulated from the body, nor are the eyes removed from their sockets; they are simply punctured in the centre of the pupil to allow the juices to escape. The skull is left attached to the vertebræ, but the brain is removed by partially disarticulating the skull from the verte-bra and cleaning out the brain cavity with a small scraper. The bulk of the muscle of the neck is removed, care being used to avoid breaking the delicate processes of the neck vertebræ. The windpipe is allowed to remain in position. After the entire skeleton is denuded of most of its flesh it is tied up in a small bag or cloth and deposited in the lake for a few days, when it is taken up, tied together as compactly as possible, and hung up in the shade to dry.

The skeleton of a small mammal is treated in the same manner, except that the skull and limbs are disarticulated from the body, the shoulder blade going with the forelimb, and all packed inside the cavity of the chest.

There are a few rules to be observed in preparing rough skeletons, otherwise it is simply a question of getting rid of the flesh and viscera. *Do not under any circumstances use a hatchet or saw in disarticulating.* Use no arsenic, salt, or other preservative upon the bones, as they materially retard the macerating and future whitening of the bones. If insects attack the skeleton, so much the better, as they simply assist in the cleaning, if they are not allowed to attack the ligaments in small skeletons.

The next morning we take the canoe and proceed up the lake on a second visit to our beaver trap. As we glide silently around a point we suddenly come into full view of a buck standing knee-deep in the water. As the canoe slows up and steadies itself, a .44-calibre rifle ball in the chest drops the buck, and he is soon hauled ashore. As we already have a good buck's skin, we shall save the head only, to mount and hang upon the wall of our workroom upon our return.

Skinning a Deer's Head for Mounting.—The skin of the neck is completely encircled with the knife well back to the shoulders in order to leave a good long "scalp," as it is called. An opening cut is made from the centre of the top of the skull just back of the horns, continuing back to the end of the neck skin. Two cuts are made from the anterior end of this opening, each reaching to the base of a horn, as in the buck already skinned. The opening cuts are thus all made on the back of the head and neck, and none below, so that when the head is mounted and hanging upon the wall there will be no seams to conceal on the under or show side of the head.

The skin of the neck is now worked off with the knife and the head detached from the neck at the first or *atlas* vertebra. In order to sever the skull from the neck vertebra, the head is turned to one side and the knife inserted between the base of the skull and the vertebra, severing the muscles and tendons. The head is now turned in the opposite direction and the flesh and tendons cut, and the head is detached. The skin is now loosened around the base of the horns with the point of the knife, and peels off easily until the eye sockets are reached. Care must here be used to avoid cutting the lids, and the skin is worked off as far as the lips. When these are reached they are cut off close to the bone and the skinning proceeded with to the end of the nose. The cartilage of the nose is severed, thus detaching the skin completely from the skull.

The lips are not cut off from the skin, but simply split with the knife from the inside to allow the salt to penetrate. The cartilage dividing the nostrils is now split in two from the inside and the nose completely inverted. The ears are turned wrong side out by detaching the skin of the back of the ear from the cartilage, clear to the very tip. This to a beginner is a rather tough job, and should the operator not possess the time or skill necessary to do it, the ears may be dipped in very strong salt brine and allowed to remain there for an hour or two, and then well rubbed with salt. This will keep the hair of the ear from slipping. The skull is cleaned of all flesh and tissue, and the brain removed with a stick through the hole in the base of the skull, and the inside rinsed out with water. The lower jaw is disarticulated in order to properly clean the lower portion of the skull, and is afterward tied in place with twine. Never hack or saw a skull, as the entire skull or its exact counterpart is necessary in mounting.

If the horns are too bulky to be conveniently carried, the skull may be neatly sawed in two lengthwise and afterward bolted together.

The head skin is thrown bodily into the lake, and all blood stains well washed from the hair and the skin wrung out.

Upon arriving at camp, the skin is well salted upon the flesh side. No alum or other preservative is necessary or half so good.

After salting, the skin is rolled up and left so until the next morning, when it is examined for soft spots where the salt, by reason of an impervious coating, has not struck in and hardened the tissues. These spots are shaved down from the inside, the skin resalted and hung up in a shady place to dry. If collecting in a warm climate, it will be necessary to paint the skin on the inside with arsenical soap, to keep out insects; but if these are not abundant, no arsenical soap is necessary.

When nearly dry, the skin is folded up, hair side in, and tied up as compactly as possible.

The skull is in the meantime simply cleaned and dried, and, with the skin, is ready for shipment.

The remaining days of our stay are spent in securing small specimens. Every trap is set, as it will certainly never catch any game while hanging up in camp.

As we have now about fifty of each of the more common species of small mammals and birds made up into skins for the cabinet, or possibly for future mounting, the balance are thrown away as trapped, while we still continue trapping in the endeavour to secure a species not yet taken.

A few of each are saved for skeletons, and these are simply punctured in the abdomen with the knife and dropped into our tank of alcohol. Alcohol of full strength is altogether too strong, and if reduced with water so as to make a seventy-per-cent solution, the mixture is strong enough to preserve turtles, snakes, birds, and small mammals for a long time. Alcohol, however, is not always perfect in its action upon the tissues of small mammals, and specimens taken from alcohol and skinned will sometimes lose their hair in spots. It is therefore safer to consider all alcoholics as material for study or skeletons. Specimens are more perfectly preserved if injected with alcohol before immersion.

A lead number is attached to every specimen put into alcohol, as ordinary writing ink will run if written on a paper label and immersed in the liquid. A lead pencil answers very well to write with, but indelible ink is preferable for this purpose.

As fish, reptiles, and crustaceans are not found in any great variety in this locality, we omit them here, but will give them our consideration in a succeeding chapter.

COLLECTING.

The day set for the arrival of our teamster having come, we take up our traps and pack our materials into the least possible space, and in due time find ourselves again in the laboratory surrounded by our friends, busily accepting their congratulations and unpacking our paraphernalia.

CHAPTER II.

I. TOOLS AND MATERIALS.

THE axiom, "A good workman never quarrels with his tools," may be made to apply to the taxidermist with great force; but, nevertheless, a good workman is seldom found with an equipment of anything but the best tools.

Common sense and ingenuity, coupled with energy, patience, and an artistic eye, are the tools which are found to require the most frequent sharpening.

In large institutions taxidermy is generally divided into three sections, with laboratories specially fitted for each. The department of birds forms one; mammals, fish, and reptiles another; and skeletons the third.

The main considerations in fitting up a laboratory are heat, light, and an abundance of both hot and cold water. Gas pipes and a gas stove should not be overlooked, as frequently the gas stove is in use for days together.

The Equipment of the Bird Taxidermist.—Leaving out such necessary articles as tables, chairs, sink, etc., the following list comprises the majority of tools and materials used in mounting birds:

Two scalpels, large and small, wooden handles.
Two pairs of scissors, large and small.
One pair of shears.
One pair of 8-inch forceps.
One pair of 3-inch forceps.
Two pairs of flat pliers, large and small.
Two pairs of Hall's cutting pliers, large and small.
Two flat files, large and small.

PLATE IV.

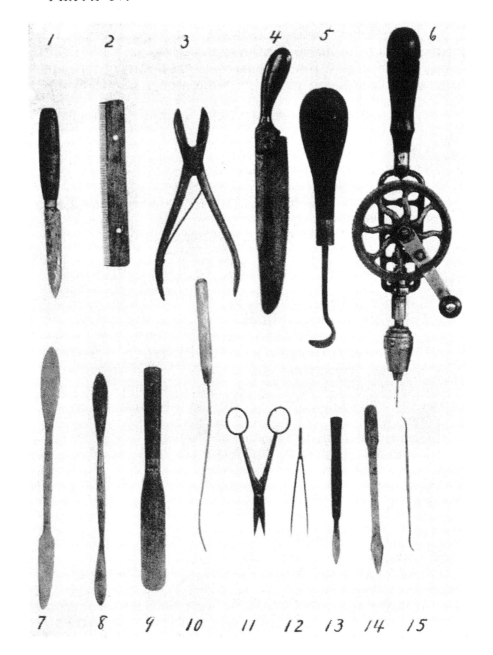

SOME OF THE TOOLS USED IN TAXIDERMY.

1. Shoe knife.
2. Steel comb.
3. Bone snips.
4. Surgeon's saw.
5. Large skin-scraper.

6. Ratchet hand-drill.
7. Plaster file.
8. Modelling tool.
9. Spatula.
10. Pusher.

11. Pointed scissors.
12. Small forceps.
13. Scalpel.
14. Large scraper.
15. Small   "

One ratchet hand drill-stock, with an assortment of twist drills from three-eighths of an inch down. For drilling very small holes through wood or comparatively soft material a three-cornered glover's needle works admirably with the drill-stock.

One brad awl with an adjustable handle, and an assortment of awls.

One tack hammer.

One surgeon's saw.

One pair of bone snips.

One small bone scraper.

One large bone scraper.

Needles and pins and various sizes of thread.

Corn meal.

Cops of winding cotton for wrapping the plumage of birds.

Beeswax and paraffin.

Tube colours ground in oil.

Brushes, turpentine, and varnish.

Fine excelsior and tow. Cotton batting.

Annealed iron wire, various sizes.

An assortment of artificial eyes, which may be ordered from the advertising sheet of the manufacturer.

Benzine.

Coarse " Michigan " plaster of Paris.

Powdered alum and arsenic, dry, in equal parts, for poisoning bird skins.

A number of T-perches, and others with the top of the T slanted, upon which to place perching birds while being mounted.

A feather duster and a flexible, flat stick a couple of feet long, to beat bird skins in cleaning.

Ground glue and coarse blotting paper for pulping, to make *papier-maché*.

A most important though rather expensive medium for fluffing the plumage of birds and the fur of mammals after the absorbing medium has been applied to the wet feathers or fur is the air compressor. This, though not absolutely necessary, is a great saver of time and labour. It consists of a large galvanized iron receiver, like the ordinary hot-water boiler of the household, into which air is pumped by means of three small air pumps, which are run by a wheel connected by a belt with a quarter horse-power electric motor. By this means a hundred pounds' pressure may be registered on the gauge, or more if necessary. A rubber hose, wire bound, is connected with a faucet or stopcock at the bottom of the receiver, and, with the full force of the compressed air, a bird or mammal skin may be thoroughly blown out and the feathers or hair fluffed in a short time.

The ordinary hand compressor in use in the large bicycle establishments for inflating tires would answer very well for this purpose on a small scale.

These tools and materials will be found to answer generally in mounting small birds. In extreme cases, and in the mounting of large birds such as the emu or ostrich, the heavier tools of the mammal taxidermist will be called into requisition.

If the bird taxidermist wishes to use the ordinary artificial milliners' leaves as accessories for his birds, an assortment of these may be kept in stock.

It is, however, far better for the taxidermist to prepare his own accessories, such as grasses, leaves, flowers, etc., directions for which will be found in a succeeding chapter.

The Equipment of the Mammal Taxidermist.—The preparation of mammals, fish, and reptiles for exhibition requires the greatest assortment of tools and materials used in taxidermy. The following comprises a partial list of them, a systematic inventory being entirely unnecessary:

An exact duplicate of the tools and materials recommended for use in mounting birds, with the exception of the perches.

A kit of carpenters' tools and a grindstone.

A set of taps and dies, one inch down to a quarter of an inch.

Two monkey wrenches, large and small.

An assortment of Norway iron rod, one inch to a quarter of an inch, with tapped or threaded nuts. Washers for same.

An assortment of bolts.

One hack saw.

One heavy vise.

Soft iron-wire netting or cloth of different size mesh.

Twist drills to fit carpenter's bit stock, three quarters to a quarter of an inch.

An assortment of screws, wire nails, and staples.

Shoe knives ground to a point for skinning and shaving down skins.

Steel combs.

Three-cornered glovers' needles, Nos. 000 to 4.

A tape measure.

Spatulas and plaster modeller's tools.

A barrel of fine dental plaster.

A quantity of white paper made of wood pulp of any kind that will pulp readily in water.

Modelling clay.

Lepage's liquid glue, ground carpenter's glue, and best French glue.

Buckets. Large, lead-lined tanks, and barrels for tan liquor.

Salt. Arsenical soap.

A large oatmeal steamer for cooking various compositions.

A glue pot.

Washing soda, shellac, lard oil.

An assortment of paint brushes.

A pair of large wooden calipers for measuring proportions of manikins.

A few pieces of rattan, three feet long, to beat fur.

Benzine, boiled oil, and white hard oil finish.

Twine. Plenty of stout pins.

Artificial eyes for mammals.

A quantity of furrier's sawdust.

A tanner's stretching frame.

A tanner's crutch or moon knife.

A tanner's shaving knife.

A tanner's shaving beam.

Lumber is generally purchased as required.

In addition to this, I recommend the mammal taxidermist to have as complete a collection of casts of dead animals, copies of sculptor's models, and photographs of living animals as lies in his power or in his pocketbook.

The Equipment of the Osteologist.—Of all branches of taxidermy, the osteologist wrongly derives the least credit for his work from the public.

THE ART OF TAXIDERMY.

To a scientific museum the osteologist is as necessary in every particular as the taxidermist; and were it not for the beautiful and immaculate skeletons turned out by the reeking maceration tub, the palæontologist would be at a loss indeed for a comparison of modern and fossil forms of animal life.

To be a successful osteologist, one requires at times a strong stomach and a wholesale disrespect for his olfactory organs.

The first requisite for the osteologist is a suitable place in which to macerate or soak skeletons, where the necessary odours which arise will not offend his neighbours.

Large wooden tubs, painted inside with asphalt varnish in order that the bones may not come in contact with iron nails, etc., will answer for this purpose. But better still are soapstone or porcelain tanks. An ordinary porcelain bath-tub makes a first-class receptacle for the maceration of large skeletons, and for small skeletons glass jars are preferable.

The tools and materials necessary are the following:

Glass jars, assorted sizes.
Brass wire, hard and soft, various sizes.
Brass nuts, washers, rosettes, rivets, and thumb screws, assorted.
Flat brass rod and various sizes of iron rod.
Tanned elk hide and felt to replace the cartilage between vertebræ.
A ratchet hand drill, with an assortment of different sizes of twist drills.
A machinist's rivetting hammer.
A set of large and a set of small taps and dies.
Two monkey wrenches, large and small.
Files, reamers, scrubbing brushes, and toothbrushes.
Quantities of benzine.
Chloride of lime. Washing soda.
Flat pliers, large and small.
Cutting pliers, large and small.
Scissors, curved and straight.
Fine forceps.
For drilling bones, etc., an ordinary turner's lathe is a

great boon to the osteologist. In addition to the foot-power attachment, which may be used in a case of emergency, the lathe receives its power by means of a belt attached to the pulley of a quarter-horse-power electric motor, upon which the speed of the lathe may be regulated with a lever and switchboard. The motor rests upon a shelf, and receives its power from the current of an ordinary incandescent bulb. A chuck is fitted on the lathe to receive any ordinary-sized drill, and, by centreing the bone properly, bores a beautifully clean and smooth hole. The lathe, with a full set of wood-turners' tools, an emery wheel, circular brushes, etc., makes this machine the envy of all who see it, and it may be well to state that other departments, at times to the discomfort of the osteologist, are apt to ask permission to use it rather too frequently.

II. COMPOSITIONS AND FORMULÆ.

No. 1.

Tan Liquor for preserving Hides in a Wet State.

Water.................................... 1 gallon.
Salt...................................... 1 quart.
Bring to boiling point to facilitate dissolving the salt.
Sulphuric acid (by measure).............. 1 ounce.

Allow liquor to cool before immersing hides. More salt, even a saturated solution, will not injure a skin.

No. 2.

Salt and Alum Pickle.

Water.................................... 1 gallon.
Salt...................................... 1 quart.
Alum (powdered or crystallized).......... 1 pint.
Bring to boiling point and cool.

No. 3.

Arsenical Soap (after Hornaday).

"White bar soap, soft rather than hard...... 2 pounds.
Powdered arsenic......................... 2   "
Camphor.................................. 5 ounces.
Subcarbonate of potash................... 6   "
Alcohol.................................. 8   "

"*Directions.*—The soap should be the best quality of laundry soap, and of such composition that it can be reduced with water to any degree of thinness. Soap which becomes like jelly when melted will not answer and should never be used. Slice the soap and melt it in a small quantity of water over a slow fire, stirring sufficiently to prevent its burning. When melted, add the potash and stir in the powdered arsenic. Next add the camphor, which should be dissolved in the alcohol at the beginning of the operation. Stir the mass thoroughly, boil it down to the consistence of thick molasses, and pour it into an earthen or wooden jar to cool and harden. Stir it occasionally while cooling, to prevent the arsenic from settling at the bottom. When cold it should be like lard or butter. For use, mix a small quantity with water until it resembles buttermilk, and apply with a common paint brush."

No. 4.

Arsenical Solution for poisoning Mammal Hides just before placing them on the Manikin.

White arsenic .... 1 pound.
Water.................................. 20 ounces.

Paint over the flesh side with a brush, stirring well while using.

No. 5.

Arsenical Solution for poisoning the Interior of the Skins of Birds and Small Mammals.

White arsenic, ⎫ ....equal parts, by measure.
Powdered alum, ⎭

Mix, and apply as a powder, with a bristle brush or fluff of cotton batting, to the inside of the fresh skin. Should the skin dry out so much during the skinning process that the powder will not cling, the inside of the skin should be slightly dampened with water and the poison applied. If desired, it may be mixed with water and painted on.

COMPOSITIONS AND FORMULÆ.

No. 6.

Bichloride-of-Mercury Solution for poisoning the Exterior of Birds and Mammals.

Alcohol.. 1 quart.
Water .... 1 pint.
Bichloride of mercury—add until it leaves a very slight deposit upon a black feather after immersion and the feather becomes dry.

For mammals this may be applied with a brush or sprinkling pot, but for birds a spray is preferable. As this is a rank poison, the mouth and nostrils should be well protected while using it. It is only necessary to use this solution in extreme cases, where insect pests can not be destroyed by means of air-tight cases and the vaporization of bisulphuret of carbon.

No. 7.

Alcoholic Solution for the preservation of Small Specimens Entire.

Alcohol.. 8 parts.
Water .... 2 "

Small mammals immersed in this solution may be subsequently mounted, if opened on the belly, and injected with the syringe previous to immersion. It unduly shrivels a specimen, however, and in time bleaches out the colours. It is also somewhat uncertain in its action, and small mammals kept in alcohol for a time sometimes lose their hair in a most aggravating way while being skinned. It is safer to consider all alcoholic specimens of small mammals as suitable only for skeletons or for anatomical study. There is no liquid preservative known in which birds, mammals, fish, or reptiles may be preserved in a wet state and hold the colours for any great length of time. The colours are retained longer if the specimen is kept in a dark place, daylight being a powerful bleaching agent.

Alcohol is, however, found to be the best liquid preserving medium for permanent use, and I am informed by Dr. E. O. Hovey, assistant curator of the Department of Geology and Invertebrate Zoölogy in the American Museum, that all specimens of marine invertebrates in the Naples Zoölogical Station are kept in this liquid. He further states that it is found that the killing of the subject has much to do with the subsequent preservation, and the medium by which the different marine animals are best killed must be learned by experience. Some are best killed by narcotizing,* some by the use of formalin, and others are best put alive into alcohol. Fish and reptiles, in order to make perfect alcoholic specimens, should be placed in the alcohol alive, and injected with alcohol soon after death.

As soon as the alcohol becomes discoloured it should be changed for a fresh supply, the alcohol and water being filtered before it is poured over the specimen.

Lizards, etc., may be posed in lifelike attitudes on slabs of plaster or cement and thus exhibited in alcohol, square jars being superior to round ones by reason of the distortion of the specimen in a round jar.

No. 8.

Formaldehyde (H.CHO).

None of the new preserving agents introduced in the past few years have been so readily accepted as formaldehyde. Its cheapness as compared with alcohol (twenty-five cents per pound in large quantities) and its condensed form were much in its favour. When first introduced, it was claimed that formaldehyde (known also as formalin, formol, formolose, etc.) would effectually preserve the colour of immersed animal forms. It is now a well-established fact that formaldehyde will discharge the colours of fish, reptiles, etc., even more rapidly than alcohol.

---

* See Artistic and Scientific Taxidermy and Modelling, by Montagu Browne; Adam & Charles Black, London, 1896, p. 26.

Mollusks, echinoderms, etc., should never be placed in formalin, as the free acid decomposes the calcareous portions, and thus changes the form and colour of the specimen. Furthermore, formaldehyde is anything but a pleasant medium to work in, the liquid literally tanning the fingers and the gas irritating the eyes and nose to such an extent as to be positively unbearable, and unhealthful to such a degree as in time to produce chronic catarrh. In spite of its bristling disadvantages, however, formaldehyde has its use as a preservative. On a collecting trip where large quantities of alcohol could not be taken, formaldehyde, although not so good, may be used instead, the specimens being transferred into alcohol as soon as possible after their arrival at the laboratory. At the Marine Laboratory at Naples formalin is used to some extent to kill certain marine forms of animal life, which are allowed to remain in the liquid for a longer or shorter time according to circumstances. The specimens are then transferred into alcohol, where they are kept permanently, the alcohol being added to delicate forms gradually from day to day, in order not to shrivel soft gelatinous bodies by plunging them directly into alcohol of full strength. For use in preparing histological specimens, formaldehyde is also of great service.

For preserving specimens—vertebrates and invertebrates —a two- to five-per-cent solution of formaldehyde is found to produce the best results. Usually one part of the forty-per-cent solution is diluted with nine parts of water, thus giving ten parts of a formaldehyde solution of four per cent. Mammals, birds, and reptiles, before being placed in this liquid, should be injected with a more concentrated solution through the mouth and the anus. For this purpose the mixture should be about four parts of water to one of formaldehyde. It is not recommended to use weaker solutions than the one mentioned (four per cent), on account of the likelihood of the growth of mould and because they produce more or less swelling of the tissues. The

6

quantity of the solution should be large—at least ten times the volume of the specimen to be preserved. It is also best to renew the fluid at the expiration of forty-eight hours. If dissecting material is preserved in formaldehyde it should be put into fresh water for three or four hours before it is wanted for dissection. A little ammonia added to the water will neutralize the irritating odour of the formaldehyde. For preserving marine specimens, such as vermes, etc., a two-per-cent solution, obtained by diluting one part of formaldehyde (forty per cent) with nineteen parts of salt water, gives very satisfactory results. For preserving reptiles and amphibians it is advisable to add to the four-per-cent solution of formaldehyde about one tenth the quantity of methyl alcohol (wood alcohol), or ethyl alcohol, and a few grains of sodium bicarbonate.

No. 9.

Wickersheimer Solution for preserving Moss, Seaweeds, etc.

Alum....................................	500	grains.
Salt........	125	"
Saltpetre.......	60	"
Potash..........	300	"
White arsenic.........................	100	"

Dissolve in one quart of boiling water. Cool and filter, and for every quart of solution add four quarts of glycerine and one quart of alcohol.

Immerse vegetable matter for at least forty-eight hours in an ordinary temperature. Wash off with warm water to remove the excess of the solution from the surface. This solution renders moss, leaves, seaweed, etc., flexible and plump for an indefinite period. It destroys the colour, rendering the object of a brownish hue. The colour is restored by painting with tube colours, and in the case of moss by sifting on powdered colours through a sieve of cheese cloth. This solution also holds the needles on fir, hemlock, etc., most effectually.

No. 10.

Papier-Maché.

Paper pulp (wood pulp), wet, with the excess of water squeezed out with the hands,
 by measure........................... 10 ounces.
Hot carpenter's glue, by measure......... 3 "
Plaster of Paris, dry "   "   .... 20 "

Work the hot glue through the paper pulp, then add
the plaster, kneading like dough. It may be coloured by
kneading in dry colour after the plaster. Stereotypers'
matrix paper, although rather expensive, is of fine grain
and makes an excellent quality of *maché*. If no other paper
is at hand, newspaper may be used. To pulp it, tear the
paper into bits and boil it in water to dissolve the size,
and afterward mush it up with the hands and squeeze out
the water by straining through cheese cloth.

No. 11.

Papier-Maché for modelling Manikins.

Water, lukewarm................... 20 ounces.
Glue (hot) or Lepage's liquid........ 1 teaspoonful.
 Mix thoroughly.

Add wet paper pulp, squeezed out with the hands until
the whole is in a mushy state. Mix in dry plaster of Paris
until the proper modelling consistence is obtained. Apply
with a spatula or flat modelling tool, and smooth while soft
by brushing over with a wet brush. The glue simply holds
back the plaster from setting, and may be left out entirely
if the batch of *maché* can be modelled into its proper form
before the plaster sets. If it is desired to have the *maché*
set very soon after it is modelled, even with the above quantity of glue in the composition, this may be effected by
simply wetting the surface of the *maché* with salt brine, or
by laying on a hide or cloth which is wet with tan liquor.

Coarse white blotting paper, reduced to a pulp by rubbing with the hands in a pail of lukewarm water, makes good pulp for this composition; but the ordinary carpenter's sheathing or lining paper, at seventy-five cents per roll, will answer every purpose. The latter, however, being red in colour, makes a reddish-coloured *maché*, which colour is not so good as a white to model in. It also works smoother if put in a bucket and pounded and punched, while wet, with a bar of wood or a pipe. The addition of gum arabic (dissolved in water) makes a very strong composition and one that will not crack in drying.

No. 12.

Javelle Water for bleaching Skeletons.

Water.................................... 1 gallon.
Boil, and while boiling add carbonate of soda. 4 pounds.
When cool, add chloride of lime............ 1 pound.

When all dissolved, decant off into a stone jug and keep tightly corked to keep out light, as the mixture decomposes when exposed to light.

No. 13.

Bleach for Corals.

Peroxide of sodium................. 1 tablespoonful.
Water............................ 1 gallon.

Dissolve the sodium in a glass or earthenware jar, and do not allow the fluid to come in contact with metal.

Add a few drops of muriatic acid. Immerse macerated corals until properly bleached, which will be in about forty-eight hours; then take out, rinse with warm water and scrub with a stiff brush, and lay in the sun to dry and bleach out. The specimens should be placed upon a plate of glass while drying, as metal or wood is liable to discolour them.

No. 14.

Wax for Casting.

As beeswax, though tougher than paraffin, shows the joints where one layer of hot wax overlaps another, paraffin wax is used instead. Pure paraffin is, however, apt to " blow " or form air bubbles when poured hot upon a cold surface. In order to avoid this as much as possible, and also to produce a firmer, tougher substance, the following is recommended :

Beeswax............................... 4 ounces.
Paraffin wax............................ 16   "
   Melt together in a water bath.*
Resin................................... 2   "
   Melt in a sand bath.

Mix the melted resin through the hot wax and the mixture is ready for casting. This wax takes a most minute impression, and is far superior in this respect to either plaster, or glue composition.

No. 15.

Wax for Mouths of Mammals, etc.

Bleached beeswax.......................... 1 part.
Paraffin wax............................. 1   "
   Melt in the water bath.

The wax may be coloured to any desired tint by the addition of tube colours ground in oil.

To Colour the Wax.—Dip up a tablespoonful of the melted wax and squeeze some of the tube colour into it. Stir the colour and wax with a small wooden spatula until

---

* By a " water bath " is meant the placing of one vessel inside of another, the lower one being filled with water, and the whole placed on the fire after the manner of an ordinary glue pot. For a " sand bath " the water in the lower vessel is replaced by fine sand, care being used that the vessels are pressed or cast, and not soldered, or the bottoms are liable to drop out. A much greater degree of heat can of course be produced with the " sand bath."

the mixture becomes so cold and stiff that it can no longer be mixed. By this time the colour will have been thoroughly ground up in the wax.

Place the bowl of the spoon into the hot wax and stir with the spatula, when the coloured wax will go off in waves and be evenly distributed through the entire body of hot wax. Repeat this process until the wax is of the requisite colour. Never place the raw colour into the mass of hot wax, or it will be impossible to get it thoroughly ground up and mixed evenly.

No. 16.

Wax for Waxed Cloth for manufacturing Leaves, Grasses, etc.

Pure bleached beeswax, by weight......... 1 pound.
Canada balsam gum, by measure.......... 1½ ounces.
   Melt the wax in the water bath and add
     the gum.
Resin, by measure...................... 1 ounce.
Boiled linseed oil, by measure........... 1   "
   Melt the resin in the sand bath and add
     the oil. Add the resin and oil to the hot
     wax, and stir well together.

This mixture is very inflammable while hot, and care should be used in the preparation and use of it. Colour as directed in formula No. 15.

No. 17

Wax Putty for finishing around the Eyes and Noses of Mammals, stopping Open Seams, etc.

Beeswax..................... 12 ounces, by weight.
   Melt in the water bath.
Resin....................... 1 ounce by weight.
   Melt in the sand bath.
Linseed oil.................. 1   "   by measure.

Add the melted resin and oil to the hot wax, and colour to any desired tint by the addition of tube colours. When cool it is ready for use.

COMPOSITIONS AND FORMULÆ.

No. 18.

Formula for making Liquid Celluloid, and Celluloid Films for the Representation of Artificial Water.

Amyl acetate	2 gallons.
Fusel oil (refined)	1 gallon.
Benzine	1½ "
Wood alcohol, ninety-five per cent	1½ "
Castor oil	1¼ pounds.
Soluble cotton (gun cotton)	2½ pounds.

Although not explosive when made up, this mixture is very highly inflammable.

Make up the liquid formula first, then put in the cotton. Stir just to wet the cotton, and then allow the whole to stand a day. Stir thoroughly, and keep in well-stoppered glass jars. Before using, strain through cheese cloth, and allow to stand about two hours to permit all air bubbles to settle out. If it is desired to use some that has stood a long time, stir well, then strain and allow bubbles to settle out, and it is again ready for use. This makes a fine transparent and permanent varnish for many purposes, and will not turn yellow with age. The solution may be coloured to any desired tint by the addition of tube colours ground in oil.

To Prepare the Film.—Take a piece of plate glass of the requisite size and wash and wipe it perfectly dry. With a wad of cotton rub the cleaned surface well with powdered talcum, and wipe off the excess.

Pour slowly enough of the liquid upon one corner of the glass to spread evenly over the entire surface when the glass is tilted up at different angles; allow the excess to drip off, first from one corner and then another, so as to equalize the thickness of the film. Set away in a dry place where no dust is afloat in the atmosphere. Do not expose to a current of air. If any air bubbles form during the operation, puncture them with a needle and they will disappear.

THE ART OF TAXIDERMY.

A number of coats will be found necessary in order to get a sufficient thickness, one day being allowed between each coat. Avoid touching the wet surface with the fingers. Before a second coat is applied the surface of the dry film should be carefully dusted. From six to ten coats will be found necessary for large areas. In case a piece of glass large enough for the purpose can not be procured, a wooden surface may be prepared. A number of seven-eighths-inch boards are glued together and planed and sandpapered down as smooth as possible. A strip may be tacked around the edges, projecting a quarter of an inch or so above the planed surface, and a corner on either end sawed out to allow for the drip. To prepare the wood so that it will be perfectly smooth, and to enable the film to draw, it will be found necessary to flow it with gelatine. This is done in the following manner:

Flow the surface of the boards with water and see that it is thoroughly wet all over, then allow the water to drain off at one corner. Make a moderately thick solution of gelatine, one pound and a half to two pounds to a gallon of water, and heat in the water bath. Strain through cheese cloth, and skim all bubbles off the surface. Allow the gelatine to cool a little and flow smoothly and evenly on one corner of the board. Incline the board so that the solution runs to the opposite corner of the same end, and then slowly down the boards to the other end. Carefully prick all air bubbles after the gelatine has partly set, and fill all holes with a little of the hot solution. Repeat the coatings until a glassy surface results. Strain the hot gelatine each time before flowing. Avoid getting dust or particles of dirt on the surface while wet, as it is impossible to remove it without more or less injury to the film.

When thoroughly dry, rub the entire surface with talcum, as directed for glass, and flow with the liquid celluloid.

Wavy glass may be used to flow the liquid over, if desired, and ripples may be represented by modelling upon the glass or wood with plaster or clay, and the whole flooded with the gelatine.

When dry, the film draws easily from the surface of the glass or prepared wood.

The film should be tacked in place in the tray or base of the group as soon as dry enough to handle, because, if allowed to roll up and become bone dry, it is almost impossible to get all the rolls out of a large sheet. The film may be tinted or coloured after it is in position in the group.

The advantages of the film over glass for representing water in bird or mammal groups, etc., are, that any number of holes may be cut or punched through it in which to place birds and accessory matter, the tips of leaning grasses, etc. A subject such as a group of the marsh wren, where it was desired to represent cat-tails, etc., growing out of the water, would be simplicity itself by the use of this film, and an utter impossibility with a sheet of glass such as is generally used for artificial water.

No. 19.

To Represent Ice.

Clear crystal ice has never to my knowledge been reproduced, and presents a difficult problem. Clear chunks of gypsum or white mica, split with a knife into thin sheets and arranged in their proper form and soldered at the joints with liquid celluloid and hot paraffin, applied with a small brush, and afterward tinted and varnished with liquid celluloid, answer the best of anything I have yet seen.

Snow ice may be readily produced by stippling on warm paraffin with a bristle brush. To produce an effect of melting snow, the flame and blowpipe are used, and the wax afterward varnished. Glass icicles may be purchased of glass blowers or dealers in taxidermist's supplies. Fluffs of cotton batting dipped in hot paraffin answer very well for this purpose. They should of course be varnished.

No. 20.

Fluffy Snow.

To build up a snow scene the following is recommended :

Take cotton batting and dip it in benzine containing a little Prussian blue—tube colour. Squeeze out the benzine and allow the cotton to dry. The cotton will be found to contain a delicate tinge of the blue colour all through it. With hot paraffin and a brush fasten the cotton to the upper surfaces of the woodwork, twigs, etc., varying the depth of the cotton according to circumstances. Heat clean paraffin in a water bath, and when melted dip out a cupful. For small groups a toothbrush may be used ; for larger groups a stiff hair brush is better adapted. Dip the brush in the cup of hot paraffin, and with a piece of stiff wire or stick of wood "spatter" the hot paraffin over the group, directing the resulting flakes so that they settle in their proper places on the upper surfaces of the cotton, twigs, etc. The snowstorm may be made as fierce or as mild as the operator chooses. If wet snow is desired, hold the brush close to the surface to be covered. The hotter the paraffin the closer it sticks and the smaller the flakes, and *vice versa.*

To give glitter, when all completed sprinkle on a very little glass frosting, to be procured of dealers in taxidermist's supplies or of a glass blower.

For very large stationary mammal groups the snow may be prepared beforehand, and shovelled into the group at leisure.

No. 21.

Rockwork.

Artificial rocks may be made in a variety of ways, either by casting or modelling.

For very large rough work modelling is preferable, but for fine work castings from the actual rocks are recommended. The latter is best accomplished by the use of piece moulds in plaster, directions for which will be found in the chapter on Casting.

To build up large masses of rock, build up a framework of wood and cover to the required form with annealed wire cloth. Upon this facing paste tow saturated with hot carpenter's glue, and before the glue chills throw on damp sand. Should the glue chill, paint on a coat of hot glue before the sand is thrown on. This material will neither shrink nor crack, and when dry is very substantial.

Another method is to model upon the netting with *papier-maché*, coat with sand while the *maché* is soft, and, when dry, colour with oil colours. The colour should be " spattered " on with a stiff brush, putting on the light colours first, and ending and toning down with the darker. The colours may then be blended by stippling with a large paint brush. It is always best to have a sample of the rock it is desired to imitate, as much better work can be done with a model than without.

The finest cliffs are, however, built up by castings.

Rock facings are cast from the natural rock, and thin slabs run out of the moulds. The slabs may be of tow and plaster, or, if great lightness is desired, they may be made in paper or paper pulp. Do not attempt to select a difficult section of the cliff and cast the actual spot. Make castings where the character of the surface is the same, and the pieces may be cut and joined together in the group in any desired form.

A framework of wood is built up to the general shape of the cliff required and covered with heavy wire netting. The slabs are arranged in position one at a time, and fastened by drilling through the slabs and wiring them to the netting. The joints are then pointed up with *maché*. When dry, the whole is coloured by " spattering " on oil colours and stippling with a large paint brush. To remove all gloss the wet colour is stippled with pumice stone or powdered clay. Dry colours may also be used over the oil colour to advantage.

"Fancy" rockwork for small groups may be prepared by using coke for a foundation, coated with glue and afterward coloured with smalt and paint. Another method of preparing fanciful rockwork for small groups is the following: Build up the rough form of the rocks in excelsior or tow and cover the entire surface, to the depth of an inch or so, with dough made of flour, plaster, baking powder, and enough water to make a good modelling dough. Place the whole in an oven and bake. When well browned remove from the oven, and the surface will be found covered with cracks, blisters, etc. This may be coloured to suit the taste of the operator.

No. 22.

Glue Composition for Flexible Casts (Montagu Browne).

"Glue (best Scotch)........................ 6 ounces.
Water.................................... 1 ounce.
Glycerine .... 7 ounces.
Canada balsam .... 2 ounces."

Break up the glue and place in the water bath with the allowance of water. Heat the glycerine and Canada balsam separately, and, when the glue is dissolved, mix. The whole should be allowed to cook for at least two hours, stirring frequently. Colour, if desired, by the addition of tube colours ground in oil. Breaking when cool is a sign of poor materials, or that too much water has been added to the composition.

Oxide of zinc—a proportion of, say, an ounce to the above formula—stirred into the composition while hot, gives a firmer and harder material when cooled.

No. 23.

To cut a Large Hole in a Plate of Glass.

Small holes may be drilled in glass by using an ordinary twist drill, lubricating with spirits of turpentine. A diamond drill is of course much better than the above.

To cut a larger hole, proceed as follows:

Place a cardboard pattern upon the glass and scratch around it with the diamond, following the edges closely. When completely encircled, start at any point on the inside of the scratch and form a spiral with the diamond, terminating in the centre. Support the plate of glass from below with cushions, and with a small pointed hammer tap the centre of the spiral from underneath until the centre is punched out. By tapping gently from below with the hammer the spiral may be followed around to the outside boundary line, knocking out a small piece at a time.

No. 24.

To make, stain, and polish a Shield for a Mounted Head.

To make a Pattern.—Take a piece of stiff wrapping paper and fold it together lengthwise, and crease the paper by rubbing the fingers over the folded edge.

Place the paper, unfolded, upon the floor and set the mounted head upon it, so that the bottom of the crease in the paper comes out of the centre of the base of the neck, and the top of the crease comes out through the centre of the back of the neck.

With a pencil, trace out on one side of the paper the form of shield best adapted for the head. Remove the head and fold the paper together on the crease, and with the shears cut through both sides of the folded paper, thus giving, when unfolded, a pattern for a shield which is uniform and evenly balanced on both sides.

THE ART OF TAXIDERMY.

To make a Shield.—For ordinary-sized heads, such as a deer's, two seven-eighths-inch pieces of mahogany board make the finest shield.

Lay the pattern down upon a piece of the board and trace around it with a pencil. As this line represents the very inside line of the shield, with a pair of compasses follow all around it, tracing a line on the board five eighths of an inch larger than the pattern.

With the compass saw, cut out the piece on the outside line, and with the spokeshave smooth up the edges. Lay this piece upon the second board and trace around it. With the compass, as before, also enlarge this pattern five eighths of an inch. Cut out this piece with the compass saw, also on the outside line, and work off the edges with the spokeshave. For the first or face piece follow all around the edges with a carpenter's gauge, marking off five eighths of an inch all around, as the groove that is to be run around the edge extends to within only two eighths of an inch of the back of the piece.

With a spokeshave cut the corner off all around, and with a gouge groove out the edge, following the inside and outside lines, and not overlapping on either. Finish up the groove and edges with sandpaper.

For the back piece simply round it off on the edge with the spokeshave and rasp, not cutting beyond either line, and sandpaper smooth. We thus have the first or face piece with a concave or grooved edge, and the second or back piece with a rounded or convex edge, the two, when fastened together, forming what is known as an " o. g." edge.

The two pieces are put in position, clamped in the vise, and a couple of screws countersunk and screwed from the rear of the back piece into the first, drawing both firmly together. The screws are then taken out, the two pieces well painted with glue—either hot or Lepage's liquid—on the adjoining faces, the pieces placed in position, the screws reinserted, and a half dozen carpenter's clamps screwed on to make the glue hold firmly. The clamps are left on overnight, when they are removed and the shield sand-

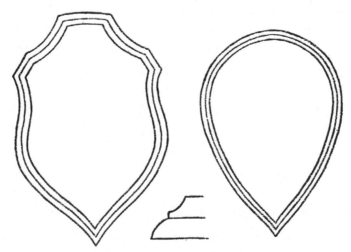

FIG. 14.—PATTERNS OF SHIELDS FOR MOUNTED HEADS.

papered and smoothed up, when it is ready for filling and polishing.

Before polishing, it is, however, better to arrange for hanging the shield upon the wall by cutting out a hollow in the back and screwing a flat piece of iron, countersunk, across the top of the hollow to catch the head of the nail or screw upon which the shield is to hang.

To finish a Mahogany Shield.—Paint with a coat of light mahogany filler, to be procured of any painter, and allow to remain for half an hour. Rub off with a bunch of excelsior. Varnish with three coats of rubbing varnish, allowing each coat to dry before putting on the next, sandpapering the first and second coats lightly with No. 00 sandpaper. Rub the last coat when dry with No. 0 pumice stone and water, applied with a piece of felt. For the final finish rub with rotten stone and raw linseed oil, using a piece of felt as before. This gives the best finish.

For a quick job, the first two coats of varnish may be replaced with two coats of shellac, which may be put on the same day. The shellac must of course be sandpapered to remove lumps, etc., as with the varnish.

To finish a shield made of white wood to imitate mahogany, stain the wood with the following:

Turpentine	1 quart.
Dry burnt sienna	1 pound.
Dry yellow ochre	$\frac{1}{2}$ "

To make the stain darker, use a small quantity of dry burnt umber. Allow the stain to remain on half an hour, and rub off with excelsior; then proceed as with the mahogany shield. A mahogany stain and filler combined may be purchased of dealers, thus saving the trouble of mixing the above stain.

To give an Ebony Polish to Whitewood.—Paint with three coats of ebony stain, to be procured at almost any paint store, sandpapering after each coat with fine sandpaper, and taking care not to cut the stain on the edges so as to whiten them. Into the first coat of varnish put a quantity of drop black. The varnishing and polishing of the remainder of the shield is carried out as previously directed.

CHAPTER III.

CASTING.

PERHAPS the simplest illustration of a crude cast would be the following:

Let the operator go off into a pasture lot and find a fresh cow track in the mud. The impression of the hoof in the mud forms what is called a "mould." Now, if a small quantity of plaster of Paris be mixed with water, poured into the mould, allowed to harden or set, and afterward be lifted out in one piece, we have what is called a "cast," or counterpart in plaster of the animal's hoof.

The process of casting varies with the object to be cast and the number of casts to be taken from the mould.

There is one supreme law to be borne in mind always when making a cast, and that is, "Will the mould draw?"

If the object to be cast is firm and immovable, the mould may be made in sections, each piece being formed and placed so that it will relieve itself from all undercuts and draw, making what is termed a "piece mould." Or the mould may be made of a flexible material, in order to come away from the undercuts without breakage to either the cast or the mould. This is performed with the gelatine or glue mould.

If the object to be cast is flexible, it will in all probability come out of a firm mould, and the cast must then be made of a flexible material, forming a flexible cast; or the cast may be made firm and the mould chipped off the hard cast and destroyed, making what is termed a "waste mould."

7

THE ART OF TAXIDERMY.

THE PROPERTIES OF PLASTER.

Dry plaster of Paris of good quality, when mixed with water, soon sets and becomes hard and firm. Plaster sets more quickly when mixed with ice water than with luke-warm water.

When plaster starts to set in the vessel in which it has been mixed, if more water is added to the batch and stirred in, the plaster will not set and become hard, and the batch is ruined.

A teaspoonful of glue, hot, or Lepage's liquid, added to a quart of water in which plaster is mixed, will hold back the plaster from setting for a number of hours. A quantity of glue added to plaster will keep back the plaster until the whole dries out, when it becomes very much harder than clear plaster, but is apt to crack in drying if too much hot glue is used. Gum arabic dissolved in the water, while making the plaster extremely hard when dry, does not appreciably retard the plaster from setting.

Common salt dissolved in water in which plaster is mixed will increase the rapidity of setting. Plaster which has been modelled into form and which is slow in setting may be made to set more rapidly by sprinkling it with salt brine. The addition of salt to plaster renders the plaster very brittle when dry; it is therefore an advantage in a waste mould, but should not be used in a cast.

Making a Piece Mould and Cast in Plaster.—For an illustration of this method of casting we will select a small boulder and proceed to cast it.

Some fine sand is procured—sawdust or meal will answer if sand is not at hand—and dampened just enough so that it will model well with a spatula or putty knife.

The boulder is studied to see where the greatest draw may be made, and partially buried in the sand, leaving the section to be covered by the first piece of the mould uppermost and exposed. With the palette knife the sand is built

up and levelled off until just the precise surface of the stone
to be covered by the first piece of the mould is visible (see
Fig. 15).

With a small brush the exposed surface of the stone is
painted thinly with lard oil.

A small quantity of water is placed in a basin and plaster sifted into it until it rises in a cone about an inch or so

Fig. 15.—First Step in Casting with a Piece Mould.

above the surface of the water, and stirred well with a spoon.
The mixture should be thinner than cream for the first
layer, which is to take the impression.

With the spoon the liquid plaster is dipped out and
poured over the oiled surface of the stone and blown stoutly
with the breath, to destroy all bridges and bubbles and to
drive the plaster into the most minute crevices of the stone.
When well covered, so that no dark places show through the
plaster by reason of thinness, this shell of plaster is allowed
to harden slightly. The remaining plaster in the basin is
thrown away, which will be but a very small quantity if the
operator has properly gauged the amount required.

When the shell of plaster has hardened enough so that
it will not be disturbed by the addition of more plaster, a
second batch is mixed in the basin, thicker than before, and
applied evenly all over the first coat with the spoon at first,
and then with a putty knife, to the depth of three quarters
of an inch. Had our object been a large one, tow would
have been mixed through the second batch of plaster to

strengthen it; but in this case clear plaster is sufficiently strong.

When the plaster has set and become quite warm in so doing, the stone, with the plaster attached, is removed from the bed of sand and the loose particles of sand dusted off the surface of the stone and the edges of the plaster.

The edges of the mould are shaved down and smoothed with a sharp knife, and holes large enough to admit the end of the thumb bored in the edges of the plaster with the point of the knife, to act as " keys " to adjust the subsequent pieces of the mould that are to rest upon it.

A quantity of clay of good modelling consistence (modelling wax is just as good) is now procured and rolled with a round bottle upon the table into a sheet about half an inch thick and cut into strips half an inch wide with a knife. The stone is placed upon the table with the attached piece of the mould and arranged for a second section of the mould.

In order to keep the liquid plaster for the second piece from covering too much area and thus producing undercuts, a wall of clay is built upon the boulder in such a way that one side of the space is taken up with the piece already on, and the balance taking in as much space as will draw after

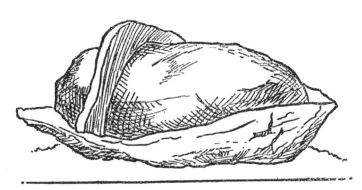

FIG. 16.—SECOND STEP IN CASTING WITH A PIECE MOULD.

the plaster sets, as in Fig. 16. When the wall of clay is properly adjusted the surface of the stone to be cast and the edge of the piece of plaster already on are painted with oil.

A quantity of dry graphite is a good thing to have on hand, as, mixed with oil, it makes a most perfect lubricant, and plaster frees from it more readily than from any other substance I know of. The stone itself should have no graphite upon it, as the graphite fills up and destroys detail. The graphite and oil mixed are used only on the edges of the moulds. A small quantity of plaster is mixed up as before and poured into the area inclosed by the wall of clay and the edge of the piece of the mould already on. After blowing, as before, to secure definition, this layer is allowed to harden up a little, and another layer of thicker plaster built upon it until this piece is of the uniform thickness corresponding with the first piece.

When this section is fully set the wall of clay is taken off, the exposed edges of the second piece trimmed and " keyed," all particles of plaster carefully brushed off, and we are ready to proceed with a third section of the mould.

This and all subsequent pieces are treated in a similar manner, the last piece being simply a filler, and not requiring a wall of clay.

When the entire boulder is incased the plaster is allowed to remain untouched until the whole mass has grown cold, when the plaster is fully set. The plaster mould is now tapped all over the outside with a mallet until the pieces chatter and show a disposition to loosen.

They are pried apart with wooden wedges, if necessary, which they should not require if properly adjusted, and each piece taken off separately and the boulder removed from the plaster casing (Fig. 17).

We now have a mould or negative of the stone (Fig. 18). The pieces may be set away and allowed to dry out, and a cast run out at any time, or they may be used at once to secure a plaster cast.

If the mould is allowed to dry out, a few hours before using it must receive a couple of coats of thin shellac, to prevent the oil that is subsequently applied from sinking into the plaster.

If it is desired to run out a cast at once, as we shall proceed to do, the insides of the pieces of the mould are well oiled. The pieces are then set in place and tied around

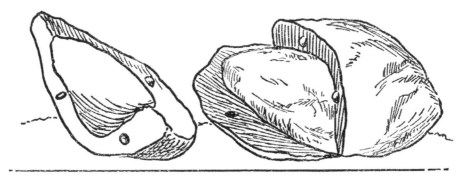

Fig. 17.—One Piece off.

with stout twine to keep them from moving, and any openings in the seams are stopped from the outside by plastering the cracks with clay. If any of the pieces show a disposition to shift, a little fresh plaster smeared on the outside over the joints will, when set, make all secure. A hole is previously bored into one of the pieces on the side of the cast which is to lie underneath when finished, or one of the

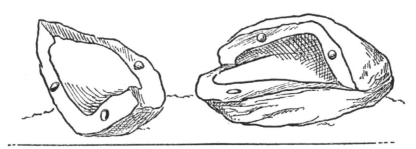

Fig. 18.—Piece Mould completed.

smaller pieces of the mould may be left off until plaster is poured in and the piece adjusted and tied into place.

When all is ready, moderately thin plaster is poured into the mould, the quantity varying with the weight desired in the finished cast, and the mould rocked about in all directions so as to distribute the plaster evenly over the interior, until the plaster is set. The cast may be made solid, or just a shell, according to the amount of plaster introduced into the mould.

In the case of moulds having one end open so that the hand and arm may be introduced, a thin wash of plaster is given to the inside of the mould, and after this has set tow or cotton batting, worked through the liquid plaster, is introduced with the hand in flat wads and the whole interior lined up with this material to any required thickness. This lining of tow gives not only lightness but great strength to the cast. For rough casts excelsior is sometimes used instead of tow. After the plaster has been allowed a sufficient time to set and harden in the mould, the outside of the mould is tapped all over with a mallet until some of the pieces rattle and loosen, when they are wedged apart and the cast relieved from the mould. We now have a perfect cast or model in plaster of the original stone.

Seams left by the joints of the mould are worked off with a knife and scraper. All holes and bubble marks may be filled with fresh plaster by first wetting the parts with a brush or fluff of cotton dipped in water and applying freshly mixed plaster. Fresh plaster should never be added to dry or partially dry plaster without first saturating the part with water, for the old plaster simply absorbs the water from the fresh, leaving the renewed portions chalky. When dry, the plaster boulder is painted with oil colours by " spattering " the colours on with a toothbrush, beginning with the lighter colours and toning down with the darker.

The mould may now be stored away and a number of casts run out at any time.

Casting with a Flexible Mould.—When but a few copies are to be taken of a complicated solid object, to save the time required to make a piece mould in plaster, or, in fact, where a piece mould would not answer, the glue mould is used.

Carpenter's glue of good quality is wrapped in wet

cloths over night or until partly jellified, when it is placed in a glue pot and heated. Too much water should not be used, otherwise the glue when cooled will not have sufficient elasticity to stretch around undercuts without tearing.

Glue composition (formula No. 22) may be used instead of the clear glue, and melted over to form other moulds at any time.

For an example we will cast a stone having a great many small undercuts and irregularities upon its surface, and which would be difficult to cast in a plaster mould.

A cardboard box minus the cover is procured, just large enough to leave about half an inch of space all around the stone. If a box of the proper size can not be procured, a cardboard box may be made by cutting the cardboard to the proper size and sewing the edges together, and afterward plastering over the seams with clay to prevent leakage.

The stone, after receiving a coat of oil, is set into the box; or, if the entire stone is to be cast, it may rest upon a couple of nails coming straight up through the bottom of the box, or upon a pedestal of clay.

When in position, the hot glue is poured into the box until the stone is covered to the depth of half an inch. The glue is now allowed to cool, and is better left overnight for this purpose.

When thoroughly cooled the glue is cut through with a sharp knife along the centre of the top to the sides of the box. The cut is continued down the sides of the box through the cardboard and glue, thus making two halves of the mould, with the cardboard at the bottom acting as a hinge.

The two sides of the box with the glue attached are now opened like an oyster and the stone lifted out.

The nails upon which the stone rested are withdrawn, the holes filled up, and the result is a perfect mould of the stone in glue.

CASTING.

To make a cast from the mould, we simply oil the inside, pour in liquid plaster, adjust the edges, and wrap the whole with twine to keep the mould in position. The mould is rocked about in all directions to distribute the plaster evenly over the inside, and when set the mould is opened and the cast lifted out.

A hole is sometimes cut in the bottom of the mould and the plaster poured in this way.

By careful handling, if the inside be previously washed with alum water, a number of casts may be taken from a glue mould before the sharpness is melted out by the water and heat in the plaster.

A glue mould should be used as soon as possible after it is thoroughly cooled, otherwise if left for any great time the water will dry out of the glue and the moulds shrink and dry. Good gelatine may be used instead of glue, and answers equally well.

In casting larger objects, instead of the cardboard box a plaster jacket is made, in the following way:

A slab of plaster is first formed large enough to clear the object vertically on all sides and allowing a few inches all around. The upper edges of the slab are "keyed." The object is then placed upon the slab and covered all over to the depth of an inch or so with crumpled tissue paper.

Clay is modelled over the paper, smoothing all. A piece mould is now made of the clay-covered object, the plaster slab at the bottom forming one piece of the mould. When set, the pieces of the mould are taken apart, the object lifted out, and the clay and paper removed from it. The reason for using the paper is to keep the object from being smeared up with the clay. Three or four holes are now cut into the upper pieces of the plaster jacket to allow the air to escape when the hot glue is poured in. The object and the inside of the plaster jacket are now well oiled and the pieces of the mould arranged around it. The hot glue or gelatine is poured into the mould, completely enveloping the object.

When the glue has cooled the plaster jacket is lifted apart, which leaves the object incased in glue. The glue is cut half in two and the object lifted out.

The cast is made as already described.

Casting with a Waste Mould.—If the object to be cast is flexible, and but one copy in plaster is desired, the waste mould is used.

For an illustration of this method of casting we will select a dead greyhound which it is desired to mount, and a cast of one entire side will be valuable for future reference in mounting.

The animal is laid on its side upon the table and properly posed. Excelsior is built around it, covered with a layer of damp sand put on with a spatula or putty knife. The sand is built up until just one half of the body and upper limbs are exposed to view.

A chunk of pork fat or tallow is tried out over the fire, and the warm oil applied to the hair with a brush and afterward smoothed down while cooling. The advantage of this fat over other oils is that it hardens somewhat in cooling, and the hair can be smoothed down so as to show every detail of the anatomy. Clay water and soapsuds are sometimes used for this purpose, but are not recommended. When well oiled and smoothed down all over the exposed or upper half to keep the plaster from sticking to and afterward pulling out the hair, everything is in readiness for the plaster.

As this is to be a waste mould, a tablespoonful of dry sienna or umber is mixed through the water in which the first installment of plaster is to be mixed. The dry plaster is sifted into the coloured water, and when well stirred is poured evenly over the entire surface of the animal. If enough is not mixed in the first batch to cover the surface intended, a second lot is mixed as before and applied.

When somewhat hardened the plaster shell is brushed over lightly with lard oil, and plaster mixed with water containing no colour is added until the mould is about half an inch thick all over.

When the whole is thoroughly set the mould is worked off the carcass, any slight undercuts relieving readily by reason of the flexibility of the flesh.

The mould may now be set aside and the cast run out at leisure, in which case the dry mould must be shellacked well inside a few hours before using it, to prevent the oil that must be painted upon it from being absorbed by the plaster.

We will, however, proceed to run out the cast at once, which is preferable.

The inside of the mould is painted over with lard oil, which by reason of the water in the plaster is not absorbed.

A quantity of moderately thin plaster is mixed and poured over the entire inside of the mould and allowed to harden up somewhat before applying more.

A quantity of tow is procured and separated into loose flat wads. These are placed, a few at a time, in the basin of liquid plaster and manipulated until thoroughly soaked.

The wads of tow thus saturated are lined up inside the mould to the depth of a quarter of an inch all over. If tow is not at hand, sheet cotton, or fine excelsior, may be used as a substitute. It is, however, necessary to thoroughly saturate cotton with water by wetting and wringing it out repeatedly until wet through, before it will take up the plaster readily. A cast thus lined up with tow is not only much lighter, but possesses greater strength than a cast made of clear plaster.

The plaster having been allowed to set in the mould is, by reason of the undercuts, bound in firmly. The mould is therefore destroyed by chipping it away with chisel and mallet.

The whole is laid upon a bed of excelsior, and piece by piece the outside layer of white plaster is chipped away in quite large chunks, relieving perfectly, by reason of the slight oiling, from the shell of coloured plaster which lies between the outside or heavy stratum of the mould and the cast. By having the thin layer of coloured plaster next the cast it is always known just how deep to cut, whereas if all were one colour clear through there would be danger of chiselling down into the cast itself.

The colours may of course be reversed, and the cast itself made in coloured plaster.

When the outside layer of the mould is completely chipped away it is but a small matter to remove the stratum of coloured plaster, and a perfect cast or counterpart in plaster of the body of the greyhound results. A wash of benzine effectually cleanses the grease from the hair of the dog.

Making a Waste Mould in Wax.—If it is desired to get a real fine impression of a delicate object, this may be accomplished by the use of the wax mould. For an illustration of this method of casting we will select a fish of a couple of pounds weight.

The fish is first washed and sponged with clear water, and then with alum water to remove the mucus and slime. After a final rinsing the fish is dried off with cloths and laid upon a table with a sheet of damp paper between to keep the wax from adhering to the wood. A wall of clay is built all around the fish to keep the hot wax from flowing away. The tail and fins are posed, and clay built under fins that are raised from the table. Casting wax (formula No. 14) is now prepared and flowed evenly over the fish, pouring on the wax slowly in order to avoid producing air bubbles. After the first layer, spoonful after spoonful of the hot wax is thrown on until a depth of a sixteenth of an inch is secured. A large flat camel's-hair brush is used with cooler wax and the wax built out around the fins. The fish now lies with the upper parts incased in a body of wax. To stiffen the wax mould, a plaster jacket of the depth of half an inch is put on by pouring plaster upon the wax. This plaster jacket is of course unnecessary in the case of small objects. When the whole mass has cooled off it is turned upside down on a layer of excelsior, and the fish drawn out of the wax mould.

Without any previous oiling very thin plaster is run into the mould, care being taken that the parts of the mould formerly occupied by the extremities are filled. When this has set, wads of tow or cotton saturated with liquid plaster are introduced into the mould to the depth of half an inch all over, and allowed to harden.

After this has taken place the whole is turned over and the plaster jacket chipped off with chisel and mallet. We now have a plaster cast of the fish incased in a mould of wax.

The wax is softened with heat by means of a gasoline blower such as is used by painters in removing paint from doors, etc. If this is not at hand, the whole may be placed in a pan and set in an oven for a time. It must be borne in mind that plaster of Paris after setting and before drying out will not stand a long-continued heat, or the plaster bakes and becomes chalky. As the wax softens it is pulled off in sheets. It is better to peel off the wax thus than to allow it to liquefy, as any dirt in the wax sticks fast to the cast.

When the wax has all been removed we have as a result a perfect and sharp cast of the fish lying upon a flat slab of plaster. After being " pointed up," the cast is allowed to dry out and is then ready for colouring. The slab may be coloured in imitation of wood, or it may be sanded, and shells, etc., glued upon its surface.

FLEXIBLE CASTS.

Flexible objects, such as toads, lizards, etc., may be rendered successfully by the use of the glue composition (formula No. 22).

In this process a plaster mould is made as previously

directed, and, after being well shellacked and oiled inside, run full of the hot composition.

After cooling, the mould is lifted apart and the flexible cast removed.

All edges are trimmed off the cast with scissors and a sharp scalpel and worked over with a hot modelling tool.

Wires may be inserted afterward in the legs and tails of lizards, etc. Objects cast in this composition will remain flexible for a long time, after they are coloured and varnished; but the main consideration is not the permanent flexibility, but the temporary flexibility which enables the cast to draw from an undercut mould.

Casting in Paper.—For very large objects where the least possible weight is desired, a cast in paper may be made. This is useful in preparing large masses of rock, cetaceans, etc., where the most minute definition is unnecessary. For complicated moulds of small objects the paper process is not recommended. The method is as follows:

A plaster mould is made in as many pieces as are necessary to properly relieve the cast.

When dry, the mould is shellacked and oiled well inside.

Stereotyper's "matrix paper" is dampened with water by pressing it for a few moments between two sheets of wet blotting paper and torn (not cut) into strips the length and width varying with the size of the mould.

Pieces of the paper, brushed over with rye-flour paste on both sides, are introduced, and pressed and well beaten into the mould with a stiff brush—an ordinary stiff shoe dauber will answer.

When covered all over with one layer, a second layer of the pasted paper is again beaten into the mould, over the first. To strengthen these, heavier brown paper is used in the same way until the whole is sufficiently stout. The paper is allowed to remain in the mould for days or weeks, according to circumstances, until the paper has dried out sufficiently, when it is eased out of the mould.

The edges are trimmed and the parts of the cast united by pasting strips of paper and cloth across the cracks from the inside. The seams are then filled with *papier-maché* and the whole coloured.

The great difficulty with this paper process is the shrinkage due to the drying out of the paper and paste. This may, however, be overcome in a measure by pasting in a few sheets at a time and allowing these to dry, and then adding more.

The following composition, though not so strong as the above, works very well and does not shrink:

Stereotyper's matrix paper is torn up and placed in a bucket of warm water and worked between the palms of the hands until reduced to a fine pulp. The excess of water is then squeezed out of the pulp by wringing it out in cheese cloth. The balls of pulp are broken up with the fingers, and gum arabic, dissolved in water until of the consistence of thin molasses, added to the pulp, making a thin mush of the whole. Plaster of Paris, dry, is mixed through the composition until a nice, easy-working *maché* results. The whole is now worked through an ordinary painter's grinding mill, to break up all lumps and refine it.

This composition is well pressed and beaten into the mould, previously shellacked and oiled, and when set may be backed or lined up with pasted paper or muslin, or tow saturated with hot glue. Should the *maché* set too quickly, a little glue (hot, or Lepage's liquid) may be added to the water in which the gum is dissolved. This will hold back the plaster from setting. If it is found necessary to make the plaster set more quickly, salt brine may be sponged over the inside after the composition is in place.

Casting in Wax.—Wax or paraffin, or a mixture of both, may be run, hot, into a plaster mould, but it is necessary that the plaster be hot to take a fine impression, and thoroughly saturated with water to keep the wax from binding fast to the mould.

The plaster mould is therefore placed in hot water and

allowed to remain there for an hour or more, when it is ready to receive the wax. After the wax has partially cooled the whole is placed into cold water to facilitate cooling, when the mould is pried apart, the cast removed, and the mould again placed in hot water preparatory to a second cast. The plaster mould, however, rapidly deteriorates under the action of the hot water, and loses its sharpness after a number of casts have been run out.

After the foregoing directions for casting, no further details of this process are necessary. The wax may of course be coloured while in a liquid state to any desired tint by the addition of tube oil-colours, and may be strengthened by using cotton batting saturated with hot wax in the same way as tow is used with plaster in the preceding processes of plaster casting.

Clay Moulds.—For rough work clay moulds are sometimes useful.

For the production of artificial limb bones for large mammals, to be used in the construction of a manikin, where the natural bones are to be used separately for exhibition as a skeleton, a clay mould can be used to great advantage. The process is as follows:

Good modelling clay is placed in a bucket with water if dry, and punched with a piece of gaspipe until the mixture is of the consistence of putty. If lumpy, these may be removed by forcing the clay through the meshes of a sieve of wire netting, using a block of wood set in a handle for this purpose. The clay goes through the netting in the form of short strings or noodles, and by the addition of water may now be reduced to any more liquid consistence. When like putty, linseed oil is added and thoroughly mixed through the clay until it no longer adheres to objects pressed into it. By forcing the clay through the sieve a couple of times after the oil has been added, with a little kneading, the oil will be found to have become thoroughly incorporated with the clay. Painters' putty, or the modelling composition ready prepared, known as " plastiline," work as well as, if not better than, common clay mixed with oil. For an illustration of the use of the clay mould, we will select a femur or thigh bone of a large mammal and proceed to cast it.

It makes no especial difference whether the bone be green or dry. A few shreds of flesh or tendon remaining on the bone will also make no difference.

The bone is well wet with water, and a piece of wire twisted about the ends of the bone to be used in pulling it out after it is embedded in the clay.

The clay is built upon the table in a solid mass, longer, wider, and deeper than the bone. The bone, front down, is pressed firmly into the clay. When the bone is nearly submerged the clay is pressed closely about the sides and made to fit the bone snugly all around, but not completely over. The projecting wires, which were previously fastened to the ends of the bone, are now twisted together, forming a loop at each end of the bone. By placing a small stick in the loops for a better grip, the bone is pulled gradually out of the clay, leaving a rough mould. If the clay has parted anywhere by reason of great undercuts, the cracks are closed by simply pressing the clay back into place. So much for the mould. Now for the cast. A piece of pine wood is cut, an inch shorter than the length of the mould, and not so thick as to come too close to the sides of the mould. The stick is placed in hot paraffin over the water bath, and submerged until all air bubbles cease to rise, when the wood is thoroughly charged with paraffin and consequently waterproofed. If this detail of waterproofing the wood is not attended to, the plaster which is to surround it will give out moisture, the wood will swell, and a cracked cast will result.

A quantity of plaster of Paris is now mixed and wads of tow worked well through it. These saturated wads are placed in the mould until a good bed is formed for the paraffined stick to rest on. When the stick is properly arranged in

8

the mould, wads of the plaster-saturated tow are tucked in all around it with an artist's camel's-hair brush, all large vacancies are filled with blocks of wood also saturated with paraffin, and tow and plaster further tucked in until the mould is filled. When thoroughly set, the clay is pulled away from the plaster, and, with a little trimming with a shoe-knife, the result is a cast of the natural bone— a rough one, to be sure, but accurate enough for the purpose for which it is designed, and much more so than the bones usually carved from wood for this purpose.

Casting Heads of Birds with Naked Head Skins, such as the Turkey, Vulture, etc.—For this operation it is of course necessary to have the specimen freshly killed and in the flesh. For an illustration we will select a domestic turkey gobbler. The skin is encircled with the knife at the ruff of feathers on the neck, and the head and part of the neck removed entirely from the body, if possible before the flesh and wattles have had time to soften.

The head is well washed to remove all blood and dirt, and a stout wire run up through the spinal canal of the neck vertebræ into the brain cavity, and the lower end stapled fast to a block of wood. The head is now posed and arranged in the position it is to occupy in the mounted bird.

A quantity of marble dust is prepared by pounding up pieces of marble and grinding them in a mortar, and sifting the dust through cheesecloth to secure only the finer particles.

This is mixed, dry, through plaster of Paris, in the proportion of one of marble dust to two of plaster.

A mould of this composition (mixed with water, of course) is now made in two pieces, each piece representing a lateral half of the turkey head, as already described, save that no oil is allowed to touch the skin or bristles of the head and neck.

To secure a fine impression, the first thin plaster is

brushed upon the wet surface of the head with a camel's-hair brush, and all small feathers or bristles allowed to stand out and not become flattened down upon the skin. The mould should not be over half an inch in thickness. When the plaster is all on, the moulds, with the head still inside, are set away in a warm place to allow the plaster to dry out and decomposition or maceration to take place in the head.

The body of the bird is now skinned and mounted in the usual way, but without a head. A single stout wire projects from the stump of the neck to fasten the cast head upon when ready.

After a lapse of several days in a warm room the two halves of the mould are pried apart, bringing with them the feathers and hair of the turkey head. Should any of the epidermis come off in the mould, this is brushed and picked out.

The bill of the turkey, with a portion of the bone at the base attached, is now cut off from the head and well cleaned and dried. When dried, the bill is dropped into hot wax, removed and allowed to cool. The bill is set in place in one side of the mould, the other half of the mould adjusted, and the two tied into place with twine.

Wax and paraffine, equal parts, are now heated over the water bath and coloured to match the light body colour of the head and neck.

The mould is placed in hot water for fifteen minutes to heat it, and also to keep the wax from sticking. A quantity of the hot wax is now poured into the mould through the open end and swashed about in all directions so as to give the interior an even coating of wax all over.

A wire wrapped about with tow is now introduced into the mould, six inches of the wire being allowed to project from the open end. The mould is run full of wax, and the whole placed in cold water to cool.

A twenty-per-cent solution of muriatic acid and water

is prepared and the whole thing submerged, where it is allowed to remain for a few hours. The outside of the plaster mould will be found decomposed and honeycombed by the action of the acid, and is easily crumbled off with a scraper, care being used not to cut or break off the protruding feathers or hairs.

The mould is again placed in the dilute acid and further softened and the surface worked off. This process is repeated until the wax cast is entirely freed from the covering of plaster. The wax and feathers are not injured in the least by the acid, and the hairs and feathers form little channels by which the acid enters the plaster and allows the gas to escape, thus freeing themselves.

When the mould is entirely removed we have a cast in wax of the turkey's head, with the bill and all feathers and bristles in position. The eye-sockets are dug out with a scraper and artificial eyes inserted and modelled in with hot wax applied with a brush, and finished with a scraper.

The final colouring is now given to the cast head, if possible using a living gobbler as a model.

When all is complete, the head is fastened upon the mounted body, the skin at the extremity of the neck having been wrapped in damp cloths previously. The neck skin is adjusted about the base of the cast and glued and pinned in position.

The above process involves a considerable expenditure of time, but the miserable mummified heads usually seen in mounted turkeys will, I think, be a sufficient justification for the enterprising taxidermist to try this method.

Stereotyper's Metal.—This may readily be procured at any type foundry, and is often useful for casting where something harder than plaster is required. This metal fuses at a comparatively low temperature, can be whittled with a knife, and is very light.

CHAPTER IV.

BIRDS.

I. The Treatment of Skins.

Bird Skinning.—If a bird is to remain permanently in the shape of a skin, it should be skinned as directed in the chapter on Collecting—that is, opened from the posterior end of the breastbone to the anus in the case of land birds, and along the back for water birds.

Birds in which the head is too large to pass through the skin of the neck should have a second opening cut made along the back of the head and the skull cleaned by inverting it through the orifice.

When a land bird is to be skinned for subsequent mounting, it is, however, more convenient to make the opening cut on the breast extend up farther. The bird may be skinned as before directed—that is, over the rump—or it may be skinned by working from the neck backward.

In the latter method the skin at the sides of the opening cut are pushed away from the muscles of the breast with the end of the scalpel handle, and corn meal liberally applied to absorb the moisture and keep the feathers dry and clean.

When the base of the neck is reached this is severed from the body inside the skin, with the scissors or bone snips. The skin is now worked over one shoulder until the base of the humerus is exposed. This is also severed close to the body. The other wing is treated similarly. The skin now peels off readily until the legs are reached. Dry corn meal is liberally thrown on during the entire process, as, especially if the bird is freshly killed, blood will flow in a greater or less degree and disfigure the plumage. The legs are disjointed at the knees, when the skin again peels off easily until the base of the tail appears. This is cut through with the scissors, care being taken to avoid cutting so far back as to injure the bases of the tail feathers, or these will drop out.

The body having now been removed, the legs, wings, and base of the tail are cleaned, and the head and neck are skinned as previously directed.

Scraping the Inside of a Bird Skin.—If the skin is that of a small bird and not fat, no scraping is necessary, and, provided no blood or grease have stained the plumage, the skin is ready to poison and mount.

If the skin is at all fat, this must be scraped off with a large bone scraper, using liberal quantities of corn meal to absorb the grease as it is loosened. Corn meal is recommended in the place of plaster for scientific specimens, as, although a more perfect absorbent, more or less plaster is apt to be retained in the feathers, thus giving them a whitish appearance. This is especially true when collecting in the field, where all the appliances for getting plaster out of the plumage are not at hand.

Scraping a fat bird skin is a tedious task, but in order to produce a perfectly prepared and permanent specimen the grease *must come out*. This should be done while the specimen is fresh, whether the bird is to be made into a skin or mounted, otherwise in time the grease will run out through shot holes or along the opening cuts in the skin and disfigure the feathers.

Very fat water birds, where heroic treatment is sometimes necessary, are cleaned as follows:

After skinning, all blood stains are carefully removed from the plumage by using warm water containing a little washing soda and applied with a sponge, brushing always from the bases to the tips of the feathers. In case the operator is not ready to proceed with the scraping, the inside of the skin may be rubbed with salt and the skin folded up and placed in a damp situation for a few days. Never apply salt to a bird or mammal skin that has blood upon the hair or feathers, or a permanent stain will result.

When ready to proceed, the skin is submerged in water, feathers and all, and the salt well rinsed out. The skin is now squeezed out with the hands in order to get rid of the excess of water, and we are ready for the scraping process.

Whether the skin has been salted or not, it is placed in a basin or bucket of benzine, and the whole inside well scrubbed with a small wire brush about the size of an ordinary toothbrush. This releases the oil, and by continuous scrubbing with the brush—scrubbing with the lay of the bases of the feathers, and not against them, or a torn skin will result—and soaking with the benzine the fat and oil are entirely removed. The skin may be left in the benzine for a day or two without deteriorating, but of course this is not necessary. As above stated, this is a rigorous measure, and need not be resorted to except in extreme cases.

Feathers, if properly handled, will stand no end of banging, and one of the first things a young taxidermist must learn is to lose all fear of handling plumage.

Skins of large birds, such as the ostrich, emu, etc., should be salted as soon as possible after removal from the carcass.

The legs of cranes, herons, etc., should have the tendons removed by making an incision in the sole of the foot after the bird has been skinned, and by working a stout awl underneath the tendons at this point, drawing them out. The insides of the legs are poisoned by injecting alum and arsenic dissolved in water, or the legs and feet may lie in salt and alum pickle (formula No. 2) for a few hours. In warm weather, if the tendons of these birds are not removed, the legs are apt to become putrid and lose their scutes. In the case of young hawks and other birds having a plump, fleshy foot—as in the osprey or eagle—not only should the tendons be removed from the legs, but each toe should be split in its entire length on the under side, the flesh and tendons removed, and their places supplied with *papier-maché* and the skin sewed up.

The legs of the ostrich, cassowary, etc., being too tough to permit of the removal of the tendons by this means, are split from behind in their entire length and the sinews, etc., removed.

If the facilities are at hand, the heads of turkeys, vultures, etc., should be cut off entirely from the neck and cast separately while fresh, as directed in the previous chapter. If this can not be done, the head is skinned in the usual way and the loose skin and wattles restored by modelling upon the dried skin in wax. The casting process is, however, more preferable. In some of the domestic fowls the combs and wattles are cut off and cast while fresh, and the wax casts afterward fastened to the dried head skin.

In the case of herons, in which the curves of the neck are angular and difficult to form, the neck vertebræ may be taken out whole, cleaned by boiling and scraping, and well poisoned with arsenic and alum. A stout wire may then be run up the spinal canal and left projecting at either end. The muscles and windpipe may then be reproduced upon the actual bones by binding tow upon them, and a well-formed neck will result. Further, this neck can only bend in a natural and angular way, and does away with the circular goose necks so often seen in mounted birds of this class.

To relax a Dried Bird Skin.—As a rule, the longer a skin has been dried the more difficulty there will be in softening it.

A number of methods have been employed to impregnate the skin with moisture and thus restore it to its original pliable state.

A box with a close-fitting lid, the whole containing a

lining of an inch or so of plaster, has been devised. Before using, the box is filled with water until the plaster is charged, when the water is poured out. The skin is then placed in the box, where the dampness from the surrounding walls of plaster relaxes it. Others have buried the skin in damp sand or sawdust. The method usually employed by professional taxidermists is to open the stitches, remove the filling, and pack the inside of the skin with pads of wet cotton batting. The bends of the wings are covered with flat wads of wet cotton, and the feet and legs also wrapped with the same material. The whole is then covered with a damp cloth and left until the skin is sufficiently relaxed to invert and scrape.

In large birds the legs and wings, which require the longest time to soak up, are wrapped with wet cotton or cloths a couple of days before the body skin is wet, as by the time the feet and wings are sufficiently relaxed there would be danger of macerating or rotting the epidermis of the body and losing the feathers.

Salt brine or tan liquor (formula No. 1) is therefore recommended for large birds, where a number of days may be spent in relaxing and scraping the skin. The flesh side of the skin is dampened with brine during the scraping process, but the feathers must not be allowed to become saturated with the liquor, as certain colours are apt to change. Were it not for this colour-changing propensity of salt brine, bird skins could be kept in a pliable state for years by simply immersing them in this liquid and allowing them to remain there until wanted.

Scraping the Dry Skins of Birds preparatory to Mounting them.—When a dry bird skin has been soaked and relaxed it is by no means ready to mount yet. The feathers are set in place as they were in the dried skin, and before these can be made to change their positions the whole inside of the skin must be scraped and the butts of the feathers loosened one from the other.

This is a tedious process, and actually requires more time than the subsequent mounting. I have seen bird skins which required three days to scrape and prepare, when but part of a day thereafter was all that was necessary to properly mount them.

In most birds it will be found that the feathers grow in ridges, overlapping and covering the bare spaces on the exterior of the body. In water birds the ridges are broader, and a much greater time is consequently required to properly scrape them.

The scraping is done with the small bone scraper, using the sharp or pointed end for this purpose, and separating

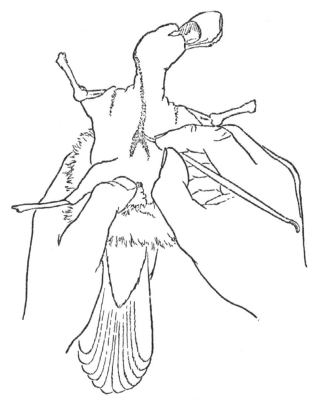

Fig. 19.—Scraping a Bird Skin.

the bases of the quills one from the other on the inside of the skin. This is best performed by first working lengthwise over the whole ridge of feathers, and then crosswise, cutting the ridge into a mass of small squares, and afterward lifting up the base of each individual feather with the point of the scraper. The whole inside of the bird skin is thus gone over until thoroughly clean and pliable. The bends of the wings and the tail quills are gently manipulated with the fingers until the wings and tail gradually open to their fullest extent.

The legs and toes are also " wiggled " in a similar manner. If the operator were to attempt to boldly force open a dry folded wing with one stroke, the wing would probably break off short at the joint. So also with the feet and legs. The dried tendons must be removed from the legs of waders, if this has not already been done. If the scraping process is not performed in one day, the skin may be covered with a dampened cloth and allowed to remain overnight, when work may again be resumed upon it.

Some very old grease-burned skins will sometimes fall to pieces upon being soaked up. If it is still desired to mount these in spite of this fact, the inside of the skin must be lined with thin sheet rubber, the pieces being sewed fast and glued with rubber cement (pure rubber gum dissolved in benzine).

Cleaning the Plumage of Birds.—When a bird is shot, the sooner blood is removed from the plumage the better. This may be accomplished in a degree by simply sponging off the blood with a wad of cotton batting. After skinning, in the field, blood stains are simply sponged off with water, and the feathers fluffed by sifting dry corn meal on the parts and beating with a toothbrush until the feathers are again dried out. Hot meal or hot sea sand work more rapidly than the above, besides having a tendency to remove any grease that may be on the plumage.

A bird's plumage is better cleaned after skinning than before, since the blood and other juices are apt to flow from the carcass and disfigure the feathers during the operation.

THE ART OF TAXIDERMY.

In the laboratory the process usually adopted is as follows:

If but a few feathers are soiled, these are washed with soda water applied with a soft sponge or wad of cotton, sponging always from the base to the apex of a feather, and not *vice versa*.

When the stain is entirely removed the excess of water is wiped off with a wad of dry cotton and the wet feathers sponged with benzine.

Before the benzine has time to evaporate the entire skin is covered with coarse dry plaster, the coarser the better, and immediately beaten with a flat stick. More plaster is added and again beaten out, when the feathers are dusted vigorously with a feather duster. If not sufficiently fluffy and dry, more plaster is heaped upon the feathers and they are again beaten and dusted.

Never under any circumstances allow wet feathers to come in contact with dry plaster without the intervening benzine bath. If benzine is not at hand, turpentine will answer.

The nicest way to dry off the plumage of small birds and the fur of small mammals is to place them, when wet with benzine, in a cardboard box with a tight-fitting cover, containing dry plaster. The box is shaken violently up and down, thus removing the wet plaster from the feathers or fur and replacing it with dry plaster. The shaking is continued until the feathers or fur are dry, when they are beaten with a stick' and afterward blown out with hand bellows or compressed air.

When a bird's plumage is badly soiled, the whole skin is better thrown bodily into a basin of lukewarm water containing a little washing soda, and well sponged until the blood is all removed. Sometimes the water requires several changes. When the blood is all removed the skin is squeezed out and thrown into benzine, where it is allowed to remain for a few minutes. It is then removed from the benzine, squeezed out, and laid in a flat tray or box containing dry plaster. Fine mahogany sawdust will answer in the place of plaster, but absorbs moisture more slowly. If the plaster has been used for this purpose before, so much the better, as it works easier provided it is dry. Fresh plaster may be added to the old from time to time as required.

With a hand scoop the entire bird is covered with the dry plaster and immediately shaken about so as to allow fresh plaster to come in contact with the feathers, in the place of the wet plaster which has absorbed all it will.

With a piece of rattan or a flat flexible stick the plumage is beaten, and more plaster heaped upon it and the beating continued. For this purpose it is better to be out of doors or in a draught or current of air, so that the flying particles of plaster may be carried off.

The plastering and beating process is carried on until the feathers resume their original fluffiness. The plumage is then finally beaten with the feather duster until no more plaster remains in the feathers. It may seem, after a continuous and hard beating, that not another particle of plaster remains, but if left thus and the skin mounted, when the bird is thoroughly dry a quantity of plaster will be found to sift down upon the pedestal. The skin is therefore better allowed to remain in the sun or in a warm place near the fire for a time, when a final beating and dusting are given. A hand bellows will also materially assist to force out the particles of plaster.

The air compressor, described on page 61, is a most complete arrangement for this purpose. It does away with the laborious beating and dusting, besides giving a much more satisfactory result by not leaving a particle of plaster remaining in the plumage, and also fluffing the feathers much better.

In all the previously described processes, where water and benzine are recommended for cleaning birds' skins, the plastering of course follows. After this the inside of the skin is well poisoned and it is ready to mount.

II. MOUNTING.

After the bird's skin has been removed from the body and properly cleaned and poisoned, it is ready to mount.

The first thing to be done is to construct an artificial body as near the shape as possible of the natural body which has been removed, but considerably smaller. If the body be made as large as or larger than the natural body, the skin will be drawn too tightly around it, and the operator is consequently hampered in the subsequent mounting. Two methods of mounting are in use. One consists in making the artificial body conform exactly in size with the natural one, no other filling being afterward introduced into the skin of the body. The second and best method is to make the artificial body considerably smaller than the natural one, and then to introduce a filling of chopped tow between the body and the skin wherever necessary to produce the proper form in the mounted bird, and also to throw out and "puff" certain feathers. With the last method the bird is under more complete control, and, although taking longer, gives more perfect results, and is therefore recommended here.

Fine excelsior or wood fibre makes the best material of which to construct artificial bodies. Cotton will not answer, as the supporting wires which are to be clinched in the body will not pass through it readily. Dry grass or other coarse fibrous vegetable material will do.

With the natural body lying upon the table for a model, a nucleus of excelsior is wound with strong thread into a hard ball. The excelsior works better and packs harder if it be sprinkled with water a short time before it is used, or else kept in a damp place. More excelsior is bound upon this nucleus until the made body is of about the same general form as the natural one, but smaller. The body should be wound as firm and hard as possible to secure stability for coupling, otherwise the mounted specimen will be shaky. A piece of annealed iron wire stout enough to support the head and neck stiffly is now cut, somewhat longer than the body and neck, and sharpened at both ends by cutting on a bevel with cutting pliers. Very large wires are pointed with a flat file.

The wire is hammered upon the table until perfectly straight. To straighten small wire, one end of a long piece may be placed in a vise or attached to a nail driven into the bench, and, by pulling stoutly on the other end until the wire stretches somewhat, it will be found to remain straight when slackened up. One end of the sharpened wire is now introduced into the wound body at the point where the neck joins in the natural body, and, by twisting and rolling between the thumb and finger, thrust into and completely through the body, coming out at the root of the tail. The projecting tail end of the wire is turned back upon itself in the form of a hook, and hammered back into the butt end of the body. This keeps the wire from turning, and gives a firm support for the head and neck.

To produce a neck, with the natural one as a model for length and girth, tow, or for very small birds cotton batting, is wound firmly about the neck wire.

Two wires are now cut for the wings and straightened and sharpened as before. These should be used in all cases, except perhaps in humming birds with closed wings.

If the bird is to be mounted with closed wings, a wire stout enough to barely support the member is all that is necessary. If the wings are to remain open or spread, a heavier wire is used, to give additional strength.

One of the wires is now introduced into the wing from the inside of the skin, the wire laying along the bone to the very tip of the wing, where it is firmly imbedded in the tissues at that point. If the wing has been opened underneath, the wire is tied fast with thread to the ulna. In any case the wire is bound firmly to the humerus near the head. The other wing is treated likewise, enough wire being allowed in each case for coupling with the body. Wiring wings is a most important factor in mounting birds, and should never be neglected, whether the wings are to remain open or closed.

Two more pieces of soft iron wire are now cut and sharpened, to be introduced into the legs. As stout wires should be used for this purpose as the skin of the tarsus will stand without breaking, in order to produce a strong, well-mounted specimen.

The wire is run up inside the leg by introducing the point at the sole of the foot, and, by rolling the wire between the thumb and forefinger, the point gradually feels its way up inside the skin of the back of the leg, until the knee joint is reached. The wire should pass here just behind the joint, when the thigh is inverted in the skin and the projecting end of the leg wire on the inside of the skin seized with the flat pliers and drawn up just beyond the end of the bone. The other leg is treated similarly.

When it is desired to represent a bird as walking, in which case the ball of the foot in the back leg is raised from the ground, instead of introducing the point of the leg wire at the bottom of the foot, the wire is started at the centre of the bottom of the middle toe at the point of juncture with the ground or pedestal.

It is sometimes necessary to run a long, slender steel awl up the inside of the tarsus in dried skins to make a passage before the wire can be introduced.

Fine tow is now wrapped around the bone and wire to replace the muscles that have been cut away, and also to stiffen the leg. The orbits of the eyes and the interior of the skull having previously been filled with tow cut up fine with the scissors, and the skin of the head and neck turned right side out, the body is inserted within the skin by running the protruding pointed neck wire up through the inside of the neck and forcing the end of the wire up through the center of the skull and out through the feathers. In the case of some long-billed birds the end of the neck wire is not forced up through the skull, but is allowed to rest between the mandibles of the bill, which when tightly closed offers a firm support.

The wing wires are now clinched fast in the body by passing the ends of the wires clear through the excelsior and then hooking them and forcing the hooks back into the hard body. When wired and coupled the heads of the humeri should occupy their normal position on the body. The legs now remain to be coupled.

The pointed end of the leg wire, which projects up inside the skin a little beyond the tow-wrapped limb bone, is forced through the body at the point occupied by the head of the femur in the pelvis of the living bird. The end of the wire is bent over into the form of a staple and driven back into the body, as in the case of the wings, thus giving a firm foundation and fastening.

The leg is now slid down on the wire and drawn out as far as the skin will permit it to go. The leg is thrown up at a right angle with the body as it lies flat upon its back, and a sharp bend made by throwing the leg down, meanwhile holding the wire firmly just beyond the end of the bone. The result of this bend is that an artificial femur

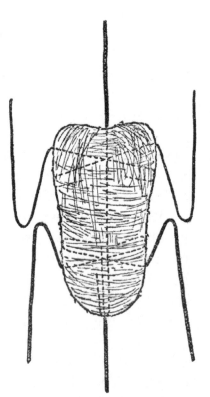

Fig. 20.—Arrangement of Wires in the Artificial Body.

9

or thigh bone of wire is produced, and if made of the proper length gives the same latitude of motion as existed in the living bird. The skin is worked loose from the end of the tibia, otherwise in adjusting the legs the skin is apt to be torn.

The other leg is treated similarly.

The head and neck, wings, and legs having now been wired, the general form of the bird is worked out before the skin of the belly is sewed together.

A T-perch is constructed by nailing a piece of round wood across the top of a second piece nailed fast to a block or square of board for a base. Holes are bored down through the crosspiece at the top and the wires projecting from the bottoms of the feet passed down through the holes. If the bird is not a percher, a flat board answers for a temporary pedestal.

The bird is now upon a perch, and the artistic part of the operation commences.

The wings are adjusted, and if they are to remain closed, see that the tips and butts are even. No further pinning or wiring of the wings is necessary from without, and here lies the advantage of wiring them from the inside. It is a difficult matter to introduce a pin or sharpened wire between the quills of a closed wing without spreading the quills more or less. Furthermore, the wings are difficult to adjust by the slipshod method of pinning from without into the hard body.

The head and neck are now bent into position, and also the legs.

A couple of pointed wires are driven from the outside through the base of the tail into the body, thus supporting this member. If it is desired to spread the tail, a single small, straight wire, sandpapered down smooth, is finely pointed and run crosswise through the base of the shaft of each tail feather, thus stringing each feather, outside of the skin, upon the wire, when they may be separated or moved nearer together at will. This wire is better introduced before the wires supporting the tail are put in.

If the tail is to remain but partly open, or closed, the tail feathers may be clamped between two strips of card-

Fig. 21.—Interior Mechanism of a Mounted Bird.

board held in position with a couple of pins driven through the cards. The feathers all over the body are now worked in place by lifting them up in little bunches with the thumb and forefinger and allowing them to fall back into position.

The form of the bird is further perfected by stuffing

small pads of tow, cut up fine with the shears, through the opening in the breast, using the forceps and a small pusher for this purpose.

The cavity at the base of the tail is filled, and the flesh of the thighs replaced with tow. When the stuffing is completed the bird is removed from the perch if necessary, and the opening sewed up with needle and thread. The bird is again set upon the pedestal, or a rustic perch, artificial rock, or such other foundation as the operator desires. Should it be necessary to change the loose filling inside of the skin, or if more is to be added to puff certain feathers of the breast or back by pressure from within, the wings are lifted up—the wires supporting them in any position in which they may be placed—and longitudinal cuts made in the skin of the body under the wings.

More tow filling is introduced through these openings, and when finished the wings are again thrown down into position. The plumage is now gone over with fine forceps and carefully adjusted by lifting bunches of feathers and allowing them to fall naturally into position. The feathers of the head are adjusted by introducing the end of a knitting needle into the orbits of the eyes and lifting the scalp upon the skull until the feathers lie properly. Tow is introduced through the mouth to fill the throat, and the cheeks and sides of the head are filled through the eye orbits. The bill is kept closed by pinning, or by drawing a thread through the nostril and tying it underneath. The toes are pinned or tied in position, and are made to properly grasp the object upon which the bird is perched.

The bird having been filled and the plumage adjusted, nothing remains but to wrap the specimen to keep the feathers in position while drying.

Wrapping a Bird.—Before wrapping a bird, each feather must lie of its own accord in the position it is to occupy permanently. Do not depend upon the subsequent binding or wrapping to hold a feather down, for sooner or later after the wrapping is removed the misplaced feathers will be found to again resume their old position. It is, however, safer to wrap all mounted birds, to keep the feathers from being displaced while drying. For this purpose the following is recommended : Long pins (insect pins, if they can be had), with a small square of cardboard strung upon them near the head, or pieces of soft wire, one end sharpened and the other end bent into the form of a hook, are driven into the body of the bird along the back, and three or four along the breast or belly. More or less of these pins or wires may be used, according to circumstances.

Fine thread, or, better still, winding cops, which may be procured of dealers in taxidermist's supplies, is now wound about the head and body of the bird, certain feathers depressed by winding them down with the thread, and where the feathers do not require binding down the thread is allowed to rest upon the cardboard or hook of the wire at that point.

When wrapped, the specimen is set away to dry, the time required for this varying from one to two weeks, according to circumstances.

The eyes are better set after the bird has dried. There is bound to be more or less shrinkage in drying, especially in fresh specimens, and eyes set while the bird is fresh will, after drying, be found to protrude in some cases. When dried out, the wrapping is cut away with scissors, the pins or wires used in wrapping are withdrawn, the wires supporting the tail are cut off short, and the neck wire protruding from the top of the head is snipped off close to the skin with cutting pliers. A small wad of wet cotton batting is introduced into the eye orbits, to soften the lids, a few hours before it is desired to set the eyes.

When the lids have soaked sufficiently, they may be further softened by scraping them through the eyelids with a small scraper. Fine *papier-maché* is now worked into the orbits with a small scraper, and glass eyes inserted, using a needle set in a small wooden handle to plump them out and arrange the lids. To give a finish to a bird's eye, a piece of black cotton thread is given a thin coat of gum arabic or liquid glue, and, with the aid of a pair of fine forceps and the needle, arranged just inside the lid around the eye, completely encircling it once, when the surplus of thread is cut off with the scissors. A little lampblack, applied wet with a camel's-hair brush, is also used to colour the lids.

If necessary, the bills and legs may be coloured, using oil colors for this purpose.

In case it is necessary to change a dry bird from one pedestal to another, the feet may be wrapped in wads of wet cotton overnight, when they will be found sufficiently relaxed to be made to conform to another surface.

Spreading Wings.—In mounting birds with spread wings, the wire is introduced from within, precisely as in wiring a wing that is to be closed, with the exception that the wire in the spread wing must be much heavier.

After the specimen is upon its pedestal and the attitude worked out, and the feathers of the body, head, and tail adjusted, the wing quills are supported by running a wire into the body at right angles and bending the end of it over the top of the first primary quill, clamping it tightly. Strips of cardboard or sheet cork are then clamped in place with pins, one strip of the cardboard being above and one on the under side of the wing, running across the quills. By this means the wing quills may be separated and held in position until dry, when the cards and wires are removed.

For very large birds, such as the ostrich, emu, cassowary, etc., the "manikin" is better adapted. The manikin is simply a dummy figure of the bird, minus head, wings, tail, and feet, over which the skin is adjusted and glued and sewed fast.

This method does away with the laborious process of stuffing, and produces a much more satisfactory result. The manikin is constructed on the same general plan as that recommended for large mammals in the following chapter.

CHAPTER V.

MAMMALS.

I. The Treatment of Skins.

Preserving the Skins of Small Mammals.—The skinning of small mammals and the method of making them up as dried skins for study specimens has already been described in the chapter on Collecting. Skins prepared thus, while being good material for study or comparison, are of second class for mounting. When soaked up they sometimes lose their hair, and are then worthless. Very small mammals, such as mice and shrews, are better mounted fresh, like birds—that is, the skin is removed, dusted on the inside with dry alum and arsenic, and wired and mounted at once.

If it is not convenient to mount them thus, the tails should have a soft brass wire, wound with cotton batting and poisoned, inserted within the tail sheaths clear to the very tip. The skin of the head, legs, and body should then be moistened with water and rubbed on the inside with table salt and poisoned. When nearly dry, the skin may be folded and laid flat, and when thoroughly dry packed for shipment. Skins of mice and shrews treated thus will always relax and mount without losing a hair. Small mammals of the size of squirrels, which are to be mounted, should be skinned, salted, covered with a damp cloth, and left rolled up overnight, when they are scraped with a large bone scraper, the inside moistened with tan liquor (formula No. 1) to further soften them, and, after receiving a coat of

124

arsenical soap on the inside, the skin is ready to mount. If it is not desired to mount the specimen at once, it may be allowed to dry up after salting and poisoning, as with the mice, and may be subsequently soaked up, scraped, and mounted.

A wire should always be placed in the tails of small mammals and left there. The wire is better wrapped with a covering of cotton or tow. If a wire is not left in the tail sheath the skin collapses and dries fast, one side to the other, and it is sometimes impossible to work a wire into the tail to the tip afterward.

If it is desired to keep the skin in a soft, pliable condition, so that it may be mounted at any future time, the skin, after salting overnight, is immersed in tan liquor (formula No. 1) and allowed to remain there indefinitely. For this purpose the feet must be well skinned down to the toes, the bottoms of the feet split open, and the tail vertebræ stripped from the sheath and a straw inserted, or the hair is liable to pull off. The tip of the tail is also better split on the under side, for an inch or so, to allow the bath to circulate freely through the tail sheath. The idea is this: Salt or other preservatives must be applied to the flesh side of a skin and allowed to strike through and bind down the epidermis in which the roots of the hair are fixed. The nature of the epidermis prevents the absorption of any preservatives from without, and if the liquor is not allowed to strike directly upon the inside of the skin at all points, these places will soon be found to have lost their hair. It is always best to clean a skin on the inside, and to remove all flesh and fat before it is placed in pickle. A skin will clean easier and better soon after the salt has hardened up the flesh and fat than at any other time, and by thus cleaning the skins before immersion the liquor is kept cleaner. All blood stains should, of course, be sponged out of the hair before immersion.

I do not, however, recommend that skins be placed in

this liquid, or in fact in any other, if they are to be used for scientific purposes, as certain colours are apt to undergo changes—some changing by immersion overnight. *For scientific purposes, the fur of small mammals should never be wet with salt or alum bath.*

To relax the Dry Skin of a Small Mammal.—If it is desired to relax and mount the dried skin of a small mammal that has been salted, it is only necessary to wrap it in a damp cloth until the skin is sufficiently relaxed to be turned inside out, when the whole inside of the head, body, and legs is scraped with the flat end of a large bone scraper, working from the tail to the head and then crosswise, wetting the inside of the skin from time to time with water or tan liquor. If a properly wrapped tail wire is in the tail sheath, this need not be disturbed, and the skin of the tail will be found to be sufficiently relaxed to bend at any angle. The face and lips require to be well scraped, the eyelids trimmed down close with scalpel or scissors, and the base of each individual " whisker " separated one from the other with the point of a small scraper, working from the inside, as in birdskins. The toes must be manipulated until they are thoroughly softened.

If the mammal skin has been made up in the field and simply cured with dry alum and arsenic, or not poisoned or cured at all, the salt and alum bath (formula No. 2) is safer to use for relaxation. If previously stuffed, the stitches along the belly are cut and the filling removed with the aid of a pair of long forceps.

As but a minimum of moisture is safest lest the hair slip, wads of cotton batting wet with salt and alum bath are packed inside the skin until it is full.

The head, feet, and tail are wrapped in flat wads of wet cotton, and a cloth also wet with clear water thrown over the whole and left until the skin is sufficiently relaxed to be turned inside out, which ordinarily requires about fifteen hours. The subsequent treatment is the same as that already described. The longer a skin has remained dry, the longer it will take it to soften.

If a dried skin absolutely refuses to soften in this way, harsh measures must be used, and if the skin spoils, it spoils. The skin is plunged bodily into warm (not hot) water and allowed to remain there until it shows signs of softening. If the skin is in such shape that it can be scraped on the inside, the scraping process should be started now, and as much of the skin gone over as possible. After scraping, the flesh side of the skin is dampened with tan liquor until sufficiently soft to turn completely inside out. The skin is now dampened and scraped until relaxed. If the hair starts, the salt and alum bath is used as a last resort; and if this does not help matters the skin is worthless, and all through the absence of salting while the skin was fresh.

The hair is cleaned and dried in the same way as already directed for cleaning the plumage of birds—that is, the benzine and plaster process. If any salt or alum crystals are upon the hair, these should be sponged off with water and the excess of water rubbed out of the fur with a wad of dry cotton. A wad of cotton is then saturated with benzine, and the hair all over well wetted and rubbed with it. The hair is now combed out, and again rubbed with a wad of dry cotton to remove the excess of benzine. This is all performed after the skin is scraped and in readiness to mount. A roll of cotton is placed inside the skin, and the opening sewed up roughly to keep the plaster from drying out the inside of the skin. After plastering and beating, the stitches are cut away and the cotton removed. After painting over the inside of the skin with arsenical soap, it is ready to mount.

Skinning Large Mammals.—The skinning of certain large mammals has already been described in the chapter on Collecting, and the same general principles are followed out in the skinning of all.

It is always better, if possible, to decide upon the attitude the specimen is to assume when mounted before making the opening cuts, and to make these where they will show the least. The process by which the animal is to be mounted should also be considered. If the plan of soft stuffing is to be used, the opening cuts on the backs of the legs are omitted, or reduced to as short a cut as is necessary to turn the leg in skinning.

Generally, in a horned ungulate the opening cuts run along the belly from the brisket to the tip of the tail, up the backs of the legs from the hoof, and when the body is reached allowing the cuts to intersect the longitudinal belly cut at a right angle. Another Y-shaped cut is made at the back of the head, the arms of the Y reaching to the bases of the horns. In a doe the arms of the Y are omitted, one straight cut being sufficient to enable the head and neck to be easily skinned. In some cases, provided the head can be inverted through the neck, no opening cuts at all are made on the back of the head or neck.

The underside of the neck of a deer should never be opened unless the animal is to be mounted with the neck stretched out along the ground, for the texture of the hair is such that the opening can never again be united so that it will not show.

In most other long-haired mammals the belly cut is extended up along the underside of the neck to a point between the angles of the jaws, and the opening on the back of the neck is consequently omitted.

All monkeys with short hair on the underside of the body are better opened along the back until the tail is reached, when the cut curves down under the tail and is continued to the tip along the underside.

In this case the opening cuts on the legs are omitted, being reduced to openings on the soles of the feet. In subsequently adjusting the skin upon the manikin, the manikin is lifted off the pedestal and the skin drawn on like a pair of trousers. A very short-haired animal, such as the horse in summer coat, is better opened along the belly, from the brisket to the tip of the tail. The backs of the legs are opened from the hoof up about a foot or so in order to clean the feet. The manikin is then so constructed that the legs all lift off. These are placed inside the skin in their proper places and the legs then readjusted to the manikin, the skin enveloping all. This method of mounting does away with the unsightly seams up the legs which are always so difficult to conceal. An adult elephant requires to have the skin divided into three pieces for convenience in handling. The opening cuts extend down the centre of the back from the neck to the tail, and, passing around this appendage, run back along the centre of the belly and underside of the neck and head and through the centre of the lower lip. Each leg is opened up behind, as in the case of a deer. The skin of the neck is then completely encircled, thus leaving the skin of each side of the body with the two legs attached, entire, making two pieces, and the head and part of the neck attached forming a third. The inside of the trunk and inside of the tail are of course split open in their entire length. A small elephant or a rhinoceros would of course have the skin removed all in one piece. Bats should always be opened on the back. The feet and hands of monkeys require to be skinned completely down to the nails, opening each toe and finger along the underside for this purpose, the opening cut on the middle toe and finger extending up the inside of the hand, or along the sole of the foot to the calcaneum.

Preserving the Skins of Large Mammals.—As soon as possible after a skin is removed from the carcass, all blood should be carefully sponged and combed out of the hair, and any surplus flesh that may adhere to the skin should be shaved off with the knife. If they are to be mounted, all mammal skins should be salted. Common table salt is the article *par excellence*, and plenty of it, although rock salt pounded up fine will answer.

THE ART OF TAXIDERMY.

If no preservative is at hand, in a dry climate thin skins if cleaned of fat and exposed to the air will dry without the application of any preservative, but they must be watched while drying to see that no folds lie in the skin, or the hair is apt to slough off in these places when the skin is relaxed. If the epidermis dries down before decomposition sets up in the skin, the hair is safe; otherwise, unless a speedy remedy is at hand, the skin is gone.

A mistake that is made by many taxidermists lies in the use of alum as a preservative for mammal skins. My advice is, *never allow a particle of alum to come in contact with a skin that is to be mounted, unless absolutely necessary to set the epidermis upon a fresh, valuable skin which is in an advanced stage of decomposition.* Alum hardens and shrinks a skin, both of which qualities are precisely the opposite of what is desired. Its great disadvantage lies in its " plumping " qualities. If an alum-cured skin is shaved and thinned down from the inside and then placed in a salt and alum bath for a day or two, the skin when removed will be found to have plumped up until nearly as thick as it was before shaving. A good proof of this is for the operator to take two freshly salted skins of the same kind of animal—the domestic cat will answer—place one in the salt and alum bath (formula No. 2) and the other in tan liquor (formula No. 1), and, after they have been there a week or more, note the difference. The alum-cured skin will be found thick and harsh, while the other will be more pliable than when immersed, and not increased in thickness. To beam the latter will of course require but a small proportion of the time taken to thin down the alum-cured skin. A great difference will also be noticed in the hair after it is cleaned out, the alum rendering the hair stiff and dry and removing the gloss.

As above stated, alum must sometimes be used in hot weather upon the skin of a valuable mammal upon which the epidermis is blistering and the hair consequently fall-

PLATE VI.

TANNER'S STRETCHING FRAME.

ing out. The salt and alum bath is applied with a sponge, and liberal quantities of salt and powdered alum used on both sides of the skin in connection with the bath. After the alum has hardened down the skin upon such a specimen it should be well washed out, and the skin treated as directed with the tan liquor alone.

A skin should be scraped or fleshed a day or two after salting, as the fat, etc., come away much easier at this stage than at any other time, the salt having hardened the tissues so that the knife will take hold.

Small skins may be scraped with the hand scraper, and the skin itself shaved down with a shoe knife, using as a beam a small half-round piece of wood screwed fast to the bench or table so as to project horizontally.

For larger hides this process of removing the flesh and fat is improved upon by using the tanner's moon knife and stretching frame. The moon knife (Fig. 22) is simply a circular steel blade clamped in a crutch-shaped handle of wood, the crutch being placed under the armpit so that the entire weight of the body may be thrown on a skin if necessary. This knife is also used in breaking up partially dry skins in fur dressing.

The stretching frame consists of two uprights connected with a crossbeam. A second crossbeam is

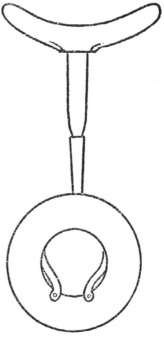

Fig. 22.—Moon Knife.

hinged at one end, and so arranged as to clamp tightly upon the first with the aid of a lever.

The skin after having been salted overnight is placed in the stretching frame and the fat and flesh worked off with the moon knife (Plate VI). The head, tail, and feet

145

PLATE VII.

FLESHING A SKIN.

are roughed off with the shoe knife. Instead of the frame and moon knife, on tough skins the large fleshing knife and upright shaving beam are used for this purpose.

The skin, if saturated with grease, should now be well washed in water containing a little washing soda, and after being wrung out placed in benzine for an hour or so. The skin is then removed and hung up to dry, and then placed in the tan liquor, where it may remain until wanted, be it a day or a year. For the first few days the skin should be moved about and its position changed, so as to give the liquor a chance to operate on every inch of the inner surface.

If it is desired to keep skins in a dry state, which is recommended if the skins are to be kept unmounted more than a year, they may be taken out, washed, painted on the inside with arsenical soap, dried, and stowed away for any length of time. When it is desired to mount them, the dried skins are simply placed in tan liquor and with a little working on the beam soon become as pliable as ever. Grease should always be cut out of any skins that are to be kept, either dry or wet, otherwise the grease will " burn " and rot them.

To beam down a Skin.—One secret of success in fine mammal taxidermy is to have the skin shaved down smoothly from the inside as thin as possible.

The skin of a rhinoceros recently mounted by the author and assistants weighed, when removed from the carcass, two hundred and seventy pounds. When the skin was shaved down and wet, ready to clothe the manikin, it weighed but twenty-seven pounds, including feet and all. For large, rough skins the tanner's fleshing knife is used (Fig. 23) to remove the bulk of the tissue, but when the skin is partly thinned down, and for all hides, such as those of the horse, deer, etc., the currier's knife is better adapted (Fig. 24).

In these processes the skin is thrown over a smooth,

half cylindrical beam of hard wood tilted up at an angle, the upper or free end coming about to the middle of the body of the operator, as shown in Plate VIII.

The currier's knife has a blade on either side, made detachable, with the edges turned over like a carpenter's steel

FIG. 23.—FLESHING KNIFE.

wood scraper. The knife works after the manner of a plane, cutting off a shaving at each stroke, thicker or thinner according to the depth of the turned edge.

The edges of the blade are turned over by first grinding it as one would a chisel and afterward giving a keen edge

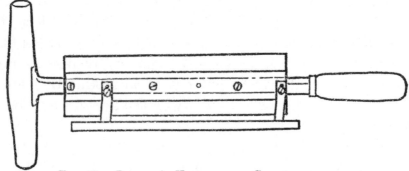

FIG. 24.—CURRIER'S KNIFE, WITH GUARD ATTACHED.

with the oilstone. The blade is then placed in the vise and the edge turned over with the turning steel which comes with the knife for this purpose.

As the crystals of salt in a pickled skin soon take the edge off a blade, the small finger steel which also accompanies the knife is used to sharpen it from time to time until the edge is again so worn off as to require regrinding. The side of the steel is run back and forth over the outer edge of the blade a number of times, and finally the point is run once or twice along the inside of the turned-over edge. Sperm oil is used with this steel, and when not in use the

10

steel is kept soaking in the oil all the time to prevent its rusting.

Much practice and skill are necessary to enable the operator to handle this knife without cutting ugly gashes in the skin. The knife must be held at just a certain angle, otherwise it will glide over the skin without cutting at all, and if tilted too high it will cut too deep. To obviate this, an adjustable guard made of brass, to attach upon the crossbar of the knife, has been invented by one of the taxidermists in the American Museum. This guard works to perfection, keeping the blade always at a certain angle. The guard going over the skin before the blade reaches the spot, removes all wrinkles and stretches out the skin, so that when the blade comes along a smooth, even surface of skin is presented.

With this tool it is therefore just a question of time to reduce a skin to any required degree of thinness, and the work when done is much more satisfactory than that done with the old-fashioned method of using an awl and drawknife. With the drawknife, the knife is drawn toward instead of from the operator, the skin being held in position upon the horizontal beam by the awl which is driven through it into the beam.

This method is not a good one, and, to make matters worse, the hide is punched full of awl holes. The head, feet, and all places which can not be reached with the currier's knife are shaved down with the shoe knife.

Most skins shave the best a day or two after having been salted and before going into tan liquor. They may, of course, be shaved at any future time, while wet or damp. When dry or nearly so, if it is desired to get a skin as thin as paper, provided it will stand it without injuring the roots of the hair and causing it to fall out, sandpaper placed over a block of wood may be used, and the skin sandpapered down as thin as desired. An emery wheel is, of course, better than sandpaper. After shaving, or during the process, a skin may be placed in and taken out of tan liquor repeatedly.

Before putting a skin on the manikin it should receive a thorough stretching on the frame with the crutch and moon knife, if at all a tight fit.

A skin which requires more stretch will be found to relax still more after coming out of the tan liquor if placed in soda water for a short time.

To relax the Dry Skin of a Large Mammal.—Salted skins of large mammals will relax readily when placed in water or tan liquor, and when beamed and stretched are ready to mount. Skins which have been simply dried without previous salting require to be placed in clear water or damp sawdust until they collapse. They are then scraped on the inside, or as much of the inside as it is possible to get at, when the skin is placed in tan liquor to complete the relaxation. If left in clear water too long the skin will macerate and the hair fall out. A dry skin will of course relax in tan liquor alone, without the previous soaking in clear water, but takes a little longer.

A tough glazed surface will be found on the inside of all sun-dried skins, and after a little soaking this must be scraped or cut away to permit the liquor to enter, otherwise the skin will never relax perfectly. After the skin is sufficiently relaxed so that it may be flattened out, it may be placed on the beam, and worked carefully with the currier's knife, and also opened up on the stretching frame, wetting the skin from time to time during the process with tan liquor. If the skin is dry and flat, it may be simply sponged on the flesh side, first with water and then with tan liquor, and worked, and the skin softened without wetting the hair, if it is desired.

To clean out the Hair of Large Mammals.—After the final beaming the skin is taken from the tan liquor, wrung out and placed in lukewarm water containing a little washing soda, say a double handful of soda to a bucket of water, and the salt well rinsed out. The skin is then wrung out with the hands and placed in benzine for half an hour. It is then taken out of the benzine and again wrung out, care being used that no fire is near, or an explosion will probably result.

Furrier's sawdust is placed in a tray and the skin well worked into it, rolling the hide over and over until the hair is completely filled with the sawdust. The skin is then shaken out, beaten with rattans, and again placed in the tray and the sawdust worked through the fur. Again the skin is beaten until the hair is as bright and clean as ever.

The air compresser recommended for birds is here useful for blowing out the residue of the sawdust and further fluffing out the fur.

As the furrier's sawdust is very fine and flies about in the atmosphere, entering the mouth and nostrils, it has been found that a drum is necessary where numbers of skins are to be cleaned.

An ordinary oil barrel fitted with an adjustable head, and placed upon an axle to which a crank is attached, has been found to work admirably. A quantity of the sawdust is placed in the barrel, the skin thrown in, the head of the barrel clamped on, and the barrel revolved so as to keep the contents continually moving. Ten or fifteen minutes will answer for the first manipulation, when the skin is beaten on the hair side with rattans, this part of the operation being done out of doors if possible, and the process is again repeated.

Hot sea shore sand will answer very well in the drum if the sawdust is not at hand. The sawdust must never be used on wet fur without the intervening bath of benzine, or the sawdust, like plaster, will cling to the hair and never come out.

All skins that are covered with hair or fur should be thus treated before going on the manikin. If it is found that the skin has dried too much during the operation, the inside should be sponged with water. The skin after having been well painted on the flesh side with formula No. 4, is ready to clothe the manikin.

To " Fur-dress" Skins, such as those of the Sheep, Fox, Dog, etc.—After the skin is removed from the carcass the blood is sponged from the hair and the skin well salted and rolled up and left overnight, when the inside of the skin is thoroughly scraped or beamed down.

If fat, the skin is placed in benzine for an hour and hung up and dried out, when the skin is placed in tan liquor (formula No. 1) for a few days. If the skin is not fat it may be placed in the tan liquor without the previous soaking in benzine. If it is desired to keep the fur dry, the tan liquor is simply sponged on the flesh side from time to time for a couple of days. If the fur has been wet by immersion in the tan liquor, the salt must be well rinsed out of the skin with clear water and treated with benzine and sawdust, as previously described. If neither sawdust nor sand are at hand, hot corn meal, or even plaster of Paris, may be used instead, after the benzine. The skin is then allowed to become partially dry, when it is " broken up " on the stretching frame with the moon knife. If this is not at hand, a piece of flat iron with square corners may be clamped in a vise at one end, and the flesh side of the skin worked back and forth over the iron until the fibre is sufficiently broken to render the skin soft and pliable. If the skin to be dressed is a dry one, it is relaxed as already described.

If it is desired to stretch a dressed skin so it will lie flat upon the floor, this is done by simply moistening the flesh side with water, and, when relaxed, tacking it out, fur side up, on a board. When dry, if the skin has been found to harden up, it must be worked again over the iron bar. When the skin is thoroughly dry it may be sandpapered down from the inside until as thin and soft as desired.

THE ART OF TAXIDERMY.

To remove the Hair from Skins.—A formula that would make hair grow upon a dressed skin would indeed be a most valuable one to the taxidermist at times; but for the benefit of those who may wish to remove what hair there is found upon a skin, the following is recommended:

Depilatory Solution.

Boiling water.......................... 1 quart.
Red arsenic........................... . . 1 pound.
Cool, and add unslacked lime............ 1   "

The solution is painted with a brush upon the flesh side of the skin, and the skin folded together and left overnight. Next morning the hair will pull readily and may be scraped off with a knife. The skin is then placed in water and washed out. This solution also works well on a salted skin. Skins thus deprived of their hair dress readily and come out as soft as a glove. They may be placed in tan liquor overnight and again washed out, when they are allowed to dry. They are then broken up on the stretching frame and remain pliable. A plump but soft skin results from a forty-eight-hours' immersion in a solution of bichromate of potash and water of moderate strength.

II. MOUNTING SMALL MAMMALS.

Mammals which are too small to be mounted by means of a manikin are stuffed by filling the skin out to the proper size and form after supporting wires have been introduced.

For an illustration of this process of mounting we will select a gray squirrel (*Sciurus carolinensis*).

The specimen having come to us in the flesh, is skinned as already described in preparing a chipmunk, and salted and wrapped in a damp cloth overnight. The next morning the inside of the skin is well scraped all over with a large bone scraper and painted with arsenical soap, and the skin lies before us ready for mounting.

Five annealed iron wires are cut. The first, sufficiently

heavy to support firmly the head or tail in any position in which they may be placed, is cut about six inches longer than the total length of the animal from the end of the nose to the tip of the tail. One end is tapered with a flat file, so that it will enter the tail sheath clear to the very tip, and this end is dipped in shellac, so that it will not afterward rust fast to the skin of the tail.

The other four wires are for the legs, and should be about eight inches longer than the bones of the leg and foot, and as stout as can be consistently used without handicapping the operator. About No. 15 or 16 is stout enough for a squirrel of this size.

The bottoms of the feet having been opened lengthwise in skinning, it is a simple matter to introduce a leg wire up into the skin of the leg and tie it fast to the bones by wrapping them together with stout thread. The wire lays along the leg bones on their back sides, and projects a couple of inches from the bottoms of the feet, the balance of the wire at the upper ends of the limb bones being left for the subsequent coupling.

The legs are bent slightly at the joints. Tow or fine excelsior, cut into flat wisps with the shears, is now bound fast with thread upon the leg bones to replace the muscle that has been cut away. It is a good plan, before removing the flesh from the legs during the skinning process, to lay a hind and a fore leg flat upon a piece of paper and trace around them with a pencil. The outline drawings thus made will be of great service to the beginner in winding the legs.

The legs must be wound firm, but not so hard that they will not bend at the joints when pressure is applied. The legs must be large enough so that they fill the skin snugly when it is inverted back over them. The two hind legs should be of exactly the same size, as well as the two front legs.

When the legs are all wound, they are coated over with

a thin layer of soft *papier-maché* (formula No. 10) and the skin of the legs turned right side out over them. The feet are now filled with the same material, and the opening cuts at the bottoms sewed up with needle and thread.

We now have a squirrel skin with the legs filled and right side out, with a couple of inches of wire for a support

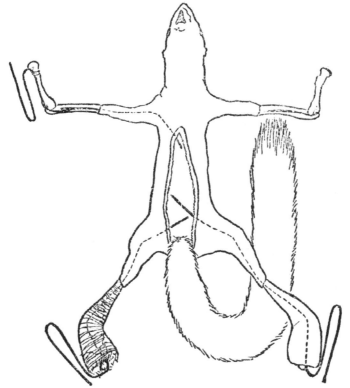

Fig. 25.—Wiring and Leg Making.

for the finished specimen projecting from the bottoms of the feet, and about six inches of surplus wire projecting from the upper ends of the legs, inside the skin.

Measuring from the tapered end of the body wire by laying it alongside of the skin, a ring is twisted upon the wire so as to come midway between the fore and the hind legs. Excelsior is now bound fast around the ring with thread, the excelsior being wound hard in the form of an elongated ball. A hole is bored lengthwise through the natural skull, entering at the back just above the orifice (foramen magnum) and coming out within the nasal cavity.

The blunt end of the body wire is pushed through this hole, thus stringing the skull upon the wire.

Long-fibred tow or fine excelsior is now wrapped around the wire at the base of the skull to the size of the natural neck. The muscles of the skull and jaws are also replaced by binding on tow.

The skull and neck are now covered with a coating of *papier-maché*.

The skull, with the neck and wire in position, is placed within the skin of the head and neck and pins driven through the skin into the skull at the anterior corners of the eyes to keep the skin from shifting upon the skull.

The front legs are now coupled fast to the ball of excelsior on the body wire, in the same way as already described under the chapter on Bird Mounting. To secure greater strength, instead of simply hooking the ends of the wires and fastening them to the excelsior in this way, both wires may pass through the excelsior and their ends be twisted firmly together. The twist is then bent down flat with the pliers so as to lie snugly along the upper end of the ball of excelsior.

The ball being in the centre of the body, the heads of the humeri are thus some distance away, and enough wire intervenes to allow for widening or narrowing the chest.

The front legs are now bent into their proper positions. Tow is wrapped about the projecting end of the body wire to the size and shape of the flesh of the tail. This is smeared with *papier-maché*, painted over with arsenical soap, and, by bending the wire almost double, the tip of the tail wire is brought up even with the base of the tail. The wire, with its tow and *papier-maché* covering, is then slipped down into the tail sheath. If desired, the tow for the tail may be wound upon the body wire before it is placed in the skin of the body.

The body wire is again straightened out, and the hind legs coupled to the ball of excelsior in the same manner as the fore legs.

The legs are now bent as nearly as possible into the position they are to assume in the finished specimen, as well as the body. Fine excelsior or coarse tow is cut up with the shears and sprinkled with water to dampen it slightly.

Soft *papier-maché*, made up with liquid glue or thin hot glue, is now prepared.

The squirrel skin is filled out with wads of the chopped tow or excelsior, each wad containing a quantity of the *papier-maché* so that it will model by pressure with the fingers and retain whatever form is given to it. The wads are introduced through the opening in the belly with a pair of long forceps, packing always against the palm of one hand, which is held outside of the skin at that point, thus getting the filling in hard and even all over without bulging the

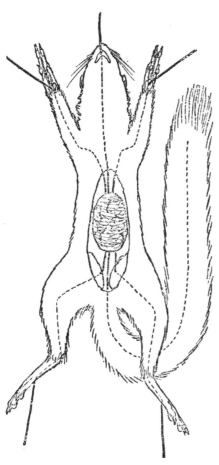

FIG. 26.—THE SQUIRREL COUPLED, READY FOR FILLING.

skin. In loose filling, material should always be used that will permit the point of the forceps or pusher to pass through it to reach any portion of the inside of the body at will while stuffing. For this reason cotton batting, or any material of fine fibre, will not answer, as it balls up and gives a specimen a lumpy appearance, like a sack of potatoes.

When nearly full, the specimen is placed upon the branch or pedestal selected for it and worked into position, varying the filling with forceps and pusher through the opening on the belly. The advantage of the modelling material (*papier-maché*) will now be evident, as with this the filling stays wherever placed, by pressure either from within or without. Excelsior or tow alone is springy, and can not be so well governed.

When the attitude is satisfactorily worked out, the squirrel is taken from the pedestal, the filling completed, and the belly cut sewed up. The specimen is again placed upon the pedestal for the last time, and wired fast by clinching the wires underneath.

Any further alterations are now made by cutting small slits in the skin just back of the fore legs, and introducing more filling, if necessary, through these openings. A fine awl is also used to prick into the skin and bring the stuffing to the surface, to fill cavities wherever they exist.

The whole specimen is now well combed out with a steel comb and the hair arranged. The wire projecting from the nose is cut off close to the bone, so as to allow the skin of the nose to pass outside of it.

Papier-maché is introduced between the split lips and about the mouth, and these parts modelled into form with the aid of a small scraper.

Glass eyes are now inserted, *papier-maché* being used to fill the sockets, and the lids worked carefully about the eyes with a needle set in a handle. When the eyes are set, to get a finished effect a little dry lampblack mixed with water may be applied to the lids with a camel's-hair brush.

After arranging the hair—much depends upon this—and placing the toes in position and pinning them there—a detail that is usually neglected, and which, if well done, will tend greatly to improve the lifelike appearance of the specimen—the squirrel is set away to dry.

For a specimen as small as a mouse, reasonably stiff *papier-maché* is used for filling altogether, and the tow or excelsior omitted. The composition is introduced through the belly opening with a small scraper until the body is full, when the opening is sewed up, the specimen placed upon a pedestal, and modelled into shape from the outside.

Some good results have been obtained on mammals of the size of the squirrel, by filling the body with dry sawdust and chopped excelsior.

The ears of a rabbit should be skinned and inverted, but the cartilage is left in, and brushed over with arsenic. A thin coating of *papier-maché* should be laid on the cartilage and the whole inside painted over with hot glue, and the ear turned right side out. The ears are modelled into shape, and will remain so permanently.

The ear of a rabbit is so delicate that it is very difficult to remove the cartilage and supply its place with any firm material, and preserve the true form of the ear in this way.

Bats are mounted without wires, by simply stuffing the body with soft filling, and, after sewing up the cut, pinning the bat upon a board, with the wings extended. When dry the wings are slightly dampened, coated upon the backs with liquid glue, and pasted upon a sheet of bevel-edged plate glass. The glass should also be well smeared with the glue upon the surface which the wings of the bat come in contact with. The glass may be suspended by drilling two small holes through the upper margin, or it may set upon a pedestal, the pedestal being slotted to receive the bottom edge of the glass.

Finishing Small Mammals.—In the course of a couple of weeks, in a warm room, a small mammal will be sufficiently dry to clean up and finish.

The pins are taken from the feet, and the specimen

blown all over with the hand bellows or air compressor to remove dust and fluff the hair. All pinholes, or other holes which may exist, are filled up with *papier-maché* or wax, and afterward coloured with tube colour. The eye-lids are also painted, and any parts which have changed colour have the colour restored. If the hair is worn off in spots, these are patched by gluing hair upon them, which process will be fully considered in the following division. If the specimen has been mounted upon a temporary pedestal, this is exchanged for a more elaborate permanent one, and the specimen is ready for exhibition.

III. MOUNTING LARGE MAMMALS.

The mounting of large mammals constitutes the most difficult part of taxidermy, for the different species of quadrupeds are so variable in form that a special study of each one is almost necessary to the turning out of faultlessly mounted specimens.

It is therefore recommended that as many sketches from life and animal photographs be obtained as possible. Plaster casts made from the carcasses of dead animals are of the utmost service as guides in mounting; and a good cast of the whole side of an animal which is to be mounted will save a great deal of time in constructing the manikin.

The term "manikin" is here applied to the modelled form or dummy figure of the animal, and which is as nearly as possible an exact counterpart in form of the body of the animal after the skin is removed. The skin is afterward stretched over the statue.

When possible, all mammals should be mounted by means of manikins, as by this method a much finer and more permanent result is attainable. To stuff the skin of a large mammal in the way already described for mounting small mammals not only involves great labour, but a most unsatisfactory specimen results.

Heretofore much has been said and written of the advantages of the excelsior manikin coated with a layer of clay, over which the skin is drawn and sewed fast. This method has a number of serious disadvantages. First, excelsior was never made to model in, and perfect angles and planes such as abound in the exterior anatomy of mammals are unknown and impossible to represent with excelsior. Would an experienced sculptor attempt to model a statue with excelsior? If not, why should the taxidermist?

The second great drawback of this method lies in the use of clay next to the skin. Clay and plaster, unless coated with a substance which renders them non-absorbent when dry, should never under any circumstances be allowed to come in contact with the skin of an animal, be it bird, quadruped, fish, or reptile. By reason of the absorbing qualities of the clay or plaster, in time every particle of the natural moisture of the skin is absorbed, and as the tension on the skin increases with the drying, either the stitches rip out or the skin cracks and tears, thus working the ruin of the specimen. I speak from experience—not only my own, but from that of other and older taxidermists, who have had faultlessly mounted specimens warp and crack out of all recognition of their former selves.

Furthermore, in the soft manikin there is nothing to hold the skin into depressions, except by sewing through from side to side, and in short-haired mammals these stitches are always unsightly. I mention these disadvantages merely to show my reasons for adopting a more perfect method of mounting large mammals; and though I by no means claim that the process here set forth is incapable of improvement, I consider it greatly in advance of the soft clay-covered manikin. For an illustration of this method we will proceed to mount an immature zebra. (E. Chapmani.)

Making a Manikin for a Zebra.—Before starting to prepare a manikin, the skin to be fitted upon it is thoroughly beamed down. The car cartilages are removed from the ears, and the hoofs and phalanges attached to the skin of the feet cut out to allow the supporting rod to lie within the bones of the feet and come out at the centre of the hoof. One secret of success in mounting mammals is to have the skin beamed down as thin as it will stand, in order to reduce the shrinkage when the skin dries.

When the skin is shaved down it is placed in tan liquor, where it is left until it is required for use in preparing the manikin. During the process of mounting, the skin may be taken out and put back into the liquor any number of times.

Now for the manikin. The dry limb bones,[*] attached at their joints by the ligaments, are placed in warm water until they are sufficiently relaxed at the joints to bend readily, when they are removed from the water, and all surplus flesh and sinews cut off with a knife. The lower hind limb bone is clamped in the vise, and with the aid of a surgeon's saw and carpenter's gouge the back of the bone is grooved out to admit the iron rod which is to be used to support the manikin. Passing on the inside of the hockbone or calcaneum, the lower part of the tibia just above is also gouged out in the same way, otherwise the rod will be in the way when the skin is clamped tightly together between the great tendon and the bone; at this point the opposite sides of the skin of the leg actually meet, and the rod must be kept out of this place at all hazards. The other hind leg is treated similarly.

The front legs are grooved out in the same manner, from the bottom to just a little above the knee joints.

Four pieces of the best Norway iron rod—in this case half an inch in thickness—are now cut with the hack saw

---

[*] In the present instance the natural bones were used for a separate exhibit as a skeleton. The bones themselves were cast in a clay mould and the casts used in constructing the manikin, as will be seen by a glance at the illustrations. The natural skull was modelled over in clay, and cast. This cast was also used in the manikin.

or cold chisel, long enough to allow about fifteen inches beyond the heads of the femur and humerus for coupling to the centre board, and about two inches below the point of the hoof, for attachment to the pedestal below.

The size of rod used is generally governed by the thickness of the tarsus or shank bone, the rod being as heavy as will conveniently fit the back of the bone without being so thick as to project beyond the sides, and thus give an unnatural thickness to the lower limbs.

A thread is run on one end of each rod about two inches in length, and, by properly adjusting the dies, two hexagonal nuts are fitted to each rod so that they will turn readily with the fingers. As the nuts will probably be taken off and screwed on a number of times, it is slow work using a wrench each time.

The attitude of the mounted specimen must now be decided upon and the limb bones arranged, lying flat upon the floor in their approximate positions.

As the threaded ends of the rods must go straight down through holes bored in the temporary pedestal, the first bend in the rods to make them conform to the backs of the leg bones begins here.

As the first bend comes as close above the thread as possible, the rod is placed perpendicularly in the vise with the threaded end projecting just far enough above the jaws so that the bend will not come in the thread on the rod, and thereby weaken it or perhaps break it off altogether.

A piece of moderately tight-fitting straight iron pipe is slipped over the end of the rod, and the rod bent by pressure to the proper angle.

The rod is adjusted to the limb bone, and the hoof, with the phalanges attached, is also placed in position on the rod.

The spot where the next bend is to come is marked with a piece of chalk, the rod is placed in the vise and again bent, using the pipe as before to make the bend come at the right point.

The rod is again adjusted to the bone, and the bend at the hock and the joint above made by bending the rod across the knee, with the bones in position on the rod.

In the case of heavier rods, all the bends are made in the vise, but a person of ordinary strength should be able to bend a half-inch rod across the knee. The other leg rods are bent in a similar manner, and made to conform perfectly and snugly with the bones in their entire length, when the bones are bound fast to the rods with twine or wire. The tops of the rods are now bent inward at right angles to the bone, just below the heads of the femurs and humeri.

The pelvis, cleaned of all flesh, is nailed fast at the proper angle upon one end of a piece of seven-eighths-inch pine board, long and wide enough to represent a section of the animal's body straight through the centre. If the board is not wide enough, a second board may be clamped fast to it to widen it.

The hind legs are now taken, and the tops of the rods again bent at right angles at such a distance from the bones as to allow the heads of the femurs to slip into the sockets of the pelvis, with the bent ends of the rods lying flat along the centre board. To keep the rod from turning in any direction when wired fast to the centre board, the part of the rod which lies along the board is bent down at an angle. A glance at the figure in Plate IX will further serve to illustrate this method of coupling, which is by no means a new one.

Before fastening on the hind legs, the body board with the pelvis attached is placed in the vise and the rear of the body board cut down with the draw-knife, first marking with a pencil the portion that is to be removed.

As the zebra slopes in a regular curve from the fore part of the bottom of the pelvis to the centre of the belly, this is marked off, the board turned upside down in the vise, and the surplus board cut away. The board is then inverted

11

and placed in the vise right side up, and the surplus board above the pelvis cut away.

The upper ends of the hind-leg rods having been bent, are now fastened into position upon the body board by drilling holes through the wood and passing stout wires through and twisting the ends with heavy pliers.

The two rods may be clamped with the same wires if convenient, although it makes no difference.

If the heads of the femurs fit snugly into place in the sockets of the pelvis, the rear part of the animal is obviously correct in height and width, provided the pelvis is properly adjusted, thus doing away with the necessity for any measurements at this point.

The measurements taken from the animal in the flesh are now looked up. The distance from the head of the femur to the head of the humerus on the same side is marked off on the centre board. The distance between the outsides of the heads of the humeri, thus giving the width of the chest, is also measured off, and the tops of the leg rods bent and coupled in accordance, in the same way as already described for the hind legs, care being taken that the elbow comes at precisely the exact point with reference to the brisket that the measurements call for, which in the zebra is about even.

A temporary pedestal is constructed of seven-eighths-inch pine boards, with a crosspiece underneath each end, about three inches in height, nailed fast.

With the centre board still clamped fast in the vise, and the limb bones attached by the rods, the legs are adjusted into the precise positions they are to assume in the finished specimen. The threaded portions of the rods are made to come down perfectly straight from every point of view, and the hocks are thrown well together. A nut is now run up on the bottom of each rod as far as the thread will permit it to go, and having four legs, our beast must be made to use them to stand upon. When all is to the

PLATE IX.

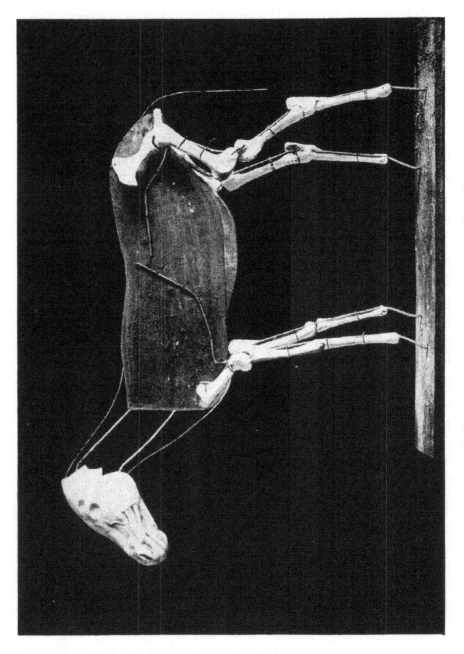

MANIKIN FOR ZEBRA, FIRST STAGE.

166

liking of the operator the frame is removed from the vise, and while an assistant steadies the frame upon the pedestal, the spots where the rods are to enter the pedestal are marked off with a pencil and holes bored through with brace and bit. The ends of the rods, with a nut on each, are now let into the holes in the pedestal. A second nut is run up on each rod from below the pedestal and screwed up tightly with the monkey-wrench. The frame of the manikin now stands alone, and if properly done remains firm and rigid.

The frame is viewed from all directions and all errors of pose, etc., corrected until everything is exactly right. If the manikin at this stage looks as if it were going to fall over frontward or backward, the finished specimen will look the same. The body board is marked off and trimmed down until it represents exactly a section of the body down through the centre. The skull is now fastened to the manikin. A longitudinal slot about two inches wide is sawed into the base of the skull underneath, the piece taken out and a block of wood, previously bored to receive a three-eighths-inch rod, fitted into the cavity. The block is held secure in the skull by means of screws running into it from above and behind. A three-eighths-inch iron rod of sufficient length to allow for the neck and also for wiring fast to the centre board is now cut, bent at the proper angle, one straight end running through the hole bored in the block in the base of the skull, and the other being attached to the centre board in the same manner as the leg rods were.

The skin is now tried on the manikin to see that the frame is not too large. The hoofs should rest easily upon the pedestal; the skin should meet across the chest and around the belly with room to spare.

The distal ends of the limb bones are raised or lowered from the pedestal by shifting the nuts on the rods. The centre board must be in exactly the centre of the body of the animal, and this may be determined by the use of a plumb line.

If the head is in just the proper position, a second three-eighths-inch rod is placed alongside of the first neck rod and also made secure to the skull and the centre board.

When the manikin is completed thus far, annealed iron wire netting, or wire cloth of moderate mesh, is procured and a piece cut off long enough to envelop the entire centre board, taking in the pelvis, thighs, and shoulders. The netting is tacked fast along the top of the centre board with small wire staples or nails, and by cutting with snips and fitting, the wire netting is adjusted as nearly as may be to the form of the body and upper limbs, and tacked fast along the underside of the body board.

The netting is held in the two natural hollows behind the fore leg and in front of the hind leg by drilling holes through the centre board at these points, passing a wire from one side of the netting through the holes to the other side, and by twisting the ends of the wires holding the netting in place.

The netting is tacked and wired wherever necessary until the body and upper limbs are built out generally to the proper form. The skin is again adjusted and fitted closely all over the manikin, and all defects remedied wherever necessary. When the netting is all adjusted on the body, the neck is attended to.

Two stout wires are cut, one to run from the top of the skull to the top of the centre board at the shoulder, and the other from the palate to the brisket. The wires are stapled fast to the centre board and bent into the outlines of the neck. Around these wires the netting is bound and fastened into place by sewing with soft iron wire. A stout tail wire is now stapled fast to the centre board above the pelvis. The whole manikin—netting, bones, and all—is now given a coat of shellac applied with a brush.

When the wire netting can not be procured, excelsior or

PLATE X.

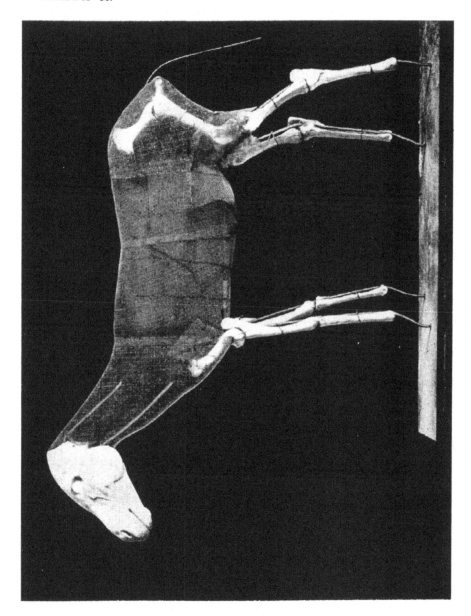

MANIKIN FOR ZEBRA, SECOND STAGE.

straw may be used instead to build out with. This may be bound on with strong thread; or burlaps or canvas may be tacked fast, as in the case of the wire cloth, and stuffed out with excelsior, etc. The netting is, however, much more substantial, easier to manipulate, and gives better results.

Now for the modelling and the artistic part of the operation.

The whole surface of the netting is given a thin coat of *papier-maché*, formula No. 11.

The *tendon achilles* is represented by drilling a hole into the top of the calcaneum, inserting the end of a stiff wire into the hole and bending the wire over until the upper end rests upon the *papier-maché* of the thigh. A second wire is bound fast underneath the first one to stiffen it. Both wires are then wrapped tightly with wisps of tow, to act as a foundation for the *papier-maché*.

If a live zebra is near at hand in captivity, study his anatomy at every opportunity and reproduce it upon the manikin. If living ones are not to be found, good photographs and casts of parts may be followed and the details worked out. If no better studies are at hand, a horse or donkey offers an excellent model for the external anatomy.

Any amount of labour may be expended in modelling the manikin. The skin is wholly or partly adjusted frequently to see what effect the underlying material is going to give when the skin is on. If the skin will not cover the model, it may be from one or two causes: either the manikin is too large, or the skin has not been sufficiently shaved down.

When fresh *papier-maché* is added to *papier-maché* that is on the manikin, and which has become partly dry, the dry portions are thoroughly wet with water before applying fresh composition. The *papier-maché* is applied with a small spatula or modelling tool and smoothed up with the hand and a flat paint brush, wet with water. If too much material has been added at certain points it may be cut away at any time.

THE ART OF TAXIDERMY.

After the *papier-maché* has set, the tendons of the fore legs may be cut in with a knife.

As much time may be given to the final modelling as is desired, and any anatomical points may be worked out. The details are of course governed by the length of hair upon the skin which is to clothe the manikin, it being obviously unnecessary to reproduce every muscle and wrinkle and then cover them with six inches of hair.

When the modelling of the whole manikin is completed, including the lower limbs, tail, the muscles of the jaws, and the mouth and nostrils, the manikin is allowed to dry out, when it is carefully sandpapered all over.

A thin sizing coat of liquid glue (Le Page's), made by dissolving two ounces by measure of the glue in a pint of water, is painted on hot all over the manikin. When dry, hot carpenter's glue of full strength is painted evenly all over the manikin and allowed to cool. Another coat of glue is given the manikin in all the depressions, when the manikin is ready for the skin.

The skin, which has been well beamed and worked on the stretching frame to insure a perfect fit for the manikin, is now taken out of the tan liquor, and a pair of artificial ear cartilages are hammered out of thin sheet lead or wire netting, using the natural cartilages, which have been skinned out of the ear and soaked up in hot water, as models.

All holes in the skin are now carefully sewed up from the inside, using a glover's needle and stout thread waxed with beeswax, sewing from within outward, with what is known as the "ball stitch." All seams are afterward flattened by hammering them upon a block of wood. Much nicety can be displayed in sewing up cuts and holes.

In a thinly haired skin the needle should go but part way through the skin, thus bringing the edges together without any stitches showing from the outside. If a piece of the skin has been cut out bodily, two V-shaped cuts are

PLATE XI.

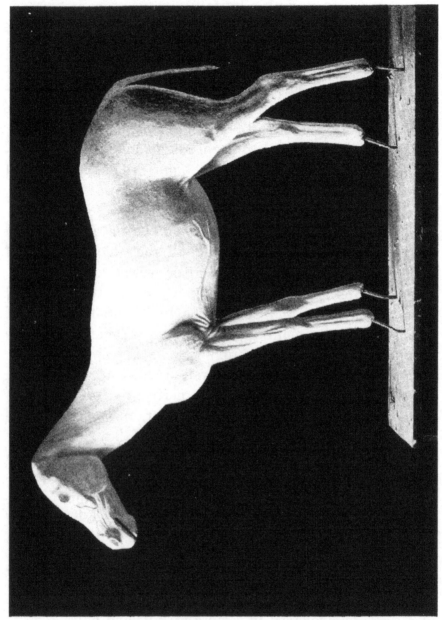

MANIKIN FOR ZEBRA, COMPLETED, READY FOR THE SKIN.

made on opposite sides of the hole, the pieces taken out and the edges, now enlarged into a straight cut, brought together. Sometimes, provided it does not interfere with the colour pattern of the hair, where a round hole exists and there is no surplus skin to spare, but one V-shaped piece is cut out at one side of the hole and the base of the V-shaped piece set back so as to occupy the space covered by the hole. The piece is then sewed into place. On a short-haired mammal sometimes the edges of cuts and holes are not sewed together at all, but are simply made to meet on the manikin, when they are glued and pinned.

The skin is now placed in warm soda water (a couple of handfuls of washing soda to a bucketful of water) and the tan liquor well washed out.

The hide is wrung out and placed in benzine for a short time and again wrung out. The hair is now thoroughly cleaned out with the furrier's sawdust, and the skin well beaten to drive out the residue of the sawdust. It is then laid flat upon the floor and well painted on the flesh side with arsenical solution (formula No. 4).

The lead or wire netting cartilages are given a thin coating of *papier-maché* (formula No. 10), and, while this is soft, painted over with liquid glue or hot carpenter's glue. The cartilages are now shoved into the skin of the ears and carefully adjusted. A few stitches are taken through the ear from the inside to the outside, and passing through the lead to keep the skin from shifting during the subsequent manipulation. The butts of the ears and the feet are now filled with *papier-maché*. The phalanges may be entirely removed and their places supplied with the composition. By the latter process a foot may be more easily modelled into shape than by leaving the bones attached to the hoof.

The skin is now placed upon the manikin for the last time. It is a great advantage to have two or three persons at work on a specimen at this stage, as the skin dries rapidly, and water applied to the skin to soak it up is liable to so soften the underlying glue as to destroy its sticking qualities.

The skin is placed in position at all points and the legs sewed up, beginning at the hoofs. The glue on the manikin offers a slippery surface upon which the skin may be worked in any direction. If too much skin is found at certain points, the surplus may be worked away and distributed over the manikin. If a stretch is required, the skin may be pulled from any direction, the operator feeling assured that by so doing he is not altering the form of the hard manikin. After the legs are sewed up, the belly cut is treated in the same manner. The ears are adjusted and made to stand in any desired position by stuffing in pads of tow and *papier-maché* mixed, through the opening of the ear with a pusher. Stout pointed wires are also driven into the skull through the ear openings, and the ears thus held in position till dry when the wires are withdrawn. If any fine wrinkling or modelling is to be done from the outside of the skin, *papier-maché* is introduced between the skin and the manikin, and the skin worked with a modelling tool.

When the skin is properly adjusted upon the manikin and all sewed up, dry sand is heated and placed in small bags, the sand, of course, not being heated enough to burn the cloth. A hot sand bag is pressed against the skin in all depressions of the manikin, and held there until the underlying glue is liquefied. The skin at this point is smoothed out with the fingers, and, if perfectly loose, will need nothing further to hold it there for all time. In places where the skin is inclined to draw away from the manikin by reason of tightness, the skin, after the sand bag is applied, is clamped tightly to the manikin by means of pins driven in with a tack hammer in the case of long-haired animals. In short-haired animals strips of leather, one side covered with hair a quarter of an inch long to act as a cushion, are cut to fit and pinned fast, hair side in. If great smoothness

PLATE XII.

THE SPECIMEN COMPLETED.

is desired, the sand bags may be used all over the specimen. The cool bags are, of course, changed for hot ones during the process. The object of pinning the skin is to hold it down upon the manikin until the skin and the underlying glue become dry, when the pins are withdrawn, leaving the skin stuck fast. The lips are modelled by introducing *papier-maché* under them, and by pinning them into place.

The artificial eyes are inserted, the sockets being filled with *papier-maché*, and the upper lid drawn well over the eye.

Care must be taken to properly adjust the eyelashes, as these hairs project downward rather than upward as is generally seen in mounted specimens. The lids are painted with lampblack mixed with water to get the expression of the eye temporarily. The hair of the entire specimen is now carefully adjusted with a steel comb.

When well pinned and everything completed, the specimen is set away to dry.

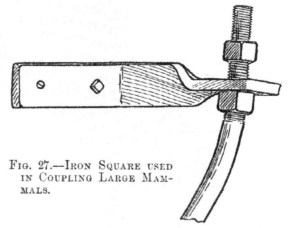

FIG. 27.—IRON SQUARE USED IN COUPLING LARGE MAMMALS.

If but one person is at work in putting the skin on a large manikin, the head may be finished first, then one fore leg after the other, and finally the hind limbs, the bulk of the skin being rolled up meanwhile to prevent its drying.

In mounting mammals by this process as much necessary detail is worked in upon the manikin as possible. In the rhinoceros, the interior mechanism of the manikin of which is shown in Plate XIII, all the folds were modelled upon the manikin, and the skin afterward glued fast, as described.

The method of coupling the leg irons to the centre board

used in the zebra is discarded in mammals requiring a rod larger than half an inch, and the iron square (Fig. 27) is used instead. This necessitates threading the rods on both ends. The latter method was used in preparing the manikin for the rhinoceros, as shown in the plate. The artificial eyes generally manufactured for taxidermist's use are much too flat, and the white corners are raised too far up on the convex side of the eye. The eyeball of an animal is a perfect sphere, and looking at a live deer from the front the eye projects beyond the lids. With a flat eye it is therefore impossible to produce this result. Half globes, painted on the inside with tube colours, using the natural eye as a model, are the best that can be procured. The best globes for large mammals are those made as in Fig. 28. These

Fig. 28.

must be made to order. Manufacturers of artificial eyes are, however, generally very obliging, and will manufacture special eyes, as a rule, when requested. Mammal eyes made in the ordinary way, but without the white corners, answer very well. The corners are best worked up in wax, and varnished after the lids are dry.

When it is found necessary to use the natural bones of an animal for a separate exhibit as a skeleton (as was done in the case of the zebra and the rhinoceros here figured), the natural bones are cast, as described in the chapter on Casting (p. 100), and the artificial bones thus produced used in constructing a manikin.

It often happens that a skin is to be mounted for which the bones are wanting. In this case bones of another individual of the same species are used as models, if obtainable. If these can not be had, artificial bones are roughly carved from wood, and afterward perfected by modelling, using the beamed skin as a guide for length. In mounting a mammal with large horns a block is fitted into the skull as usual, but the neck rods must be so arranged that the head can

PLATE XIII.

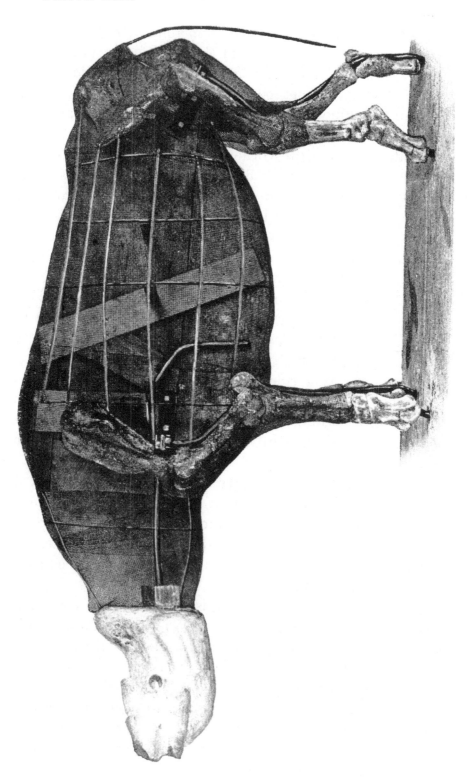

178

slide off and on the rods. In fitting the skin the head is taken from the manikin, placed inside the skin of the head through the opening cut at the top, and slid up over the neck rods and the skin adjusted on the body.

Very short-haired mammals are best mounted by constructing a manikin in which all the legs lift off.* For this purpose the animal is skinned by allowing the opening cuts on the backs of the legs to run up no farther than is absolutely necessary to turn the leg skin inside out, in order to save the unsightly seams on the legs of the mounted specimen. In the case of a dog, on the hind leg this would be to about halfway up to the calcaneum from the bottom of the foot. The belly cut extends from the brisket to the tip of the tail, as usual.

The manikin is then constructed on the same general principles as those already described, except that the leg rods, instead of being wired fast to the centre board, are flattened on their upper ends, and holes are drilled in the flattened portions to receive two wood screws for each rod. The rods are then bent so that their flattened ends lie snugly lengthwise along the underside of the centre board, the screws running up into the board and holding the rods secure.

The modelling of the body and upper parts of the leg is then performed as usual.

The limb bones are then sawed through about even with the lower line of the body. A sheet of waxed paper, slightly oiled also, larger than the circumference of the leg at this point, is now introduced into the slot formed by sawing the bone in two and allowed to remain in a flat position. The legs are then modelled as usual, plenty of dilute gum arabic being used in the *papier-maché* modelled on at the

---

* A zebra would ordinarily be better mounted in this way; but as the skin of the legs had been cut all the way up to the body in skinning, this method was obviously unnecessary.

point of separation, as this material becomes very hard when dry.

When all modelled and allowed to set and dry, the screws running up into the centre board through the tops of the leg rods are unscrewed and the legs all lifted off the manikin body, coming away where the paper was inserted.

In putting on the skin, the artificial legs are slipped down into the skin one at a time, and when all are in position the skin is thrown over the body and the leg rods screwed fast from below, working the screwdriver through the belly cut of the skin. The adjoining faces of the modelling material of the legs are coated with hot glue before they are finally screwed into position. After the skin is on, should there be any tendency to turn in the lower leg, this may be remedied by making a short cut in the skin, drilling a hole so as to pass from the lower into the upper part of the modelled leg and driving in a stout piece of wire. Instead of using a pedestal to construct the manikin on, a raised block is used for each foot, each leg thus being independent of the other. The blocks may be screwed fast to the floor or a board if necessary. It takes a little longer to construct a manikin in this way, but much time is of course saved in sewing up the leg openings afterward, and, best of all, there are no awkward seams to conceal.

Finishing Mounted Mammals.—The finish of a mounted specimen is an important point, and all the time the specimen demands should be put in on finishing. I have seen many a really finely mounted specimen which looked very ordinary because of the lack of finish. A monkey especially may be made or ruined according to the finish it receives.

When thoroughly dried out, a mounted mammal is gone over and all pins drawn out with flat pliers. Skins mounted by the method described will be found to remain where placed and not shrunk out of depressions. The seams will

PLATE XIV.

FINISHED RHINOCEROS.

not open—in some instances even though the edges of the skin are merely drawn together and pinned without sewing —nor will the eyelids draw away from the eyes in drying. The whole specimen is then well beaten with a rattan to loosen all dust and dirt, and the hair blown out with the air compressor. If this is not at hand, the cleaning is done by beating alone. Steel combs are used on some specimens to help clean out the hair, but in specimens with curly or long, matted hair, such as the American bison or some sheep, a comb should never be applied. Short-haired mammals may have dried glue removed from the hair along the seams by the use of a wire brush.

Should the skin have been placed on the manikin wet, and the hair be dirty or greasy—a thing that should never be done—the hair may be cleaned out by first dampening it with water and then applying benzine and furrier's sawdust or hot sand, and beating it out with the rattan as already described under the head of treating skins.

When the hair is well cleaned, all holes and cracks and the insides of the nostrils are modelled with *papier-maché*, using a small scraper for this purpose. The *papier-maché* is sandpapered and shellacked when dry and then painted with tube colours. Should there be any spots from which the hair has been worn or lost, these spots must be repaired by gluing on hair taken either from another skin or from other parts of the same specimen. Hair is best glued fast or "set" with rubber cement (raw rubber dissolved in naphtha or benzine), which may be readily purchased all dissolved from any rubber house or bicycle establishment.

The cement is painted thinly over the spot to be covered with hair, and small bunches of hair, their bases touched with some of the liquid cement, applied with the aid of forceps in which the hair is grasped. The bunches of hair after being glued on are arranged with a needle set in a handle. Hair setting is very slow and difficult work, and requires great patience and much practice to do it well.

Natural bare spaces require to be painted with oil colour applied with a brush, using plenty of turpentine with the colour. Glossy places, such as the nose of a deer, will require a coat of varnish over the colour. If a " dead finish " is desired, as in the case of a monkey's face and callosities, the colour is stippled upon the skin, the lightest colour first, and the gloss deadened by stippling on dry powdered clay or plaster. The deeper colours are then stippled on and again gone over with the powder. Hairless mammals, such as the rhinoceros, are coloured all over in this way, after receiving a coat of shellac. Skin which is covered thinly with hair so that the skin shows through, as in the under parts of some monkeys, is coloured in the same way, the plaster absorbing the colour that catches on the hair and is removed with the dry plaster when brushed and beaten. The inside of the ears of deer are also best coloured in this way. Without the use of a dry powder after the colour is applied, more or less paint will adhere to the hair and thus change its colour.

Horns should never be polished for mounted specimens or heads, but should receive a light coat of linseed oil rubbed on with a piece of waste or cotton cloth. Open mouths of mammals are finished after the specimen is mounted by modelling the interior in *papier-maché* and painting over it with hot, coloured wax (formula No. 15) applied with a flat camel's-hair brush. Different coloured waxes may be used, one over another, where desired, and the wax finished off with a modelling tool and smoothed by polishing it with the side of a round needle. The whole inside of the mouth is then varnished with spirit varnish or liquid celluloid.

Should the specimen be received in the flesh, the roof of the mouth may have a mould taken of it in plaster and a wax cast run out of it of the proper colour. The cast may afterward be fastened to the roof of the mouth, thus doing away with the longer process of modelling it. The tongue may also be treated likewise, but instead of casting the

PLATE XV.

Fig. 1.—First stage.

Fig. 2.—Second stage.

MOUNTING A MOOSE HEAD.

tongue in clear wax, pieces of cotton batting saturated with hot wax are laid into the mould until the mould is full, thus adding greatly to the strength of the cast tongue. The cotton should project beyond the base of the cast tongue, and just before the tongue is placed in the head the projecting ends of cotton are dipped in hot wax and the tongue placed in position, the wax cooling and thus gluing the base of the tongue fast. The tongue may be further fastened into place by painting hot wax around it.

Where it is desired to make wax blend off into hair, the hot coloured wax is painted upon the skin and the excess absorbed by laying a piece of blotting paper on the wax and running over the paper with a hot modelling tool.

The insides of nostrils and the eyelids are also worked up in hot wax, and afterward tinted with oil colours and varnished. Discoloured teeth are whitened by painting on slightly diluted muriatic acid with a brush, and after a few seconds removing the acid with another brush dipped in water. The acid, if left on too long, will cut the enamel and decompose the tooth.

Mounting a Horned Head.—The process of skinning a horned head and the treatment of the skin having already been described, no further instructions will be found necessary.

The entire skull, with the lower jaw, should always be kept for mounting, but for an illustration of the method of building out a skull where all save the plate of bone connecting the horns has been cut away by an inexperienced collector, we will select the head of a bull moose—one of the largest and noblest of the game animals of the world.

A stick of two by four clear pine scantling, or joist, is placed in the vise at the proper angle, one end cut so as to conform to the inside of the bony plate connecting the horns, and the plate firmly attached to the scantling by means of large screws. A piece of seven-eighths pine board is nailed fast to the scantling, as shown in Fig. 1, Plate

XV, and the upper edge of the front of the board cut off to conform to the general outline of the moose's nose. The framework of the head is now fixed in the vise in the exact position the mounted head is to assume, and a plumb line dropped from the end of the most backward point of the horns, crossing the centre post. The post is marked off with a square just where the plumb line crosses it.

If the scalp that is to be placed upon the manikin is a very short one, and a neck is to be constructed as short as possible, allowance can be made for the neck board and shield that are to be used, and their thickness deducted from the length of the centre post. In large horns, obviously the higher the backs of the horns are tilted the shorter the neck required. The object of plumbing the horns at this stage is to find the length of neck that is required to permit the finished head to hang upon the wall without the ends of the horns touching.* The centre post is now sawed off neatly on the line marked upon it.

To get at the length of the neck board a wire is laid from the top of the skull and supported at the other end, and the wire bent to just the curve of the outline of the back of the neck. A second wire is placed underneath in the same way, and bent to give an outline of the bottom of the neck. The folded edge of a piece of stiff paper is placed across the distal ends of the wires, and marked where the wires touch it. This gives the length of the neck board.

With the paper still folded together lengthwise, the outlines of the neck board are marked off on one side of the paper and both thicknesses of the paper cut through with the scissors, following the pencilled outline. When the paper is unfolded we have a pattern for a neck board.

A piece of one-and-a-half-inch pine board of the required

---

* In the accompanying photographs, by reason of distortion, a line drawn from the base of the centre post to the tips of the horns will pass much inside the tips of the horns, but in the actual mounted head such was not the case.

size is now procured, the paper pattern laid down upon it and traced around with a pencil.

The neck board is roughed out with a hatchet and finished with drawknife and spokeshave. The neck board is now fastened with three large screws running from the back of the neck board into the centre post. The neck wires are stapled fast at both ends, when we have the head finished as far as represented in Fig. 1, Plate XV. Another piece of seven-eighths-inch board is cleated fast to the first piece and cut out to the general outlines of the nose.

A third piece of board is now cut to the shape of the throat, to get the lateral diameter or cross-section of the head at this point, and nailed fast to the post, as shown in Fig. 2, Plate XV.

Another piece of one-and-a-half-inch plank is now cut and screwed fast from behind into the neck board. This last piece is only temporary, and in the finished head will be replaced by the shield.

The head is supported in the vise by gripping the bottom of the temporary shield, or the whole may be hung upon the wall at a convenient height for work.

The whole head and neck are now enveloped in annealed wire netting, which is worked into the general shape of the head, and holes are cut in the netting where the mouth, nostrils, and eyes are to go. The netting is, of course, stapled fast to the neck board all around and along the centre board of the head. The netting is given a coat of shellac. Excelsior may be bound on instead of using the netting if desired, but netting is preferable.

Papier-maché (formula No. 11) is now used as a modelling material, and the head modelled as already directed for building manikins. All the details of the nose and mouth are worked out carefully, enough room being allowed between the lips for the skin to slide in. The skin is tried on from time to time during the process to insure a proper fit when the manikin is complete, as in Fig. 1, Plate XVI.

12

When the modelling is completed the manikin is set away and allowed to dry out thoroughly. When dry the manikin is coated with glue and the skin adjusted, as already described in mounting the zebra.

The head of an animal of the size of a Virginia deer does not need to have a wooden neck block inserted, and in fact it is a decided disadvantage. A three-eighths-inch iron rod is used instead, the upper end of which is run through a hole bored lengthwise in a block of wood which is screwed fast into the brain cavity of the skull and the rod bent around underneath the block and stapled fast.

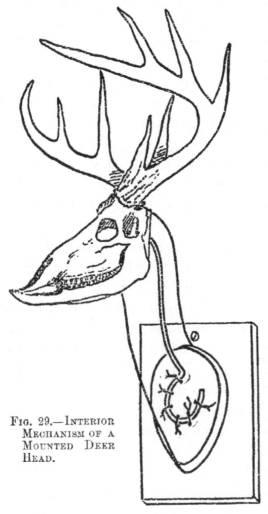

FIG. 29.—INTERIOR MECHANISM OF A MOUNTED DEER HEAD.

Neck rods or sticks should never be fastened into a skull with plaster, as the plaster not only adds to the weight of the head, but the rod or stick will shake loose. The other end of the rod is fastened by drilling holes through the neck board, and twisting wires which run from behind the board through these holes over the rod, as shown in Fig. 29. If wire netting is not at hand for covering the manikin, tow or excelsior may be bound upon the frame with thread and worked into the general form of the

Fig. 1.—The manikin completed.

Fig. 2.—The finished head.

MOUNTING A MOOSE HEAD.

neck. The modelling material may then be used as with netting.

Casting Heads.—Taxidermists who have a great number of heads of one species of animal to mount in the course of a year might save the time required to model each individual head by making a careful model manikin, of a deer's head, for instance, and making a heavy piece mould of it in plaster and casting the head in paper or other compositions. A number of moulds of the same model may be taken. If a variety of poses is desired, one may be made with the head straight, one looking to the right, and the other to the left. In the casts the whole head and neck are formed, including the modelling of the nose, all ready to slip the skin over. In the model the neck is better made long, the casts then having the neck shortened to suit the scalp which is to adorn it. At least three sizes of each style would be necessary to allow for the variation in size of individual deer heads. The horns are of course sawed out of the skulls of the originals, leaving them attached with a triangular piece of the skull. A paper head is then cast as follows:

After drying out, the inside of the mould is shellacked and when dry oiled with lard. Ordinary carpenter's sheathing or lining paper is then dampened with water and torn, not cut, into strips a couple of inches in width by five or six inches in length. One side of the paper is coated with good thick flour paste (rye flour boiled in thin glue water), and piece by piece pressed into the mould with the pasted side upward so that the paste will not cling to the mould. Paper of another colour is now taken, pasted on both sides, and the interior of the mould given a second layer. The first colour of paper is then introduced into the mould again, pasted on both sides, and so on alternately until the mould is lined up with six or eight layers of paper. A block of soft pine wood is now introduced into the mould to come just underneath where the horns were sawed out of the skull. The block of wood is securely fastened in place by pasting strips of paper and muslin across it in every direction, the ends being pasted fast to the surrounding paper on the inside of the mould.

The paper may be left inside the mould until it has dried sufficiently to be removed, when the mould is taken apart and the paper head taken out. If it is desired to remove the paper cast from the mould at once, a quantity of plaster is poured inside the mould with the paper in position, and the mould rocked about until a thin layer of plaster is deposited all over the inside of the paper cast. The excess of plaster is poured out. When the plaster has set, the paper is sufficiently rigid to come out of the mould. In some respects the thin lining of plaster is an advantage, as it tends to keep the paper cast from warping out of shape in drying. Instead of the paper, plaster of Paris mixed with water containing gum arabic to strengthen it is used with tow for lining up the mould. The tow in long flat wads is dampened and saturated with the liquid plaster, and the excess of plaster is squeezed out of the tow by drawing it between the thumb and finger. The inside of the mould is thus lined up all over. The block of wood for the attachment of the horns is now placed in the mould, the block being previously soaked in hot paraffin to prevent its swelling from the moisture in the plaster and cracking the cast.

The cast is made about half an inch in thickness all over. When set the cast is relieved from the mould and the inside of the cast lined up with tow saturated with hot glue. The plaster and tow process is much quicker than the paper and fully as strong.

A neck rod or stick is unnecessary, as the neck is stout enough without one.

The neck board is fitted as usual, stout wire nails being driven into the neck board all around through the paper or tow.

The paper heads are shellacked when dry. This is unnecessary with the plaster heads.

The antlers are screwed fast to the top of the cast, the screws running down into the wooden block on the inside of the cast skull. The skin is adjusted as already described.

By casting the manikins in this way they may be run out at any time when work is slack and be in readiness for the fall trade, when most of the work upon the head will have been already accomplished and the head may be delivered within a week after it is received by the taxidermist.

CHAPTER VI.

FISH, REPTILES, AND CRUSTACEANS.

MOUNTING FISH.

MOST fish are better reproduced by casting than by skinning and mounting the skin. It sometimes happens, however, that a fresh specimen is not at hand, so both methods will be considered.

Very large fish, as well as cetaceans, are best represented by a cast in paper. By this method a piece mould is made in plaster, the mould dried out and shellacked with two or three coats of shellac, and oiled well with lard oil.

Stereotyper's matrix paper is then dampened and beaten with a stiff brush, such as a blacking dauber, into every crevice and detail of the mould. The paper is torn into strips, one side painted with rye flour paste, and laid inside the mould with the unpasted side downward. A coarser quality of brown paper is now used. The layers of paper, pasted on both sides, are lined up inside the mould three ply and left for a few days to dry out. The edges of the paper are allowed to lap over on the edges of the mould and stick fast, to prevent the paper from drawing away from the sides and edges of the mould in drying. More paper is now pasted into the mould and again allowed to dry out. The process is continued until a sufficient thickness has been obtained to secure strength. In a wet climate the moisture in the atmosphere greatly retards the drying out of the paste, and artificial heat is necessary.

When sufficiently dry the edges of the paper are trimmed and loosened from the mould, and the paper cast eased out. The two half casts are joined together by adjusting a centre board to reach along the inside of the cast in its entire length, and nailing the edges fast. The fins, or flippers, are cut off and cast separately, and afterward joined on the paper cast, the joints being filled with *papier-maché*. The whole is then shellacked and painted and varnished in imitation of the original.

For smaller fish, where more minute definition is desired, the paper must be discarded, at least for a first coat.

Plaster of Paris, mixed thin and containing a proportion of dilute gum arabic, is first poured into the mould, and the mould rocked about in every direction until the whole inside is covered with a thin layer. When set, this is backed up with a *papier-maché* composition made in the following way:

Stereotyper's matrix paper is reduced to a pulp by rubbing it between the hands in warm water. The excess of water is then squeezed from the pulp, and a quantity of gum arabic, dissolved in water to the consistence of thin molasses, is placed in a basin and the pulp mixed through it until the whole is in a soft, mushy state. Plaster is now well worked into the pulp until it is of a soft, modelling consistence. The mass is then run through a painter's grinding mill, when it is ready for use. The pulp is laid into the mould over the plaster lining to the depth of a quarter of an inch, and well pressed with the fingers. Soft wire netting, shellacked, may now be introduced into the mould if great strength is desired, but ordinarily this is unnecessary. Flat wads of tow saturated with hot glue are lined up inside the mould over the pulp lining, and this when dry renders the cast exceedingly stout.

For a real fine cast, where but one copy is desired, the wax mould described on page 96 is the best.

When the plaster cast is dry, if small enough the cast is

placed bodily into hot paraffin, or if a vessel can not be procured large enough, the cast is warmed in an oven or on a radiator, and hot paraffin is painted upon it to give it a surface that will take colour better than the plaster itself.

Any excess of paraffin may be removed by rubbing with a piece of waste wet with benzine. The cast is then coloured with thin oil colour stippled on, using if possible a fresh specimen of the same species as a model. If a fresh specimen can not be procured, the same one, or its skin, may have been kept in alcohol and now used as a guide.

When the paint is dry the cast is varnished with liquid celluloid (formula No. 18), two coats being applied. If the fish is silvery, the silvery appearance may be reproduced by applying aluminum powder with a fluff of cotton to the celluloid before it dries. The gold powders or bronzes are used in the same way. These powders should never receive a coat of varnish of any kind, as the brilliancy is ruined thereby. Manufactured dyes are sometimes used for colouring fishes, but these lack permanency.

Mounting the Skins of Fishes. Skinning.—If but one side of a fish is to be seen in the finished specimen, an opening cut is made on the side which is most damaged, reaching from the gill to the tail. If both sides of the fish are to be exhibited, the opening cut extends along the belly, keeping to one side of the belly fins. The skin is then removed from the body, detaching the fins and tail on the inside of the skin.

The gills are removed and the skull cleaned out. The eyes are removed from the outside. The bases of the fins and tail are then cleaned of all flesh, when the skin is well washed, salted, and treated in other respects as the skins of mammals already described. A fish skin after salting, if at all oily, should be placed in benzine for several hours, or longer if necessary, to remove the oil. The tarpon should always be treated thus.

FISH, REPTILES, AND CRUSTACEANS.

Mounting Fishes.—If the fish is received in the flesh by the taxidermist, the fish is posed and a rough plaster mould made of it, exclusive of the head, fins, and tail.

A block of wood is roughly shaped to lie loosely into the mould. This block is boiled in hot paraffin to render it waterproof. When thoroughly charged, the block is used as a nucleus for the mould, and tow saturated with plaster is packed around it. When the plaster sets, the mould is knocked off the cast. After the scale markings are sandpapered off the cast, a perfectly formed manikin results, over which to mount the skin. The manikin is of course coated with hot glue in the same manner as already directed for mounting mammals. Soft *papier-maché* is placed at the bases of the head, tail, and fins before the skin is placed on the manikin. The fins are spread and clamped in position by means of pieces of cardboard until they are dry, when the cards are removed. When dry, the fish is painted, varnished, etc., and, if desired, screwed fast to a panel from behind, or mounted on an upright support. If the scales, should any exist, show a disposition to curl up when drying, the outside of the fish is given a coat of thin, hot glue, and the scales brushed down with the flat of the hand. If only the skin of the fish is received by the taxidermist, a manikin is modelled, using a block of paraffin-saturated wood as a nucleus, so that the fish may be screwed into from behind if necessary and rigidly supported. Modelling composition (formula No. 11) is used for modelling here, as in the case of mammals.

The great objections to mounted fish are the shrinkage and mummification of the fins and head in drying. A fin which in a fresh specimen is an inch wide will when dried be found reduced to less than half that width in some instances.

THE ART OF TAXIDERMY.

Mounting Reptiles.

Snakes.—As with fish, snakes are sometimes better cast than mounted. The size of the snake and the intricacy of the colour pattern should determine whether a snake is better cast or mounted. Large snakes, in which the pattern is simple, so that the colours may be readily painted in, should be cast. A large snake with a very difficult pattern to represent, such as the boa constrictor shown in Plate XVII, is better mounted, the colour pattern remaining in the skin after it is dried and the colour restored by painting. As with fish, if the specimen is received in the flesh by the taxidermist, the snake is posed properly and a waste mould made in plaster. The mould is then dried out, shellacked, and oiled; or, if used while wet, painted on the inside with lard or lard oil. Modelling composition (formula No. 11) is then lined up inside the mould. Soft wire netting is placed inside the mould to secure strength, and more of the composition placed over the netting to secure it in the mould. When the composition is set, the mould is broken away with chisel and mallet and a manikin results, which, when sandpapered and modelled further, is ready for use. The object of thus casting the snake is to secure a perfectly formed manikin by process work in a short time without going to the extra trouble of modelling one. The snake's skin, previously removed by opening along the belly and skinning as usual, is treated as with mammals, being glued upon the manikin as directed. When dry, the specimen is painted with oil colours. If the skin only is received, a manikin must, of course, be modelled, the skin being used as a guide for length and girth. The natural skull may be used if it is desired to represent the specimen with the mouth open, but the skin should be entirely removed from the skull in skinning, as with mammals. If the mouth is to be closed and the skeleton saved for a separate exhibit, as was done in the boa shown on Plate XVII, the skull must, of course, be dispensed with in the mounted skin and a cast used. All small snakes should be cast, preferably in plaster, using the wax mould. For this purpose the dead snake, as fresh as possible, is posed upon a piece of natural rock, the face of the rock being wetted slightly. The casting is then done as described on page 96, casting with a wax mould. Snakes are also successfully cast by the use of the gelatine mould.

Frogs and Lizards.—Frogs and small lizards are best represented by casting. Large lizards may be mounted on properly constructed manikins. If a plaster cast is desired, the wax mould is preferable. The wax is softened by heat and pulled away from the cast after the plaster has set in the mould.

Glue composition (formula No. 22) is found to work admirably on frogs and small lizards. The frog or lizard is placed in the desired position and a mould made in plaster. The creature is then withdrawn and the mould allowed to dry out.

The mould is then given a coat or two of shellac, oiled thinly with lard oil, slightly warmed, just so the plaster will not chill the warm composition and destroy definition, and the hot composition run into the mould. When cooled, the cast is eased out of the mould and the edges trimmed off with scissors or a sharp knife. The legs and tails of lizards and the legs of frogs are strengthened by running a pointed wire up the inside after they are taken out of the mould. The cast is then colored with oil colors and varnished.

Turtles.—Turtles may be cast entirely and a separate exhibit made of the skeleton if desired. In the case of the large leather-back turtles a cast should always be made. Ordinarily turtles are better mounted.

If the specimen is brought in alive, the nicest way to kill it is to place it in a tight box containing a wad of cotton saturated with chloroform. Turtles are very difficult to poison, and I have seen a land tortoise. that had received several hypodermic injections of prussic acid, alive and seemingly enjoying life the next morning. Snakes or frogs are also quickly killed with chloroform.

In skinning, if the plastron or under shell is large enough to admit of it, as in Fig. 30, a square piece, as large as can be cut without materially weakening the remaining corners, is cut out with the aid of a surgeon's saw. The viscera are then removed.

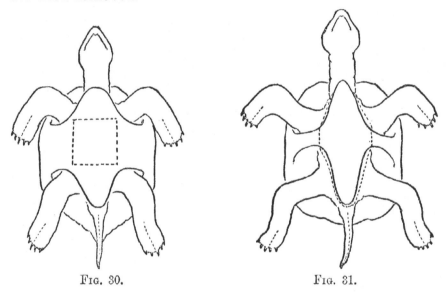

Fig. 30.   Fig. 31.

The head and neck, legs and tail, are then skinned through this hole, the bottoms of the feet and the under-side of the tail being split open to facilitate skinning these members.

The head is skinned over as far as the muscles run, but the skinning must stop where the skin grows directly upon the skull. The turtle is then salted and placed in tan liquor for a day or two, when the skin is well scraped on the inside, the whole washed with clear water, and painted with arsenical soap.

If the plastron is too small to have the piece cut out, as in Fig. 31, the bridges at the sides of the plastron are sawed through and the under shell is partly detached from the upper, being connected by the skin about the fore legs. The skin from the back of the fore legs is cut through all around the plastron and afterward united by sewing. A wire is then placed in each leg and bound fast to the limb bones. The legs and tail are treated as already directed for small mammals.

A piece of wire is now taken for the head and neck and bound with tow to the proper size. This is coated with *papier-maché* and the neck placed in position inside of the skin, the end of the wire projecting from the mouth, which is afterward cut off short, so as to allow the jaws to close.

Medinm-sized turtles are coupled as already described for small mammals. Large turtles are coupled by using a block of wood inside, through which holes are drilled, the wires being passed through the block and stapled fast on the opposite side.

To make all secure, wads of tow saturated with hot paraffin are laid inside the turtle and wrapped about the wires. When cooled the paraffin hardens and holds the wires inside perfectly rigid.

The square of plastron which has been sawed out is finally set back in place and secured by drilling holes through the edges and wiring. The seams are then filled with *papier-maché*. The soft parts when dry will require to be coloured with tube colours, and the whole painted with thin varnish.

Alligators.—Small alligators may be mounted by the method described for mounting small mammals. Large saurians should be mounted by means of modelled manikins, constructed on the same general principles as the ones already described for large mammals.

Crustaceans.—Lobsters and crabs are always mounted, the hard shell if properly handled retaining its original form.

Each leg and claw is detached from the body, the flesh removed by means of hooked wires, and the inside of the body cleaned out. When thoroughly cleaned, the whole is placed in tan liquor overnight, or longer if necessary.

The specimen is then well washed in clear water to remove the salt and allowed to dry out partially, but not so much as to dry the ligaments. Should this happen the whole may be wrapped in a damp cloth, or the ligaments softened by brushing with water. A soft wire is then placed in each leg or claw, the member bent into its proper position and the limb run full of hot paraffin. When the paraffin has cooled, the limbs, etc., are placed in position on the body with the wires simply projecting loosely into the cavity of the body. Cotton batting saturated with hot paraffin is now placed inside the body, wad by wad, and arranged with a camel's-hair brush. The paraffin when cool will make all secure, when the specimen is placed upon a pedestal. The joints are painted over with hot paraffin and modelled with a scraper.

The colours are restored by painting with tube colours and varnishing with liquid celluloid.

This makes a good, firm preparation for crustaceans and does away entirely with the warping and brittleness of specimens which are simply dried without filling, or filled with plaster of Paris.

CHAPTER VII.

SKELETONS.

Roughing out Skeletons.—The process of roughing out the skeletons of birds and mammals having been described in the chapter on Collecting, it will not be necessary to again describe it here.

The process is simple, the idea being to clean off as much of the flesh as possible, disarticulating the bones wherever necessary in large specimens, and leaving the bones attached by their ligaments in small ones. Mammals of the size of a fox or under, in which the bones are so small that drilling and subsequent wiring into position is a difficult matter, are left ligamentary. All birds except the largest species, such as the ostrich, emu, etc., are left ligamentary, except that the skull, wings, and legs are detached from the body. Snakes, lizards, etc., are always mounted as ligamentary skeletons. As soon as possible after a skeleton is roughed out, it should be placed in water for a few days, in order to soak out the blood. A little salt added to the water will materially assist its removal. Blood which is allowed to dry into bones is much like that dried into feathers or fur, and always requires much more labour to remove it after it has once dried in.

After soaking, the skeleton may be simply dried and kept indefinitely; or it may be cleaned and mounted at once by the following processes. No salt, arsenic, or other preservatives should be put upon a fresh skeleton, as these all materially retard the subsequent maceration and whitening of the bones. If insects attack the specimen, allow them to proceed, so long as they do not injure the bones nor ligaments of small skeletons. If absolutely necessary to keep insects from carrying off a ligamentary skeleton bodily, dry arsenic may be dusted over it.

Preparing a Small Mammal or Bird for Mounting as a Ligamentary Skeleton.—If it is desired to mount the bird or small mammal as quickly as possible, without regard to the quality of the preparation, the whole skeleton may be placed in boiling water and cooked until the flesh is sufficiently loosened to be removed with a bone scraper. Skulls of mammals designed for study and comparison are usually treated in this way, the form of the bones being the end sought. The best method of preparing a ligamentary skeleton is as follows: The skeleton is placed in water, at an ordinary temperature, in a vessel containing no iron or other metals, the oxidation of which is liable to stain the bones, and is allowed to remain there for a few days, until the flesh is sufficiently softened, so that it may be removed with a stiff toothbrush and bone scraper. The skeleton should not soak long enough to allow the ligaments at the joints to macerate, or the bones will fall apart. In scraping, the scraper is always worked from the joint toward the other end of the bone, in order to thin down the ligament on the bone, and run it off to nothing. After the bulk of the flesh is removed, and maceration has gone far enough, the skeleton is placed in a vessel of water, containing a proportion of borax—about half a teaspoonful to a quart—and kept there until the scraping is completed. The borax retards maceration. After scraping, the skeleton is allowed to dry and is then treated with javelle water (formula No. 12), to remove all small particles of flesh and membrane that may adhere to the bones. The bones are simply immersed in the javelle water and allowed to remain there for a few minutes; they are then removed and scrubbed with a toothbrush and warm water. The skeleton is now allowed to dry, and if the bones are at all greasy they are placed in a jar of benzine or naphtha, with a close-fitting glass cover. The jar should not be over three quarters full of benzine, as, if fuller, the jar is apt to crack. The whole is placed in the sun, the jar being turned from time to time, so that the sun's rays may strike and bleach every side of the skeleton. A false bottom of wood is previously fitted into the jar, perforated with holes, and placed an inch or so from the bottom, so that the bones will not lie in the grease which soaks out of them. This answers during the summer months only. In cooler weather the jar is placed on a radiator or in a warm room, where the temperature is up to about 80°. Very greasy bones will require to have the benzine changed from time to time, as it becomes too much saturated with grease. The time required to degrease by this method of course varies with the size and quality of the bones, and may take several months. Ether or chloroform, although very expensive and explosive, if used in the same way, will remove the grease more rapidly than benzine. The expense connected with the use of ether may, however, be greatly reduced by redistilling the grease-charged ether, and using it over and over again. Warm water is used to vaporize it, when the vapour is of course condensed in a coil, producing the clear liquid. The great expense connected with this method of degreasing, however, renders it practically useless for extensive osteological preparations.

After the grease is out of the bones the skeleton is well rinsed in warm soda water and allowed to dry. If the bones are not white enough, they may be bleached by immersion for half an hour or so in a warm solution of chloride of lime and water (a tablespoonful in two quarts of water). The skeleton is then rinsed off with hot water and dried. If some of the bones are still not white enough, they may be again treated with the chloride bath. It will be borne in mind that chloride of lime while bleaching the bones also corrodes and decomposes them, and if the bones

13

are allowed to remain in the solution too long they will disintegrate and soften. The ligaments will also be destroyed.

The skeleton is now ready for mounting, which process will be described farther on.

Macerating Large Skeletons.—In large specimens, where every bone is taken apart and afterward drilled and wired into position, maceration or continuous soaking is resorted to in order to soften the flesh and tendons adhering to the bones, so that they may be scrubbed and scraped off clean.

Before maceration, all the large limb bones are drilled from the ends at such points as are covered by adjoining bones in the mounted skeleton. One good-sized hole in each end is sufficient. These bones are filled with marrow and animal matter, and this must be extracted in order to produce a good preparation.

When drilled, the bones are placed in a vat or tub of water, care being taken that no iron or other metals which are liable to rust come in contact with them. Small bones may be wrapped in cloths and tied up securely if it is found best to keep them separate. This is a good plan in order to keep them from being lost. They may be macerated separately—preferably in a large glass jar. For very large skeletons, a porcelain bath tub fitted with a cover, makes a first-class receptacle for maceration. Rain water is the best for maceration, but any fresh water will answer. The temperature has a great deal to do with the length of time necessary to complete the maceration, between 80° and 100° F. being a fair medium. If the temperature of the room can not be kept up to this point in cold weather, a steam coil may be placed about the tank, if practicable.

The bones are allowed to remain in the water for two or three days, when it is changed for a fresh supply. A little salt added will materially assist in soaking out the blood. Should the second bath become too bloody in the course of a few days, this should also be changed, as filthy maceration water is liable to stain and discolour the bones. The bones are allowed to macerate until the flesh becomes slimy, and decomposition, and plenty of it, takes a good hold on the tissues. The process of renewal of the water should be continued as often as necessary, as the nicest way to keep bones white is not to allow them to become stained by dirty maceration water. The changes, of course, retard the maceration, and they should not be made oftener than necessary.

When the flesh becomes slimy and the bones are sufficiently macerated, which may take several months' time, they are removed from the maceration water and placed in a tub of hot water containing a few handfuls of washing soda. They are then scrubbed with a wire brush and scraped until every vestige of soft tissue is removed from the exterior of the bone. The insides of the drilled bones are cleaned out with a hooked wire and syringed. The bones are again soaked as before and then finally well scrubbed.

After the final washing, the bones are allowed to dry out, when they are ready for drilling and degreasing.

The sternum, or breast bone, is ordinarily simply dried and not macerated, as, being largely cartilaginous, it is liable to fall to pieces during the process. When dried it is soaked in soda water for a day or two and thoroughly scraped, when it is ready for degreasing.

Degreasing and bleaching Large Skeletons.—After the skeleton is macerated and dried, the bones are drilled as subsequently directed under the head of Mounting Skeletons. The bones are better drilled before the grease is removed, as the holes offer channels for the exit of the grease. For degreasing large skeletons after they have been macerated and dried, in large institutions a machine is used which degreases by the vaporization of benzine. If the preparator does not wish to go to the expense of constructing such a machine, and which is altogether unnecessary where but a few skeletons are to be degreased, the grease may be extracted by simply placing the bones in benzine, as already described for ligamentary skeletons. This process is slow but sure, as the results obtained are beyond criticism. After removal from the benzine the bones are well scrubbed with warm soda water and a brush, and are then bleached by immersion in chloride of lime, as already directed. The length of time necessary to bleach bones may be several hours or several days, according to circumstances. The solution should not be made too strong, or it will corrode the bone and ruin the small processes. After removal from the chloride bath the bones are washed off in warm water and allowed to dry, when they are ready for mounting.

Mounting the Ligamentary Skeleton of a Small Mammal.—When the skeleton has been cleaned, bleached, and dried, as previously directed, it is ready for mounting. The skeleton is placed in water and allowed to remain there until the ligaments soften. The body is first taken. A piece of galvanized iron wire is worked down through the neural canal of the vertebral column and the distal end anchored firmly in the sacrum, thus stringing all the vertebræ upon the wire, enough of the wire projecting beyond the first vertebra or atlas to allow for attaching the skull. The backbone is now bent into position. Two pieces of stiff brass wire, heavy enough to offer a firm support for the skeleton, are cut to the proper length for standards. One end of each rod is heated and plunged into cold water to soften the metal at this point. The rods are placed in the vise, and with the hack saw split on the softened end down the centre far enough to form a U of the proper size to receive the vertebræ, one at the axis and the other in the lumbar region. A thread is cut on the other end of each rod an inch or so in length, and a brass rosette screwed upon it.

The rods are now adjusted upon a temporary pedestal by boring two holes through it for their reception. A nut is screwed up from below on each rod, which holds them firmly in an upright position. The axial skeleton is now placed in position upon the rods, and the tops of the U bent over the tops of the vertebræ. The ribs are spaced by tying a double thread to the neck vertebræ, and, twisting the thread, taking a turn around each rib, from the first to the last, and thus holding them in position. The ends of the thread are tied to the lumbar vertebræ. To give the chest cavity its proper expansion, braces of wire are placed inside across it. If the tail has been removed, this is wired as in the case of the vertebræ, by running a small wire lengthwise through it. The projecting end of the tail wire is then forced up inside the cavity of the sacral vertebræ, the adjoining faces coated with liquid glue and the tail placed in position. The body, with the exception of the skull, is now complete. The legs are adjusted to the skeleton one at a time, and the proper pose of each determined. The legs, in the exact position they are to occupy in the finished specimen, are laid flat upon a board, as in the accompanying illustration (Fig. 32), and pinned in position. They are allowed to dry thus, when they are ready to attach to the mounted body.

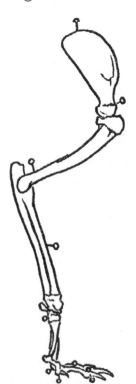

FIG. 32.—LIGAMENTARY LEG OF A SMALL MAMMAL, PINNED DOWN TO DRY.

The hind legs are fastened on by drilling a small hole through the heads of the femurs, and also through the sockets of the pelvis. A small brass wire is passed through each hole and the legs thus held in position.

In placing the fore legs it will be borne in mind that in the living animal the scapula is separated from the ribs by layers of muscles, and this is consequently placed a little distance from the ribs in mounting the skeleton.

A piece of brass wire is run across the skeleton, through the second or third dorsal vertebra, and out through each scapula. A piece of coiled spring is placed between the scapula and the vertebra, on the wire, to keep the scapula

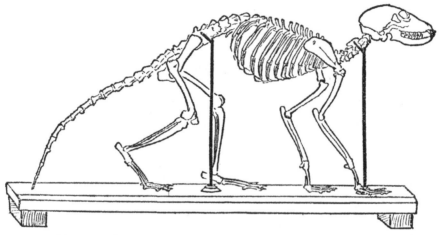

FIG. 33.—LIGAMENTARY SKELETON OF A SMALL MAMMAL.

in its proper position. A hook is made on each end of the cross-wire, outside of each scapula, to keep it from slipping off. The skull is fastened on by fitting a piece of cork into

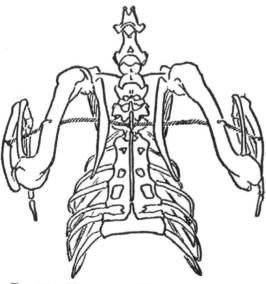

FIG. 34.—METHOD OF WIRING A SKELETON WING.

the occipital opening (foramen magnum) and piercing a hole through it to receive the wire projecting from the vertebræ. The cork is run down the wire, fitting snugly into the cavity of the atlas vertebra. The skull is then placed upon the wire, the cork offering a firm foundation for its support.

If any bones have been broken they are now repaired. The best way is to first glue the broken bones, and then fill in the cracks with a little paste made of liquid glue and plaster. If a rib has become detached, coat the points of attachment with liquid glue; and then, with a little cotton batting cut up fine with the scissors, mixed with liquid glue, construct a false ligament, which when dry will hold the rib firmly in place. When thoroughly dry the skeleton may be transferred to a permanent pedestal and the uprights gilded or painted with black shellac.

FIG. 35.—LIGAMENTARY SKELETON OF A BIRD.

The same general principles will apply to the mounting of ligamentary bird skeletons. Figs. 34 and 35 will give an idea of the methods of wiring the wings and attaching the upright support.

Mounting a Disarticulated Skeleton. Drilling.—For an example of this method of mounting we will select an adult male of the Indian antelope (*Antelope cervicapra*).

After the bones have been macerated, scraped, and dried as already described, they are ready to be drilled for the reception of the wires in the subsequent mounting.

We start with the vertebral column. Commencing with the sacrum, the vertebræ are arranged upon the table in their proper order. With pen and ink the last lumbar vertebra is marked on its anterior articulating surface No. 1. The next lumbar vertebra is numbered 2, and so on, until all the vertebræ have been numbered.*

The last lumbar vertebra is now marked on both the anterior and posterior articulating surfaces with two dots, one on either side of the neural canal, on the body of the vertebra. The bone is drilled through from front to rear at the points indicated by the dots. Placing this vertebra in its proper position on the sacrum, the latter is marked to drill by passing a drill or pointed wire through the holes already bored and revolving it. The sacrum is drilled at the points indicated in such a way that both holes come out on the underside of the bone. The drill, in this case, should be just large enough to bore a hole to receive easily a No. 18 wire. The second lumbar vertebra is now marked in the same way, by placing the bored vertebra in position on the one preceding it and marking the points on the bone where the holes are to be drilled. This process is continued, alternately marking and drilling, until all the vertebræ except the first or atlas has been drilled. This bone is attended to later on and attached separately. The next to the first vertebra (the axis) is, like the sacrum, drilled in such a way that the holes come out on the underside of the bone. Since in the living animal the vertebræ are separated one from another by a cushion of cartilage, artificial cartilages are cut out of felt, or, better still, tanned elk hide. The posterior surface of a vertebra is laid flat upon the leather and traced around with a pencil. The piece is then cut out and numbered to correspond with the vertebra. The outline of the body of each vertebra is treated in this

---

* As it is next to impossible to describe the process of mounting a disarticulated skeleton without the use of more or less of the technical names of the bones, I advise the osteological student to procure a copy of Flower's Osteology. (An Introduction to the Osteology of the Mammalia, by William Henry Flower. Macmillan & Co., 1885.)

way, the holes previously bored through the vertebræ being continued through the artificial cartilages.

The next step is to cut a piece of brass wire about three times the length of the spinal column, and somewhat smaller than the holes drilled through the vertebræ. The wire is doubled and straightened; the ends are passed up through the holes in the sacrum and drawn tight. The vertebræ are then strung upon the wires in their proper order, the wires passing through the drilled holes. When the wires are pulled tight, and the bones are all adjusted one to the other, to get the outline of the spinal column, the whole is laid flat upon a piece of plain paper, or a board, and properly posed. A line is drawn upon the paper along the underside of the spinal column in its full length.

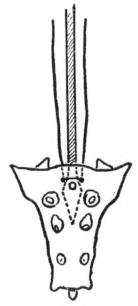

FIG. 36.—TREATMENT OF THE SACRUM.

A square rod of iron is now selected, a foot or so longer than the spinal column, which will pass easily through the neural canal of each vertebra. One end of the rod is flattened into the shape of a spear head and fitted snugly into the spinal canal of the sacrum. A hole is drilled through both sides of the sacrum, up and down, passing through the flattened end of the rod. A brass bolt is placed in the hole and a nut adjusted, thus firmly securing the sacrum to the rod (Fig. 36). The rod is now bent to conform to the outline of the spinal column traced upon the paper. The vertebræ are strung on the rod, the wires also being in position; and if they fit properly they are taken off preparatory to drilling for the attachment of the ribs. The rod is given a couple of coats of black shellac and allowed to dry. The ribs are arranged in pairs, with the dorsal vertebræ to which they attach. The foremost pair of ribs is first taken. A hole is bored, with the lathe or hand-drill, through the centre of the articulating surface of the tubercle of the rib, directing the drill so that it will come out on the outside. Another hole is drilled through the head

of the rib (Fig. 37). The rib is fitted to the vertebra, and the articulating surface marked, by passing a drill or pointed wire through the holes bored in the rib. The vertebra is drilled at the points marked, and the opposite rib of the pair is bored in the same way. The ribs are all drilled in this way. The distal end of each rib should have a small hole bored through it, for attachment to the sternum, the cartilage of the sternum having first been drilled at the points of attachment with the ribs. The feet and legs are drilled, as shown in the accompanying cuts.

FIG. 37.—WIRING THE RIBS.

MOUNTING.

After the skeleton has been drilled, degreased, and bleached, it is ready for the final mounting.

The false, intervertebral cartilages which have been cut out are tacked fast to the vertebræ by driving a small wire nail through the centre into the body of the vertebræ.

The ribs are arranged in pairs in their proper order and fastened to the vertebræ to which they articulate by passing brass wires through the drilled holes and clinching the ends outside. The vertebræ, with the ribs attached, are strung upon the double wire already arranged, and placed in position on the iron rod, the rod being suspended horizontally with cords. The "cage" of the skeleton is then completed as shown in (Fig. 38). To tighten the vertebræ a screw-driver is worked between the bottoms of each vertebra, beginning with the last lumbar and working up toward the head, thus crowding them into their proper positions, which will be accomplished when the articular faces are seen to fit accurately. When the axis vertebra is reached, the wires are twisted tightly together underneath, thus keeping the vertebræ in position one upon another.

The sternum is next placed in position by wiring it fast to the ends of the ribs through the holes already drilled. The ribs are now to be spaced off. To do this properly a piece of thin, soft, brass wire about three times the length of the dorsal vertebræ is taken; it is first doubled and attached to the inferior process of the last cervical vertebra.

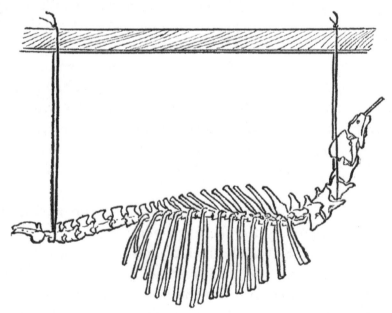

FIG. 38.—THE VERTEBRAL COLUMN IN POSITION, WITH THE RIBS ATTACHED.

In the next step the free ends of the wire are twisted together until the first rib is reached, when one wire is allowed to pass inside the rib and the other on the outside, and the wires again twisted together until the next rib is reached, and so on across all the ribs of that side. The ends of the wires are finally attached to the transverse process of one of the lumbar vertebræ. The ribs on the opposite side are treated in a like manner.

For larger skeletons a strip of flat brass is used, holes being bored through each rib and at the same time passing

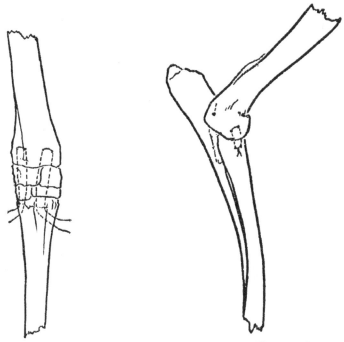

FIG. 39.—KNEE JOINT OF FORE LEG, FRONT VIEW.

FIG. 40.—ELBOW JOINT, SIDE VIEW.

through the rod. Each rib is then riveted fast to the rod, the rod being on the inside of the chest cavity.

In some cases the ribs are drilled and a brass wire passed through all, the ribs being spaced and held in position by means of pieces of coiled spring strung on the wire between the ribs. When the ribs are properly spaced, the points of attachment between the ribs and sternum are modelled over with coloured *papier-maché*, and when dry, with the entire sternum, given a couple of coats of red shellac.

The atlas vertebra is now to be attached to the axis bone. Two holes are drilled on each side of the anterior articulating surface of the axis. Through these holes a pointed wire is passed ,the atlas vertebra placed in position, and the point marked on the posterior articulating surface of the atlas where the holes are to be drilled.

A double wire is passed through the holes and twisted tightly together underneath the axis. The pelvis is next attached to the sacrum by drilling two holes through each side at the points of attachment and passing double wires through and twisting the ends together inside.

The tail is next attended to. Each vertebra is drilled lengthwise through the centre, and artificial cartilages are used to separate them, as in the larger vertebræ. The cau-

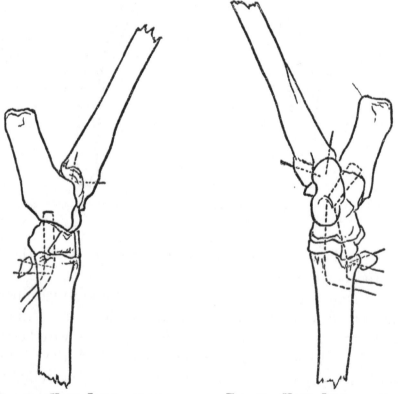

FIG. 41.—HOCK JOINT, VIEWED FROM OUTSIDE.   FIG. 42.—HOCK JOINT, VIEWED FROM INSIDE.

dal vertebræ are then all strung upon a brass wire and the wire attached to the sacrum.

The legs are now wired together, the wires passing through the holes already drilled.

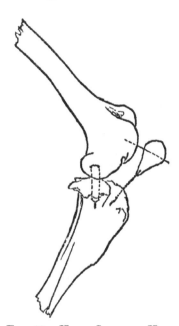

FIG. 43.—KNEE JOINT OF HIND LEG, SIDE VIEW.

A hind leg is attached to the pelvis by boring a hole through the head of the femur at such an angle that when continued it passes up through the socket of the pelvis. A brass bolt with a nut or thumbscrew on one end is used to hold the leg in position. The first phalanx of each foot is drilled and a wire pin driven down into the temporary pedestal which is now provided.

The scapula or shoulder blade is attached to the humerus by means of three brass pins. It is best to get the exact position of the scapula with reference to the ribs before fastening it to the humerus. The scapula is fastened to the body by two brass bolts which pass through it, one going through a rib and the other through the spinous process of one of the dorsal vertebræ. The scapula is held at the proper distance from the body by means of pieces of brass tubing which encircle the bolts between the scapula and the body. Coiled springs are sometimes used for this purpose instead of tubing.

The skull is now to be adjusted. The rod projecting from the vertebral column is cut off with the hack saw to the proper length and the skull placed in position, the end of the rod resting within the brain cavity. Two brass pins are passed through holes bored in the atlas vertebra and continued on through the occipital condyles of the skull. These hold the skull firmly in place. The lower jaw is articulated by means of brass springs, which allow for opening the jaws in order that the teeth may be examined at

PLATE XVIII.

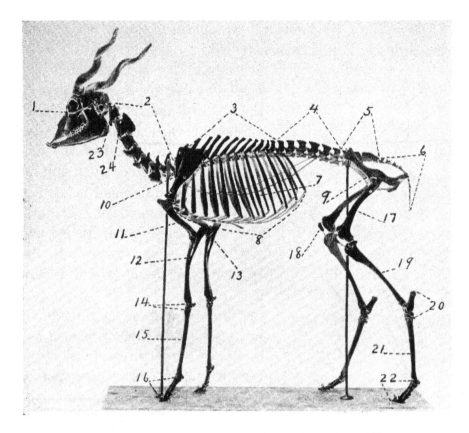

SKELETON OF AN INDIAN ANTELOPE.

1. Skull.	13. Ulna.
2. Cervical vertebra	14. Carpals.
3. Dorsal "	15. Metacarpals.
4. Lumbar "	16. Phalanges.
5. Sacral "	17. Femur.
6. Caudal "	18. Patella.
7. Ribs.	19. Tibia.
8. Sternum.	20. Tarsals.
9. Pelvis.	21. Metatarsals.
10. Scapula.	22. Phalanges.
11. Humerus.	23. Atlas vertebra.
12. Radius.	24. Axis "

any future time if desired. The hyoid bones are finally wired into position.

Two standards of iron rod are now prepared to support the skeleton. One end of each rod is split with the hack saw for a few inches and the ends bent to form a U. The tops of the U are rounded off with a file, and a hole is bored through the ends to receive a bolt which is to keep the vertebræ that they clasp in position. Brass rosettes are screwed upon the other end of both rods. The rods are then adjusted to the pedestal and the skeleton placed in position upon them.

The skeleton may now be transferred to a permanent pedestal, preferably a black one, the rods, nuts, bolts, and all exposed wires gilded, and the skeleton is ready for exhibition. All iron or other metals should be first painted yellow, and when dry the gold liquid should be painted over this. Gilding done in this way is much more permanent than if the gold paint is placed directly upon the metal.

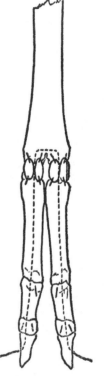

Fig. 44.—Bones of the Foot, Rear View.

CHAPTER VIII.

THE REPRODUCTION OF FOLIAGE, ETC., FOR GROUPS.

I. BIRD GROUPS.

BEFORE constructing a bird group, with nest and eggs, it is better, if possible, for the preparator to have seen the proposed group in a state of nature, rather than to trust to the imagination, or to the descriptions of other people.

For an illustration of the methods employed in constructing a bird group, with artificial foliage modeled in wax and cloth, in close imitation of the natural plants, we will select the nest of the Wilson's thrush (*Turdus fuscescens*), as this will include the making of grasses, leaves, and flowers.

Presupposing that the whereabouts of the nest is already known to us, we consider what tools and materials are necessary to collect and properly transport the actual sod, with the plants, etc., that are growing upon it, to the laboratory.

Since it will be necessary to box and ship the group, we first decide upon the area of the base, and get out the stuff for a box of seven-eighths-inch pine boards, two feet long by two feet wide by eighteen inches in height. The boards are sawed out and prepared to nail together, including a cover; but since we are to carry the box into the woods with us, it is more convenient to take a hammer and nails along, and put the box together there. Other materials necessary are the following:

A small surgeons' saw.

A stout butcher knife.

A ball of twine.

A two-foot rule.

A notebook and pencil.

A tin box with a tightly fitting cover, or, better still, a botanist's collecting can.

A small spade, and, if possible, a photographic camera.

If the birds themselves are to be collected, as is usually the case, a shotgun with the auxiliary barrel will of course be included.

Collecting a Bird Group.—Upon arriving at the nest, the birds, male and female, are first secured, if possible, when the nest and surroundings are closely inspected. Should the nest prove to be all that is desired for a group, the sod upon which the nest is situated is squared off and measured with the rule, and cut all around with the spade. Should any roots connect the square with the surrounding earth, the saw is called into requisition, and for smaller roots the butcher knife. Should the sod, after the surrounding growth is cut away, seem too bare, there is no objection to enhancing the beauty of the group and supplying vacancies by transplanting other species of plants that are found close by, or duplicates of those already found upon the sod. Too great an assortment of species should not be placed in one small space. The amount of labour required to model certain plants should be taken into consideration, and those that present too difficult a problem may be omitted altogether, or their number cut down and replaced by other species which are found in the same situation.

The eggs are now removed, with the nest, and carefully packed with cotton in a small box.

The height of the nest from the ground, the size and number of each species of plant, with notes on the colours, form, etc., are all entered in a small book. A rough sketch

14

is then made, and finally a series of photographs is taken from each side.

As the sod contains a wild rosebush, this is sawed off close to the ground on a long bevel, so that it may be spliced fast again when fitted up with artificial leaves. As this is the only plant upon the sod which has a rigid stalk and which would be liable to break if bent over too far, the others are allowed to remain in position. The entire sod is now loosened from the surrounding earth, with the spade, saw, and butcher knife. Some of the box boards are shoved under the sod lengthwise, and a couple of others crosswise under the ends of the first. By lifting on the ends of the bottom boards the whole sod is lifted bodily from its position. The boards are then nailed together and a cushion of green ferns or leaves placed in the box, and the sod allowed to rest upon them.

The flexible plants are now gently bent over, and ferns or leaves packed in over them until the box is full. The cover is then placed upon it and nailed fast, when the sod is ready to ship. Larger groups will of course require to have some of the plants shipped separately. Duplicates of the plants to be represented are now secured, care being taken to select specimens with perfect leaves, and leaves having as strong veining as possible. A number of flowers of the species to be represented in the group are also secured, which in this case are the dandelion, swamp buttercup, and wild violet. These, with the duplicate plants, are placed in the air-tight tin box, where they will keep well for a number of days, provided the box is kept out of the sun. If the box be kept on ice the plants will last much longer.

We will now proceed to the laboratory and commence work upon the group.

Unpacking the Sod, and Preliminary Work upon the Group.—The sod is unpacked as soon as it arrives, by knocking off the top and sides of the box and removing the packing materials. The plants are straightened up, and the whole sod is well sprinkled with water to keep the plants green and fresh while work progresses upon the group.

The birds are first mounted and the eggs blown. The wild rosebush is then placed to soak in Wickersheimer solution (formula No. 9), to keep it from drying out and becoming brittle. Pieces of green moss, such as were found growing upon the base of the bog upon which the nest was situated, are also placed in the solution, to render them always plump and flexible. All mosses, seaweeds, branches, etc., should remain in the solution for at least forty-eight hours, for without it these growths soon assume a miserably dried and shrunken appearance, and become so brittle that it is almost impossible to handle them without breakage.

Duplicate plants of the violet and dandelion * are now taken from the tin box, and a half dozen typical leaves with sharp, strong character selected from each plant, and placed in a basin of cold water. The leaves range from the smallest to the largest in size. Where a large bush is to be fitted with leaves, upward of fifty moulds are sometimes taken from different leaves. The flatter the leaf the easier it is to reproduce in wax.

Casting Leaves.†—A newspaper is laid flat upon the table, and a small quantity of cold water is placed in a bowl. Plaster of Paris is slowly sifted into the bowl until the plaster rises in a small cone above the surface of the water. The plaster should be mixed rather thicker than

---

* The leaflets of the wild rose, being so small, are modelled without moulds, as afterward directed. The leaves of this buttercup are also best made without the use of moulds.

† The methods here described are essentially the same as those used by Mrs. E. S. Mogridge and Mr. H. Mintorn in the preparation of the series of bird groups in the American Museum of Natural History, New York, the United States National Museum at Washington, and the South Kensington Museum in London. I am indebted to Mrs. Mogridge and Mr. Mintorn for my first lessons in this art, which have enabled me to continue the work at the American Museum.

necessary and then reduced by the addition of more water while stirring, rather than to have the mixture too thin, and try to thicken it by the addition of more plaster, as the latter is apt to produce lumps. The liquid plaster is well stirred with a tablespoon, one of the leaves taken from the water and the excess of water shaken out of the leaf. The stem is cut off close up to the leaf with the scissors, and, holding the base of the leaf with the thumb and forefinger of one hand, a spoonful of plaster is poured over the face or front of the leaf and blown with the breath, to send the plaster into every line of the leaf. Another spoonful is poured over the face or plastered surface of the leaf as a second coat, when the leaf, with the plaster upon it, is laid, plaster side up, upon the newspaper, care being taken that no folds or deep creases exist in the leaf.

The flatter the leaf is when cast, the flatter the resulting mould, and consequently the easier it will be afterward to press wax into every detail with the thumbs. If the natural curl of a leaf is desired in the mould, this may be accomplished in small leaves by simply pouring the plaster upon the face of the leaf as described, laying the leaf down upon the paper in its natural position, resting upon one edge or plane. The plaster is allowed to stiffen up, when a second coat is poured on with the spoon, the leaf itself not being disturbed. If the leaf lies perfectly flat, a sufficient thickness of plaster to complete the mould, say about half an inch all over, may be poured upon the leaf at once. But when the first layer of plaster, by reason of the curl in the leaf, would be broken down by the weight of more plaster if added in a quantity, the plaster is added little by little until the mould is thick enough.

Large flexible leaves are laid in position on a bed of clay or sand, and cast thus.

Leaf moulds should be made quite thick and heavy at the edges, otherwise in the subsequent pressing of the wax they are apt to crack off.

PLATE XIX.

LEAF MOULDS IN PLASTER.

When the plaster has hardened up just enough so that it will hold together when picked up from the paper, any plaster that may have accidentally run over the back of the leaf is carefully scraped off with a knife blade, and the edges cleaned, so that the whole leaf is exposed to view from behind.

The mould is then left to harden up, when the leaf is removed and the edges of the mould carefully trimmed to the outlines of the leaf.

Not more than half a dozen leaves should be in process of casting at once, as, if a greater number be taken, the plaster that runs over the backs of the leaves will set before it can be scraped off, and give trouble. When a sufficient number of moulds have been made to insure a good assortment of sizes and shapes, the moulds are set aside until the plaster has become thoroughly hardened, when the leaves are stripped off, leaving a perfect mould or reverse of the face of the leaf.

The moulds are then placed in the sun to facilitate drying out. When thoroughly dry, the moulds are placed in hot paraffin until they stop bubbling. This is to harden the plaster and keep it from cracking and wearing away during the subsequent manipulation. The moulds are taken out of the paraffin, the excess from the face being removed by means of a piece of blotting paper. The moulds are now ready for use.

Preparing Cloth for the Backs of the Artificial Leaves. —While the moulds are drying out, the stock of sheet wax, ordered from the sample card of the manufacturer, is inspected, and the colours selected which come nearest to the ground colours of the leaves—if anything, a trifle lighter.

A quantity of silk *crêpe de lisse*—a fine transparent fabric, to be purchased at the larger dry-goods houses or department stores for about seventy-five cents a yard—is now procured. The cloth is cut into strips three or four inches wide with a knife and straight-edge, and ironed out smooth with a hot flatiron.

While the fabric is being cut into strips, wax formula No. 16 is prepared and coloured. In this formula the best Madras white wax should be used, if it can be obtained, for the finest work. Unbleached beeswax will answer for rough work, but ordinarily American bleached wax is used.

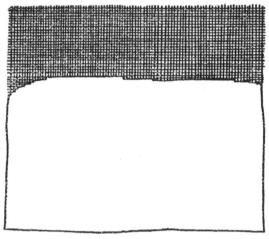

FIG. 45.—A PIECE OF CLOTH PARTLY COATED WITH WAX.

A piece of *lisse* is dipped into the wax and drawn out slowly, thus giving the fabric a coating of wax. The wax should be coloured, so that when the cloth is coated it will be of a colour to match the backs of the leaves to be imitated. The backs are generally several shades lighter than the faces of leaves.

A strip of *lisse* is now taken, rolled up into the form of a cylinder and placed into the hot wax, keeping hold of the end of the fabric with the thumb and finger. The cloth is now slowly drawn out of the wax, receiving a deposit or coat on both sides. The cloth is moved backward and forward to facilitate cooling, when the sheet is hung over a tight cord or wire, while a second piece is being coated.*

---

* Mrs. Mogridge has never, to my knowledge, allowed one of her pupils to see this process, nor would she ever explain how the cloth was coated. The above is therefore the outcome of my own experiment, and works equally well with cloth supplied by her. Mrs. Mogridge is always willing to supply pupils or others with not only waxed cloth, but sheet wax of a quality greatly superior to any manufactured in this country.

Enough of the strips of cloth are thus waxed to cover the backs of what leaves are to be made. A greater quantity may be prepared than is desired for immediate consumption, as it keeps well for at least a year. Beyond that time the wax is liable to become brittle and crack in handling by reason of the evaporation of the oils.

When a sufficient quantity of the fabric has been coated, the ends of the cloth where the wax has clotted are torn off, and the sheet stretched in all directions to remove the wrinkles and smooth it. In stretching, if the room be at all cold, the cloth must be held before a fire to warm, or the wax is apt to crack more or less. Wax works best at a temperature of about 75° F., and the room in which the work is to be done should be kept at about that temperature.

The heated wax may now be allowed to cool, and when solidified turned out in a block, by warming the vessel. The block is stowed away for future use. The same wax may be used again at any time, and the colour changed, if desired, by the addition of more colours.

In preparing white waxed cloth for petals, etc., of flowers, care should be used not to put in too much tube white, or the whole mess is liable to froth and be ruined.

Should the colours not dissolve readily, by reason of poor quality, the wax may be strained through a piece of *lisse* and the undissolved portion discarded.

Another batch of wax is now heated, and coloured to the ground colour of the base or lightest portion of the long grass found in the group. For this grass a heavier cloth is used for greater stiffness, although the same cloth may be made to answer by doubling it. A cloth known as *Mousseline de soire*, is better adapted for long tapering grasses, being stiffer, and also considerably cheaper.

The cloth is cut into strips as before, and again cross-cut into sections the length of the grass to be made. Each section is dipped into the hot wax separately, drawing it out as quickly as possible, thus leaving a heavier deposit of wax upon the bottom end of the cloth, which is to be the base of the grass.

Having prepared some of our working materials, we will see what other materials and tools are necessary to enable us to model artificial foliage.

Tools and Materials.—An assortment of silk-covered wire on spools, No. 26 being about the average size used for leaves. Nos. 40 and 60 are also used for small flowers and fine work.

A small scalpel.

A pair of fine scissors, both blades pointed, and cutting clear to the very tips.

A pair of stouter scissors for cutting fine wire.

A pair of small cutting pliers.

A pair of small flat pliers.

A half dozen ladies' hat pins, with porcelain or glass heads ranging from one eighth to one quarter of an inch in diameter.

An assortment of stiff iron wire, Nos. 17, 19, 21, 23, and 25.

A three-cornered needle set in a handle, for drilling small holes, and a very large three-cornered needle, also set in a handle, for grooving blades of grass.

An assortment of powder colours, to use with water.

An assortment of Winsor and Newton's pan colours.

A half dozen stippling brushes, those with the bristles set in a quill being recommended.

A half dozen small sable brushes.

Making Grass.*—We will first prepare a blade of the bog grass, about eight or nine inches long, which hangs over and droops from the bog upon which the nest is situated.

---

* In preparing groups, the flowers, being the most perishable, are usually first made up; but, for the sake of convenience, in writing this chapter, the grasses and leaves, being more simple in construction, are taken up first.

One of the pieces of heavy waxed cloth is taken and laid flat upon a smooth pine board upon the table.

A quantity of the powder colours, Prussian blue, cadmium yellow, and a dash of burnt sienna, are mixed together with water in such proportions that when painted upon a piece of the waxed cloth, the colour matches that of the natural grass. A little gum arabic dissolved in water, and a few drops of glycerine to keep the batch of colour from drying in the dish, are added.

The end of the cloth that received the thinnest coating of wax is now painted on both sides, lengthwise, using

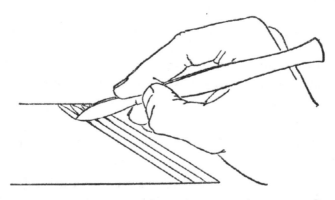

Fig. 46.—Cutting Waxed Cloth to make Artificial Grass.

a stippling brush, and painting from the thick end of the cloth to the other, so that the heaviest deposit of colour lies at the thin end. The blades of grass are now cut out with the scalpel, the cloth lying flat upon the board. A glance at the illustration (Fig. 46) will give an idea of the direction of the cuts.

In this way the blades of grass are coloured and cut. They can, of course, be cut out first, and each blade coloured separately afterward, if desired, but this takes more time. The grass is now grooved lengthwise, to stiffen it, and also to give the character, in the following way:

A blade of the wax grass is laid lengthwise of the forefinger, and a large three-cornered needle, set in a handle, is pressed into the blade lengthwise, forming a groove, as in Fig. 47.

The needle is moistened by drawing it through the mouth as often as is necessary to prevent its sticking to the wax. It will be remembered that all tools when used with wax must be kept moist, or the wax will cling.

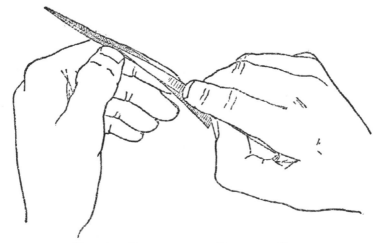

FIG. 47.—GROOVING THE BLADE OF GRASS.

The sides of the blade are now bent toward each other by drawing it through the thumb and forefinger, thus creasing the blade lengthwise and producing a sharp back.

A V-shaped groove is cut in the board with a small V gouge or with a knife, the groove gradually becoming less toward one end until it runs out to nothing. The groove is moistened with water and the creased blade laid into it, with the tip just at the small end of the groove. The large three-cornered needle is now run back and forth, lengthwise, up and down the blade of grass resting in the groove, thus straightening the edges. The blade is then lifted out of the groove.

A downward curve of the tip of the blade is now made by drawing the blade, face up, between the thumb and forefinger. A piece of iron wire two or three inches long, and previously waxed by placing one end of a long piece in the vise and rubbing it smartly with a piece of wax, is now put in the groove at the base of the blade, and the blade welded fast to the end of the wire by revolving it between the thumb and finger, pressing firmly. The blade of grass is now ready to set into the bog. The bottom of the piece of wire is subsequently coated with liquid glue and thrust into the natural sod, dried, the wire offering a firm support for the blade of grass.

A board drilled full of small holes is kept on hand, in which to set the blades of grass temporarily until ready to place in the group.

Any final colouring or blotching with sienna or Vandyke may be done now, using a sable brush and pan colours for this purpose. Having prepared a few blades of this grass for working models, following the natural grass for form and colour, notes are made on just what colours and materials were used, so as to enable us later on to manufacture all of this kind of grass that we wish for the group.

The long grass which towers above the nest for a distance of eighteen inches is now taken in hand. This grass grows up with a long stalk, having the blades arranged alternately up and down the stalk. The method of manufacture will therefore be different from the preceding. The blades are also flat, and not grooved lengthwise, so a wire will have to be introduced into each blade to support it.

Since a wire is necessary, the thinnest waxed cloth is used.

For a pattern of the shape of the blade, a natural blade is laid upon a piece of white paper, held in position with a pin, and stippled over with any dark colour. The blade is then removed, leaving a stenciled outline. Using the pattern as a guide, the blades are cut out as before, except that the wax is unpainted. A duplicate set of blades of this same length, but narrower, are also cut.

Thin silk-covered wire (No. 40) is now cut into pieces

with the scissors, each piece being somewhat longer than the blade of grass, to allow for a support at the base.

A quick way to cut wire into short lengths, where a great number are desired, is to fasten one end of a long piece to a nail driven into the wall, and stretching the wire out from the other end and removing the kinks. The distant end is now made fast to the same nail and the doubled wire again stretched from the end. This end is again looped over the nail and the wire redoubled on itself until the lengths grow short, when the ends of the wire that are fast to the nail are snipped off with the scissors. The wires, in a bundle, are now cut with the scissors into their proper lengths. By stretching the wires in this way they are also straightened.

One of the broad blades is laid flat upon the wetted board, and a piece of the silk-covered wire pressed lengthwise along the centre, one end of the wire being at the tip of the blade, the other projecting from the base.

One of the narrow blades is now placed over this so that the edges come just inside the edges of the first piece.

The upper piece is pressed with the fingers to secure it to the lower one, when the two are firmly united by rubbing them lengthwise with the ball of the modelling pin (hat pin), using care to rub the edges of the blade down thin.

The two pieces, welded fast with the wire between them for a support, are now lifted from the board.

A paper of fine needles, set in a handle, is run lengthwise over the upper or face surface of the blade, the points of the needles scratching small equidistant grooves in the wax as are found in the natural grass.

The blade is now coloured by stippling with the powder colours mixed with water, gum, and glycerine, as before directed.

If it is desired to moisten water colour to secure a little upon the brush, do not dip the bristles in the water. Dip the end of the handle, to which a drop or two will adhere.

The drops thus secured are placed on the edge of the batch of mixed colour, the brush reversed, and the bristles coated with the colour.

After a number of artificial blades have been made, enough for a model, one whole stalk is constructed as follows:

A piece of annealed iron wire, long enough to represent the stalk of the grass, is rubbed smartly with a piece of wax. The base of one of the artificial blades of grass is wrapped partly around the end of the wire and rolled with the thumb and finger, and afterward with the side of the modelling pin, to weld it fast.

A narrow strip of waxed cloth of the colour of the stalk, and cut on the bias, is now wrapped about the heavy wire and also the fine silk-covered wire projecting from the base of the blade, binding the two together. The cloth is wrapped smoothly and evenly down the wire, twisting and rubbing with the thumb and finger, and also with the side of the pin, to secure smoothness. The stem is built up in this way until a second blade is ready to be bound to the stalk.

The second blade is fastened on in the same way, and so on down until the whole stalk is built up. Sheet wax is sometimes used instead of the waxed cloth for binding, as a smoother stem can be built up with it. Should one wire not be heavy enough to support the whole, when wrapped part way down the stalk may be strengthened by placing in additional wires alongside of the main wire and binding them fast. In this way a stalk of six feet or more in height may be built up, if necessary, the thickness of course increasing toward the base.

It will be noticed that at the junction of each blade with the main stem the stalk makes a bend in the opposite direction. This character should be preserved always in making artificial grasses, if found in the original. In the preparation of foliage, as in all branches of taxidermy,

THE ART OF TAXIDERMY.

Nature must always be closely scrutinized from all directions, and followed as nearly as possible in every detail.

A combination of the two foregoing methods of preparing grasses is sometimes resorted to, as, for instance, in making lawn grass. The blades are made of single, painted cloth, grooved with the three-cornered needle on the forefinger, and the edges folded together by drawing and compressing them between the thumb and finger. The blades are then mounted on pieces of iron wire, enough of the base of the blade being allowed to lap over on the wire to twist around it and thus form the main stem, instead of wrapping or binding fast with a separate strip of cloth or wax, as already described in the second process of grassmaking.

Very long, slender grass is better dried in sand, by laying the green grass in a box in layers and sifting fine dry sand over each layer. The grass when dry is painted with oil colour and run through hot coloured wax. It is then mounted by binding the bases to short pieces of wire cut on the bevel with a pair of cutting pliers to sharpen the end. A piece of waxed cloth is used for binding, the cloth when so used being always cut on the bias for greater strength.

Rushes are made in the same manner as the blades of grass described in the second process, by placing the broadest piece, or the piece representing the face of the rush, upon a dampened board, the board being marked or scratched lengthwise, so that the face of the rush will be grooved when pressed down upon the board.

Narrower pieces of heavy waxed cloth are welded fast to the first, by rubbing with the ball of the modelling pin until a sufficient thickness results; a wire may be placed inside before the last piece is put on. The rush is afterward painted.

"Timothy" and "red top" are best represented by drying the natural plant and running a small wire up the inside of the hollow stalk, as near to the top as possible. Artificial blades are then prepared and fastened upon the stalk as already directed, the whole stalk being wrapped with wax.

Working models of all the grasses for the group having been completed, we will now proceed to make some leaves of the wild violet.

Making Leaves.—The moulds having been prepared for work, the *lisse* for the backs of the leaves all coated, or a sufficient quantity to enable us to make up our model, the

Fig. 48.—Cutting Out Pieces of Cloth for Winding Stems.

first thing to be done is to manufacture midribs or "stems" for the leaves. These are prepared as follows:

Waxed cloth, in this case light green in colour, is cut with a scalpel into long V-shaped pieces, as in Fig. 48, the lengths varying according to the length of the stem required. Silk-covered wire is now cut in pieces long enough to reach from the tip of the leaf to and a little beyond the base of the stem, to leave room for attachment. The point of one of the V-shaped pieces of cloth is then placed across the end of one of the pieces of silk-covered wire, and the cloth wrapped around the wire by twirling between the thumb and finger until the end is reached. The stem is then smoothed by drawing it rapidly through the clamped thumb and finger a few times. Some practice is required to enable the beginner to wind a smooth stem, but, as with many other things, it is simple enough when the knack is acquired.

The stem being long in this instance, and the leaf to be made being too heavy to be supported by one thickness of wire, when the wire is wrapped with the cloth part way down a second wire is laid alongside of the first and bound fast to it.

A number of wires may thus be used in a stem if desired, to stiffen it. It is much better to wrap stems thus than to use one heavy wire, as the heavy wire does not allow for tapering. In some instances, for very nice work, where a clear, transparent stem is desired, sheet wax is used instead of the cloth, but is more difficult to handle owing to the breaking of the wax. Tendrils are made in the same way, and wound or coiled about a piece of round wood and the wood withdrawn, leaving the tendril coiled in the shape of a spring, when it may be twisted into any desired position. Very fine midribs, or, for the purposes of this work, "stems," are made by using a pig's bristle, cut from a paint brush if necessary, instead of silk-covered wire, and wrapping it with a piece of sheet wax.

Having wound enough stems to enable us to go on with our models of the violet leaves, we will proceed to press the leaves. Using the natural leaf as a model, sheet wax is selected, of the colour that comes nearest to the lightest body colour of the leaf, and large enough to cover the face of the mould. The mould should be slightly warmed— placing it in warm water for a time will answer, provided the water is not warm enough to melt the paraffin in which the mould has been boiled. If the temperature of the room is well up, the mould will be warm enough for ordinary work, and will not require extra heat.

A piece of thin waxed cloth large enough to cover the face of the mould is torn off, and a stem placed in readiness.

The sheet of wax is laid over the wet face of the mould —the moisture, as a rule, being supplied by licking the face of the mould with the tongue. The wax is now well pressed and kneaded into every detail of the mould with the thumbs, wetting the thumbs from time to time with the mouth. The stem is now laid on in its proper position in the centre of the leaf, with the point well up in the apex, and slightly pressed to keep it from shifting. A sheet of waxed cloth is now laid on and pressed and kneaded all over with the thumbs as before, until the sheet of wax and the cloth are welded fast, with the stem between. Care must be taken that the wax does not shift on the mould, or a double impression will result and spoil the leaf. No pressure should be applied directly over the stem, or this is apt to be forced to one side. The edge of a square piece of soft rubber is used to press close along the side of the stem. When sufficiently pressed, the whole is lifted off the mould.

The wax is now trimmed off with the scissors all around the edge of the impression, and the notches or serrated edge cut in with fine-pointed scissors, as hereafter described. After notching, to thin down the edges of the leaf, and also to weld them fast so that there will never be any possibility of the two layers of wax and cloth separating, the leaf is turned back up on the forefinger or in the palm of the hand, and the edge rolled with the ball of the modelling pin (Fig. 49). The side of the pin is then pressed into the face of the leaf just at the base where the stem joins it, to secure a perfect unison of the wax and stem at this point. As the stem all the way down from the base of the leaf is grooved on the upper side in this species, the stem is pressed upon the

15

finger lengthwise with the side of the modelling pin, thus forming a groove.

The leaf is now ready for its final colouring.

Directions for preparing large fleshy leaves will be given further on, under the head of Casting Leaves.

Moulds that are too large to be covered by one sheet of wax may be cast, or two sheets of wax may be used and their edges joined neatly along the stem.

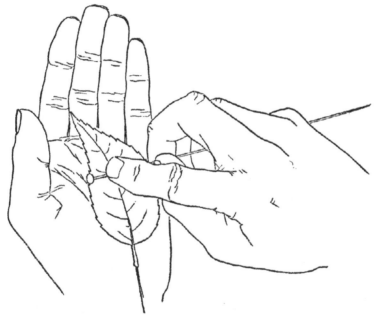

FIG. 49.—ROLLING THE EDGE OF A LEAF.

Beautiful effects in autumn leaves may be produced by using two sheets of different coloured wax, say a red and a yellow, one overlying the other, with a sheet of waxed cloth at the back. The stems of these may also be made up of red or yellow wax as desired.

Some leaves, such as those of the little *Antennaria* and the button ball, having a velvety surface, may be produced by stippling the sheet wax on the face side with dry dextrine and pressing as before, only the mould must be dry.

For very fine colouring, the gloss must be removed from

239

sheet wax, as it interferes with delicate tinting. The wax should be pressed for a few moments between two sheets of blotting paper wet with turpentine, and then allowed to dry off, when the wax will be found to have a perfect mat surface.

A variety of notches or serrations of the edges of leaves will be found. These are all imitated with the scissors

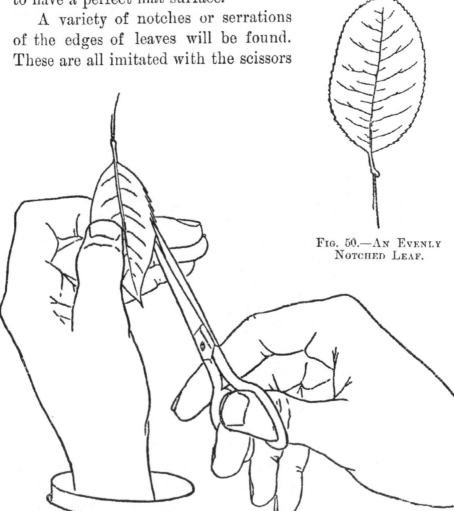

FIG. 50.—AN EVENLY NOTCHED LEAF.

FIG. 51.—SNIPPING THE EDGE OF A LEAF.

on the edges of the wax leaves. The regular notch (Fig. 50) is made by making short straight cuts in the edge of the leaf, pointing toward the base, allowing the tips of the scissors to close with each cut (Fig. 51).

The little ends thus produced are then broken off by pulling with the thumb and finger, as in Fig. 52.

The irregular notch is made in the same way, the cuts being made to vary in length and in the distance between the cuts.

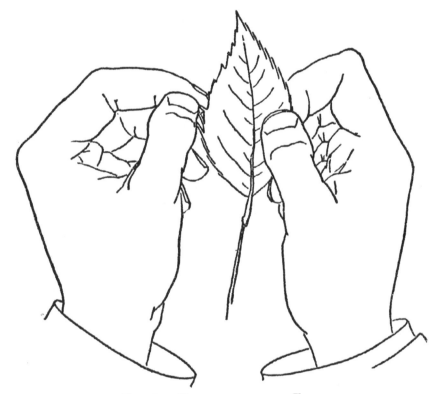

FIG. 52.—BREAKING OFF THE ENDS.

The pieces that are too big and wide to be broken off with the fingers are again snipped across the base with the scissors.

A regular curved notch, such as is found in the chestnut leaf, is best made by punching the edges of the leaf at intervals with a harness-maker's punch, thus filling the edge with round holes (Fig. 53), and afterward snipping out the piece between the holes, leaving the pointed ends connected by a circular base.

After notching, the backs of the edges of the leaves are

rolled with the head of the pin, as previously described (Fig. 49), and are then ready to colour. Dry colours are mixed with water, and a few drops of gum water and glycerine added to the batch to keep it from caking, and also to make the colour spread more evenly on the wax. A flat-ended stippling brush, preferably one with the bristles set in a quill, is used to apply the colour. The end of the handle is dipped in a cup of water, and the drops that adhere are placed at the edge of the mixed colour in the dish. A small quantity of the colour is taken up with the brush and stippled upon the face of the leaf. Should too much colour adhere to the brush, it is wiped off with tissue paper.

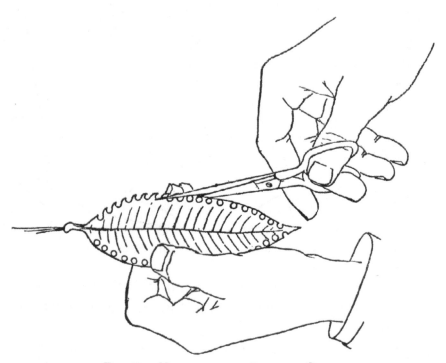

Fig. 53.—Notching the Chestnut Leaf.

The colouring of the leaf is seldom finished in one colour. The lighter colours are stippled on first, and the darker ones over them.

Veinings are painted on afterward, with a finely pointed

sable brush, using Winsor and Newton's moist pan colours for this purpose.

If the leaf has a polished surface, such as the ivy, the gloss is imparted to the wax after the paint is dry by breathing upon the surface of the leaf to moisten the colour slightly, and then polishing by rubbing with a soft brush. That used to brush the hair of infants, for sale at all apothecary shops, is admirably adapted for polishing.

Leaves with a highly glossed face, such as the young leaves of poison ivy, are coated with spirit varnish after colouring.

Red-clover leaves, which have a light-coloured, kidney-shaped marking in the centre, are made by stencilling on the colour. The leaf is pressed in the light-coloured wax, and a paper pattern, the shape of the marking, laid upon the face of the leaf in its proper position and held fast with a pin. The darker green is then stippled over the leaf and the paper pattern removed. The edges of the marking are then stippled over lightly to reduce the hard lines.

Worm holes are made in artificial leaves by cutting out a small piece with the scissors and running a red-hot wire around the inside of the hole, thus producing a ragged edge. The edges of the hole can be coloured with Vandyke or sienna applied with a sable brush.

Very small leaves are made without the use of moulds, being cut out with the scissors, and the veinings marked on the face by pressing the wax on the finger with the modelling pin. The leaves of the buttercup and wild rose are made in this way. Very large fleshy leaves are made by casting, as follows:

A mould of the face of the leaf is made as previously directed, except that a hooked wire is inserted in the plaster at the apex of the leaf mould by which to hold the mould in the subsequent manipulation. The mould is simply allowed to dry without being boiled in paraffin. It is then placed in hot water for ten or fifteen minutes before being used, and the wax heated and coloured as directed for coating the cloth. The mould is removed from the water, and while hot held over the vessel containing the hot wax, and the wax poured evenly over the face of the mould with a cup. If the vessel is large enough to accommodate the mould, it is better dipped bodily into the wax, and the covering of wax afterward removed from the back and sides of the mould and remelted. If the apex of the mould is held uppermost, as it should be, the wax in running down leaves a heavier deposit at the base, which gives a stronger leaf. The stem is then placed in position, and the waxed cloth pressed on for backing, as usual. In making very large, long leaves, a piece of sheet cotton large enough to cover the mould is sometimes used, being dipped in the hot wax, laid upon the face of the mould, and, when partially cooled, pressed with the thumbs to thin it down.

Fruits and berries are cast in the same way, except that piece moulds are made in plaster.

Cactus plants (prickly pear) have been nicely reproduced by pulling the spines out of the natural leaves, making two-piece moulds and casting the leaves in coloured wax, the wax being mixed half and half with paraffin for greater cheapness. The natural spines are then glued back into the wax leaves, and the leaves joined one to the other by drilling and inserting wires and painting hot wax in at the joints.

Modelling Flowers.—The making of the flowers, although the most perishable vegetable matter in our group, and therefore usually first made, are, for the purposes of this chapter, left until the last.

Modelling the Violet.—One of the violets is now taken and a model prepared as follows: A few sheets of white waxed *lisse* are prepared. It is better to make this up in small quantities from time to time as wanted, as it is apt to grow yellow with age. One of the flowers is pulled apart to see how it is constructed. We find that it is, for our purposes, divided into a centre, five petals, and a little bag-shaped affair at the back covered by the calyx.

The centre is first made by taking a piece of stout silk-covered wire and turning over one end into a knob to keep the wax from slipping off.

A strip of light-green sheet wax is cut, and one side folded back upon itself three or four times. The strip

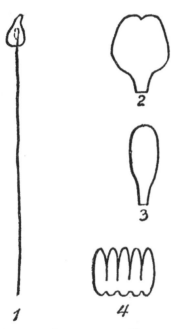

FIG. 54.—DIAGRAM FOR VIOLET.

of wax is wound tightly around the end of the knotted wire, making a small reversed cup (Fig. 54, 1), and the tip coloured with a little cadmium and chrome. The stem is now neatly wrapped with light-green wax and rolled with the thumb and finger to the size of the model stem. Petals are cut out of the white cloth by using stencilled patterns from the natural ones, making one petal for the bottom of the flower as in Fig. 54, 2, and four as in Fig. 54, 3. The petals are coloured by mixing violet and white, applied dry by rubbing the petal between the thumb and finger. The colour is not applied to the bases of the petals, as they are afterward to be welded fast at this point, and colour keeps the wax from sticking. Moisture will do the same.

The petals are now modelled into proper form by placing them, one at a time, in the palm of the hand and working them with the head of the modelling pin. The fine veinings of the petals are painted on with a small sable brush, using violet and crimson lake applied wet.

The petals are welded fast to the centre by rolling their bases with the side of the modelling pin. The little bag at the back is now made by rolling a piece of waxed cloth into the proper form, leaving the ends loose for welding fast to the body of the flower. The bag is welded fast in the same manner as were the petals, and the joint concealed by colouring. The calyx is cut out of green cloth, after the pattern (Fig. 54, 4), and coloured slightly with violet. The calyx is also modelled with the head of the pin and welded fast to the body of the flower by wrapping it around the base and modelling with the pin. The stem is given its characteristic crook, coloured with pan colours after the natural stem, and the flower is complete.

The leaves are now arranged about the flower, and the bases of the stems united by rolling them together with the thumb and finger, inserting a short piece of stout wire, and wrapping all firmly together with a piece of waxed cloth. The plant is now ready to be placed in the group.

Modelling the Buttercup.—We will now proceed to make up a specimen of the swamp buttercup. A flower is pulled apart, as in all cases, to see how it is constructed. We find it composed of four parts, independently of the stem. These are the head or foundation (carpels), the fringe of stamens surrounding the centre, the petals, and lastly the calyx at the back formed of five distinct points (sepals).

As with the violet, the foundation is first made by winding a ball of light-green wax over the knotted or turned-over end of a piece of silk-covered wire. Fine points are made on the top of the ball to represent the carpels, by pricking the wax with the point of the modelling pin (Fig. 55, 1).

The stamens are made in the following way: The tip of each stamen broadens out into a little flattened head called the anther, upon which the pollen is deposited. To produce this enlarged end, a piece of chrome-yellow waxed cloth is cut into a strip and one side turned over upon itself twice, and the finger run along it to weld the folds together. With the scissors the piece of cloth is chopped into fine pieces, each cut being as long as a stamen, and the pieces cut being just as wide. The cuts do not run all the way across the strip, thus leaving each artificial stamen attached one to the other at the base (Fig. 56). The stamens of the flower are counted, and the same number used in the reproduction. The stamens, attached at their bases on

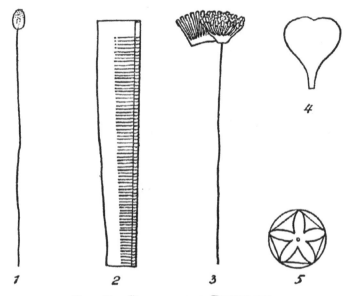

FIG. 55.—DIAGRAM FOR BUTTERCUP.

the strip (Fig. 55, 2), are now wound about the foundation (Fig. 55, 3) and given a natural set with the point of the pin. The pollen is reproduced by painting on powder colour mixed with just enough water to bind it.

The petals (Fig. 55, 4), are now cut out of cloth which is coated with the second shade of chrome-yellow wax, and painted with a very little orange and chrome. The petals are then modelled, and welded fast to the foundation, from behind, one at a time, when the flower is ready for the calyx. This is better made in one piece. A circular disk is first cut out of the cloth, and the edges are trimmed off with the scissors, so as to produce five points upon the disk to act as guides in cutting out the calyx (Fig. 55, 5). The calyx is then cut out, coloured, and modelled with the pinhead in the palm of the hand. With the

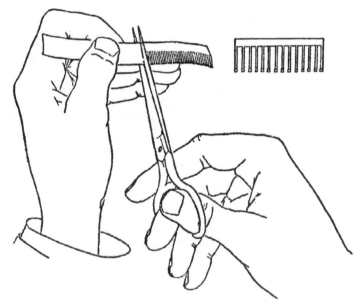

FIG. 56.—SNIPPING STAMENS.

point of the pin a hole is punched in the centre of the calyx, and the calyx slid up the wire stem from below and welded fast to the bottom of the flower. The petals are now given their gloss on the upper surfaces by painting them with spirit varnish applied with a camel's-hair brush.

The leaves of the buttercup are made by pressing a piece of thin silk-covered wire or a white hog's bristle between a sheet of wax for the face and a piece of waxed cloth for the back. The leaves are then cut out with the scissors according to stencilled patterns. After a number of leaves have been made the patterns may be discarded if desired, and the leaves cut out by the eye. The leaves are then modelled with the head of the pin, and the backs of the edges rolled, to keep the wax from separating and to thin down the edge. The leaves are then coloured and built upon the wax-covered stem, following the natural plant for a model. When completed, a piece of iron wire is bound fast to the base of the stalk to give a firm support for the plant when set into the sod.

Modelling the Dandelion.—A fresh specimen is procured as a model, as this flower closes up soon after being plucked.

Yellow waxed cloth is prepared of a colour to match the flower stamens. These are cut out of the cloth in long strips and wound about a wax foundation on the turned-over end of the wire (Fig. 57, 1). The stamens are cut very fine for the centre, and coarser and V-shaped for the middle tiers (Fig. 57, 3). The outer ones are cut with nearly parallel sides with notched ends, as in Fig. 57, 2. The calyx is

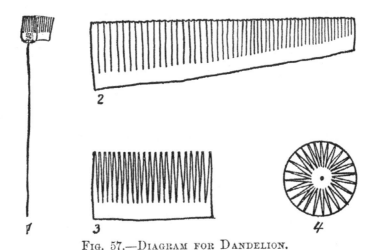

FIG. 57.—DIAGRAM FOR DANDELION.

cut out of one circular piece of cloth, as in Fig. 57, 4. The centre is punctured and the calyx slid up the wire from below and welded fast to the back of the flower, as in the buttercup. The stamens are then arranged with the point of the modelling pin and coloured. The wax leaves, previously pressed and coloured, are now bound fast to the base of the flower stem, and the plant is ready to place in the group.

Preparing the Wild Rosebush.—The leaves of the wild rosebush being very small are prepared in the same manner as already described, by simply cutting the leaves out of the wax and cloth pressed together, without the use of moulds. A fine bristle or silk-covered wire is used for a stem, the bristle or wire being clamped between the cloth and wax. The leaves are arranged in small sprays by using wire as a base, and binding the leaflets fast with a strip of waxed cloth cut on the bias. The natural plant is of course used as a guide for form and colour.

The woody stalk, having been through the Wickersheimer solution to toughen it and keep it from shrinking, is now trimmed of the fresh growth, and holes drilled through the stems at the points where the sprays are to be adjusted. The holes are best drilled with a three-cornered needle set in a handle. The wires projecting from the bases of the sprays are twisted together and run through the holes. A little liquid glue is applied to the base of the artificial stem, and the stem drawn up tight to the twig. The wires are now clipped off short on the opposite side of the wood and bent over and clamped tightly with pliers. When the twigs are too small to be drilled, the ends are whittled down to a point. The spray is bound fast to the pointed twig with a silk thread, and covered with strips of waxed cloth, bound down firmly and smoothed out with the thumb and finger. The twigs are then coloured. In this way, instead of making up the woody stalk, which is entirely unnecessary, we preserve it, and simply restore the perishable parts, namely, the leaves and finer twigs or stems.

The plants that were found growing upon the sod when collected having all been reproduced in wax, the sod is now prepared to receive them. All the larger plants, and the bulk of the green grass, are removed from the sod, enough being left to represent the dead growth of the preceding year. The sod is then exposed to the hot sun until thoroughly dried out. When dried, the sod is placed in an airtight box containing a quarter of a pound of bisulphuret of carbon, and allowed to remain closed up tightly for a day or two to kill any insects that may exist in the sod. If an oven large enough to receive the sod is at hand, the whole may be placed inside and baked, killing all insects and their larvæ at once, and thus doing away with the bisulphuret of carbon.

A wooden tray is now made, of the dimensions previously planned, and a three-cornered bevelled strip constructed to tack upon the top of the tray all around. The strip should be ebonized and polished, and fastened in place when the group is nearly finished. The sod is now trimmed down until it fits snugly into the tray, in such a way that the inner edge of the strip will fit nicely to the sides of the sod. If the sod is to be raised at any point, peat moss, dried, or excelsior, is introduced underneath for a foundation.

The larger plants are now set into the sod, liquid glue being used on the bases. The nest is placed upon the top of the bog and held in position by driving wires down through it into the bog. The grasses and flowers are finally set in position—frequent reference being made to the sketches and photographs of the group when collected. The moss which was found growing upon the sides of the bog, having been placed in Wickersheimer solution, rinsed off, and dried, is coloured by dusting powder colours over it, and fastened into position with hot paraffin, which is painted on the back. While the paraffin is hot a bunch of moss is held in position until the wax chills, thus gluing the moss firmly to the bog. *Papier-maché* should never be used for this purpose, neither should hot glue, as the glycerine in the moss holds back the water in the glue from drying out, and the glue rots and mildews.

The blown eggs are now placed in the nest, the birds introduced, and the group is complete, save casing. The group should be covered with tissue paper, and left for a week or so to insure its being perfectly dried out before cas-

PLATE XX.

THE FINISHED GROUP.

ing. The case is usually a square one, with rosewood edges, and made to set down over the group. The case should be practically air-tight, and charged with bisulphuret of carbon when it is finally adjusted, to kill any insects that may chance to appear with time.

As the reader may at some future time wish to prepare the daisy and the pond lily, two of our most attractive wild flowers, brief directions are here given.

Modelling the Daisy.—As with all flowers, the centre is first made, and the petals, etc., built upon it. The daisy centre is successfully made in the following way: Take a small flat button and run a piece of silk-covered wire up

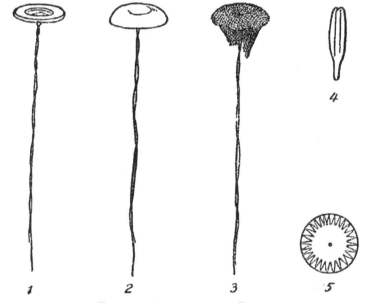

FIG. 58.—DIAGRAM FOR DAISY.

through one hole and down through another and twist the ends together underneath, for the flower stalk (Fig. 58, 1). Coat the button with liquid glue or dilute gum arabic and then with a layer of green sheet wax, pressed on smoothly with the fingers. Build upon this with yellow wax to the form of the daisy centre (Fig. 58, 2). Cover the whole with one piece of yellow sheet wax, allowing the ends to come underneath, where they are all pressed smoothly together. A piece of strong white lace or net with hexagonal holes is now covered over the whole, allowing the ends to come below and leaving room enough to pull on. Dip the whole in hot water and pull on the bottom of the lace. The result is that the warm wax squeezes through the holes in the lace, producing a centre cut up into a mass of small rounded points (Fig. 58, 3). The first covering of green wax shows through at the bases of the points, giving a very natural effect. The dip or hollow in the centre may be made by taking a stitch down through the centre of the wax before the wax is heated, and pulling on the ends of the thread from below at the same time the net is drawn down. The net or lace is now cut away around the underside of the head, and the whole allowed to dry out before the petals are put on. The petals are made of two thin sheets of white fabric pressed together, between which a fine bristle is clamped lengthwise for a support. Dry arrowroot and flake-white powder colour are mixed and rubbed on the petals before they are modelled, care being taken to keep the powder off the bases of the petals. The longitudinal lines of the petals are produced by rolling or creasing them lengthwise with the head of a large pin, the petal meanwhile resting along the finger (Fig. 58, 4). The calyx is prepared and placed in the same way as already described for the buttercup (Fig. 58, 5). The bases of the petals are slightly coloured with light green after they are in position on the flower.

To the beginner in colouring I recommend Ridgway's Nomenclature of Colours, mentioned on page 7, as a guide.

Modelling the White Pond Lily.—The pistil is first made by rolling a ball of chrome-yellow sheet wax upon the turned-over end of a piece of heavy wire. The wax is then pressed and modelled with the curling pin after the natural pistil (Fig. 59, 1). Colour with orange and chrome,

powder colours. The stamens are now made. Four rows
are cut, the inner row being finer than the one next to it—
the outer row being very coarse—each row being long enough
to reach once around the centre (Fig. 59, 2 and 3). The

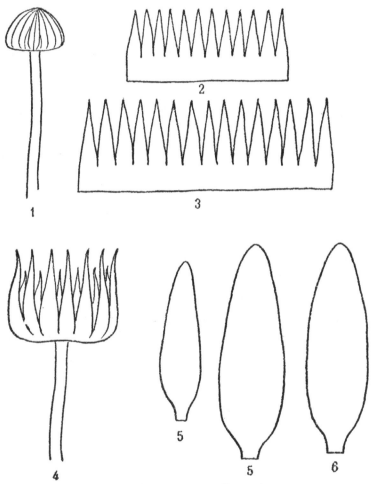

FIG. 59.—DIAGRAM FOR POND LILY.

rows are cut out of doubled thick waxed cloth, white and
light yellow pressed together and afterward coloured, the
rows being made richer in colour toward the centre. The
stamens are wrapped around the pistil and modelled fast
with the pin (Fig. 59, 4). The petals are now modelled.
Using the stencilled patterns for models, artificial ones are

16

cut out of white sheet wax with a piece of white cloth at the back for the inside petals, and double white cloth for the outer ones (Fig. 59, 5). As the petals are all quite thick, the cloth should be heavily coated with wax by drawing it quickly through the hot wax. A heavier quality of cloth may also be used. After the petals are cut out they are rubbed between the thumb and finger with arrowroot, to remove the gloss and also to whiten them, when they are modelled into form by laying them one at a time in the palm of the hand and pressing heavily with the thumb to dish them. They are then rolled lengthwise with the head of the modelling pin until they assume the proper shape. When all are modelled, the petals are welded fast to the centre with the modelling pin, being arranged in fours. Four petals are placed so as to oppose each other, and then four more similarly arranged between the first four, and so on. The calyx (Fig. 59, 6) is made in the same way, of three thicknesses, the first being white cloth, the next green, or two sheets of green if not heavy, and the third white cloth again, all pressed together before cutting out. After modelling as before, the outside of the calyx is coloured with light green stippled on, followed by a deeper shade of green, and then by a tinge of crimson lake on the edges and on the inside. The outside is then polished with the brush, slightly stippled with crimson lake and again polished. Spirit varnish may be used instead of polishing. The calyx is then arranged in place. The stem is wound a short distance down and a long wire lashed fast. The whole stem may be made up of wax, but rubber tubing made in imitation of pond-lily stems, sold by manufacturers of milliners' articles, answers very well. The tubing is simply placed over the wire and welded fast at the top, thus giving a long flexible stem, which may be arranged in any position and held there by the wire inside.

The leaves and stems of some plants are covered with a downy substance. This may be produced artificially by the use of manufactured " down," to be procured of dealers in wax-flower supplies; or it may also be made readily by clipping up a piece of coarse white flannel very fine with the scissors. The down may be coloured to any desired tint by the admixture of dry colours. The leaves or stems to be coated are painted over with dilute gum arabic or honey, and the down sifted on with the fingers, enough adhering to give the desired effect.

When the stamens of a flower are few, instead of clipping them out of one piece of cloth, as was done in the case of the buttercup already described, they may be made separately of waxed thread. The white bases of moose hairs answer admirably for some stamens.

II. MAMMAL GROUPS.

In preparing groups of large mammals there are so many details and effects to be taken into consideration which can not be foreseen, that groups should always be carefully designed, and each individual specimen in the group modelled on a small scale in clay before the specimens are mounted. The relative positions of the models may then be shifted until the desired effect is obtained.

There should be a front and also a " point " to every group. In order to have a front, and one only, it is of course necessary that glass should be in but three sides of the case, leaving the back to build against.

In my opinion, a square case with four plate-glass sides to it is the ruination of every large mammal group that was ever constructed. In a four-sided case the group must look well from all directions, and three of these sides must of necessity detract from and limit the view from the fourth, or front of the group. For instance, to represent a group of deer as being startled at some imaginary object, and all looking intently in one direction, would be an impossibility with a square case exposed on all sides, as the back would of necessity be anything but attractive.

THE ART OF TAXIDERMY.

If a landscape is painted with one show side and one back, why should a mammal group be constructed otherwise?

Therefore I say, have a back to a group, and a light-coloured one. By a back I do not mean a painted background containing a scene, as on the curtain of a theatre. Let the background be pale blue, and build up against it with rocks, trees, or whatever the scene is intended to represent.

In collecting the accessories for a group of large mammals, the plan of the group is kept in mind and the materials collected in accordance with the design. There are many difficulties in the way of finding a piece of ground that is perfectly adapted in every respect for representation in a large group, and, if found, it would be impracticable to attempt to take up and ship the natural sod, etc., with every identical tree, rock, etc., upon it, as in the case of small bird groups.* Such trees, shrubs, etc., are selected as will best serve to represent the character of the flora of the locality, care being used that too great an assortment of species is not introduced.

Trees, if large, are cut into sections, on a bevel, for convenience in shipping, and the parts afterward united. All trees or twigs which are to have the foliage reproduced upon them for representation in a group should go through the Wickersheimer solution to toughen the twigs and keep them from shrivelling, and also to kill any insects that may exist in the wood. The twigs when dry are drilled with a three-cornered needle set in a handle, and the artificial leaves attached by running the wires through the holes,

---

* An exception to this rule occurs in prairie scenes where the actual sod is necessary for a base. In a group of bisons at the American Museum, and, I believe, in the bison group in the United States National Museum at Washington, enough sod to cover the floor of the case was actually dug up and transported from the localities represented to their destinations, and installed in the cases.

touching the bases of the stems with liquid glue or gum arabic and drawing them down firmly against the twig. The excess of wire is then cut off the opposite side of the twig and the balance turned over and pressed firmly against the wood. The natural twigs should always be used, if stout enough, in preference to making them up artificially in wire and wax as this involves a great deal of labour.

Mosses should always be treated with the Wickersheimer solution. If dry, the moss should be wet before going into the liquid, as the dry moss sucks up a great quantity of the solution, which is somewhat expensive by reason of the proportion of glycerine it contains.

Artificial logs may be constructed of wire netting—which enters largely into the foundations of all large mammal groups—and the netting covered with pieces of bark and mossed over. Moss that has been through the Wickersheimer solution should never be attached with glue. The base of a bunch of moss is dipped into hot paraffin and at once placed in position upon the object it is to cover, and held there until the paraffin chills, when it is stuck there for good.

Flat lichens, such as are usually found growing upon rocks and tree trunks, should also never be glued on. The dry lichen should be wrapped in a damp cloth until relaxed, when the back is painted over with hot beeswax. While hot, the piece of lichen is laid upon the surface it is to cover and pressed with the fingers, and modelled into the crevices of the bark or rock by means of a hot scraper or modelling tool. In this way the lichen is made to conform to the surface it covers, as it does in Nature, and the edges may be kept down flat—an impossibility with glue.

APPENDIX.

*Addresses for purchasing Tools and Materials used in
Taxidermy.*

Absorbent cotton, for wrapping bird skins:
Dennison Manufacturing Company, 198 Broadway, N. Y.
Agassiz tanks, for alcoholics, copper, with screw top:
C. Muller & Son, 731 Seventh Ave., N. Y.
Artificial eyes, for birds and mammals:
J. Kannofsky, 369 Canal St., N. Y. Demuth Bros., 89
Walker St., N. Y. F. B. Webster, Hyde Park, Mass. J.
W. Critchley, Providence, R. I. Globes for hand paint-
ing: F. Schumacher, 74 Maple St., Jersey City, N. J.
Artificial flower makers' materials:
George J. Kraft, 85 Chambers St., N. Y. Benjamin Rosen-
stiel, 28 West 3d St., N. Y.
Artists and modelers' tools and materials:
Devoe, Raynolds & Co., corner of Fulton and William
Sts., N. Y.
Auxiliary barrel for shot gun (Fig. 1):
F. B. Webster, Hyde Park, Mass.
Bird skins, dry:
Ward's Natural Science Establishment, Rochester, N. Y.
M. Abbott Frazar, 93 Sudbury St., Boston, Mass. J. W.
Critchley, Providence, R. I. F. B. Webster, Hyde Park,
Mass. W. W. Worthington, Shelter Island, N. Y.
Books of reference on birds and mammals:
L. S. Foster, 33 Pine St., N. Y.
Cases for large bird or mammal groups:
B. and W. B. Smith, 220 West 29th St., N. Y.

Clay, for modelling :
    Stewart Drain-pipe Works, 540 West 19th St., N. Y., and
    259 Wabash Ave., Chicago, Ill.
Combs, steel :
    A. Eickhoff, 381 Broome St., N. Y.
Composite clay, for modelling :
    C. H. Chavant & Co., 75 Rutgers Ave., Jersey City, N. J.
    Devoe, Raynolds & Co., N. Y.
Cops, for winding birds after mounting :
    F. B. Webster, Hyde Park, Mass.
" *Crêpe-de-lisse,*" for manufacturing artificial foliage :
    Arnold, Constable & Co., 881 Broadway, N. Y. R. H. Macy
    & Co., Sixth Ave. and 14th St., N. Y. Stern Bros., 38
    West 23d St., N. Y.
Excelsior, very fine :
    John B. Taylor, 261 Canal St., N. Y.
Formaldehyde :
    Kny-Scheerer Company, 17 Park Place, N. Y.
Furriers' sawdust, for dressing out fur :
    J. B. Le Claire, Jr., $552\frac{1}{2}$ West 52d St., N. Y.
General purchasing agents :
    H. A. Welch & Co., 647 Greenwich St., N. Y.
Glass frosting, for snow scenes :
    Demuth Bros., 89 Walker St., N. Y. J. Kannofsky, 369
    Canal St., N. Y. F. B. Webster, Hyde Park, Mass.
Glass icicles, for snow scenes :
    Demuth Brothers, 89 Walker St., N. Y. J. Kannofsky,
    369 Canal St., N. Y. F. Schumacher, 74 Maple St.,
    Jersey City, N. J.
Glass jars, for alcoholics etc. :
    Kny-Scheerer Company, 17 Park Place, N. Y. Whitall,
    Tatum & Co., 46 Barclay St., N. Y.
Glass shades, for covering small bird groups :
    Nicholas Wapler, 50 Barclay St., N. Y.
Glass shades, square, with oval centres for wall pieces :
    Charles K. Reed, Worcester, Mass. F. B. Webster, Hyde
    Park, Mass. J. W. Critchley, Providence, R. I.
Hand scrapers, for cleaning small mammal hides (Plate IV,
    Fig. 5) :
    F. B. Webster, Hyde Park, Mass.

APPENDIX.

Labels and tags:

Dennison Manufacturing Company, 198 Broadway, N. Y.

Mammal skins, dry:

Ward's Natural Science Establishment, Rochester, N. Y.
W. W. Hart & Co., 5 West 3d St., N. Y. J. Murgatroyd,
18 North William St., N. Y. F. Sauter, 3 North William
St., N. Y. Charles K. Worthen, Warsaw, Ill.

Moth-proof cans, for storing bird and mammal skins:

C. Muller & Son, 731 Seventh Ave., N. Y.

Needles, all shapes and sizes:

A. Shrimpton & Sons, 273 Church St., N. Y.

Oölogists' supplies:

F. B. Webster, Hyde Park, Mass. Frank H. Lattin, Albion, N. Y.

Paper, for pulping, to manufacture *papier-maché*—in quantity only:

Henry Lindenmeyer, 20 Beekman St., N. Y. Small quantities of pulp may be procured of F. B. Webster, Hyde Park, Mass.

Papier-maché heads, for rugs:

J. Kannofsky, 369 Canal St., N. Y. J. Murgatroyd, 18
North William St., N. Y. F. B. Webster, Hyde Park,
Mass.

Paraffin:

Devoe, Raynolds & Co., corner Fulton and William Sts.,
N. Y.

Pins, very stout, for mammals:

The "Puritan" blocking pins, Nos. 15, heavy, and 17, lighter, American Pin Company, 441 Broadway, N. Y.

Scrapers, large and small (Plate IV, Figs. 14 and 15):

Tiemann & Co., 107 Park Row, N. Y. F. B. Webster,
Hyde Park, Mass.

Stereotypers' paper, for making paper casts:

B. and O. Myers, 16 Beekman St., N. Y.

Surgical instruments:

Kny-Scheerer Company, 17 Park Place, N. Y. George
Tiemann & Co., 107 Park Row, N. Y.

Tanners and curriers:

A. Bowsky & Sons, 220 East 51st St. N. Y. J. Meseritz &
Sons, 47 Bogart St., Brooklyn, N. Y.

Tanners' and curriers' tools and supplies:

Mulford, Cary & Conklin, 34 Spruce St., N. Y.

Taxidermists' tools and supplies:

F. B. Webster, Hyde Park, Mass. Kny-Scheerer Company, 17 Park Place, N. Y. F. H. Lattin, Albion, N. Y. J. W. Critchley, Providence, R. I.

Tow and flax, for use in mounting birds and small mammals:

"Dutch hackle" grade. The Elm Flax Mills, 90 White St., N. Y. Factory, corner 57th St. and 11th Ave., N. Y.

Traps:

"Climax" mouse traps, "Climax" rat traps, J. R. Schuyler & Co., Bloomsburg, Pa. "Cyclone" mouse traps. Lovell Manufacturing Company, 30 Warren St., N. Y. Out-o'-sight" mouse traps, "Out-o'-sight" rat traps, Animal Trap Company, Abingdon, Ill.

Wax, sheet wax, all colors:

Theodor Leonhard, Paterson, N. J. "T. L." bleached wax, round cakes, for coating cloth in making artificial foliage, etc. Devoe, Raynolds & Co., corner Fulton and William Sts., N. Y.

Wax-flower supplies:

Devoe, Raynolds & Co., corner Fulton and William Sts., N. Y.

Wire, cotton or silk covered, for use in making artificial foliage:

Devoe, Raynolds & Co., corner Fulton and William Sts., N. Y.

Wire netting (wire cloth) annealed:

Estey Wire Works, 65 Fulton St., N. Y. Williams Wire Works, 85 Fulton St., N. Y.

Other books from CGR Publishing at CGRpublishing.com

1939 New York World's Fair: The World of Tomorrow in Photographs

San Francisco 1915 World's Fair: The Panama-Pacific International Expo.

1904 St. Louis World's Fair: The Louisiana Purchase Exposition in Photographs

Chicago 1933 World's Fair: A Century of Progress in Photographs

19th Century New York: A Dramatic Collection of Images

The American Railway: The Trains, Railroads, and People Who Ran the Rails

The Aeroplane Speaks: Illustrated Historical Guide to Airplanes

The World's Fair of 1893 Ultra Massive Photographic Adventure Vol. 1

The World's Fair of 1893 Ultra Massive Photographic Adventure Vol. 2

The World's Fair of 1893 Ultra Massive Photographic Adventure Vol. 3

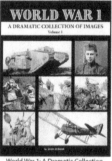

World War 1: A Dramatic Collection of Images

Magnum Skywolf #1

Ethel the Cyborg Ninja Book 1

1901 Buffalo World's Fair: The Pan-American Exposition in Photographs

How To Draw Digital by Mark Bussler

The Complete Butterfly Book: Enlarged Illustrated Special Edition

Other books from CGR Publishing at CGRpublishing.com

Ultra Massive Video Game Console Guide Volume 1

Ultra Massive Video Game Console Guide Volume 2

Ultra Massive Video Game Console Guide Volume 3

Ultra Massive Sega Genesis Guide

Discovery of the North Pole: The Greatest American Expedition

Chicago's White City Cookbook

The Complete Book of Birds

The Clock Book: A Detailed Collection of Classic Clocks

Oceanography and Sailing in the 19th Century: The Water World

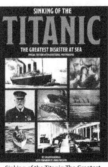
Sinking of the Titanic: The Greatest Disaster at Sea

All Hail the Vectrex Ultimate Collector's Guide

Dante's Inferno: Retro Hell-Bound Edition

The Art of World War 1

The Kaiser's Memoirs: Illustrated Enlarged Special Edition

Captain William Kidd and the Pirates and Buccaneers Who Ravaged the Seas

Gustave Doré's London: A Pilgrimage Retro Restored Special Edition

Made in the USA
Coppell, TX
11 March 2023

14142256R00149